The 25 GREATEST MOMENTS IN
Camp Randall History

BY MIKE LUCAS

PRODUCTION CREDITS

ISBN: 0-9758769-5-3

Published By:
KCI Sports Ventures, LLC
1402 Quail Run Drive
Savoy, IL 61874

Cover photo courtesy of David Stluka

Editor: Peter J. Clark
Photo Editor: Molly Voorheis
Dustjacket Design: Terry Neutz Hayden
Booklayout and Design: Terry Neutz Hayden

Photos Courtesy of University of Wisconsin Sports Information, University of Wisconsin Archives, Madison Capital Times, Craig Schreiner, John Maniaci and Joe Jackson of the Wisconsin State Journal, University of Minnesota Sports Information, Ohio State Sports Information, David Stluka and Neil Ament.

Printed and bound by Worzalla Publishing, Stevens Point, WI.

The 25 GREATEST MOMENTS IN
Camp Randall History

CONTENT

Mike Lucas (l) and Matt Lepay.

ACKNOWLEDGEMENT

Thanks to all the players, coaches and fans who have created the memories, and the great moments. A special thanks to Peter Clark, who was the driving force behind this project and patient enough to put up with the whims and belly-aching of the author. Also thanks to Matt Lepay, a trusted friend and the Voice of the Badgers, Dave Vitale and Jonathan Utz; Justin Doherty and Steve Malchow at the UW; and Adam Mertz, Ron Larson, and Dennis McCormick at the *Cap Times* and Madison Newspapers. And, finally, a heartfelt thanks to Tom Butler, a mentor to the kid, who's still fighting that growing up thing.

DEDICATION

To my wife, Peggy, a survivor, whose commitment and total dedication to a cause, Gilda's Club of Madison, has been an inspiration. I love you, Peg.

To my mother, Marika, a survivor, whose perseverance — during a hard transition without the man in her life — has been an inspiration. I love you, mom.

To the spirit and memory of my father, Gus, a battler, whose unmatched work ethic — and zeal for doing the right thing — has been my inspiration. I miss you, dad.

FOREWORD   PAT RICHTER

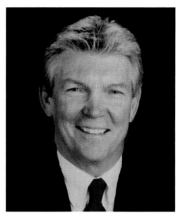

I was probably 10 years old when I saw my first game at Camp Randall Stadium. Let's put it this way - that was the first time I got in with a ticket. Occasionally, we would sneak in. But it was harder for us living over on the east side of Madison to get over there than it was for the guys from Edgewood and West. We didn't live close enough, and you'd have to bus. So, for the most part, we'd play our games in the park, and listen on the radio.

But I do remember seeing Ohio State in 1951. They had Vic Janowicz, who went on to win the Heisman, and the Hard Rocks did a number on him that day. It was a 6-6 tie. I remember watching players like John Coatta and Alan Ameche and Rollie Strehlow.

I grew up on Rutledge Street, east of the Yahara River, just before Rutledge turns into Lakeland Avenue. And Gary Messner, who was a center on those Ameche teams, lived about four houses down from us. Back in those days, Gary would have some of the guys over — Ameche and Hulaska and Hutchinson — and you'd hang out with them.

There was more accessibility to college football players back then. It wasn't as structured as it is today. And they didn't have as many demands on their time. I remember the autograph signings at Wolf Kubly on the square. It was a big deal for us. And I think the Badger players got a kick out of it because it was a big deal to them, too.

I don't remember much about the first game I played at Camp Randall other than it was against Marquette, and they had a big defensive end, George Andrie. I think the following week we beat Purdue in the Big Ten opener. It was Dad's Day at the stadium.

I remember that because my dad was in the hospital and couldn't make it to the game. And I remember going over the middle and catching kind of an awkward pass that was real low and I was kind of thinking after the catch, 'Dad, wish you were here to see it."

We played Michigan for Homecoming, and I needed just one catch to tie the school record (for receptions in a season). I made the catch, but I also broke my collarbone.

I was supposed to have my first date that night with Renee (Sengstock, who would later become his wife). She likes telling the story that she was sitting at the game next to somebody else that I had given tickets to. I'm not sure that's true. But I'll take her word I had given tickets to two different girls for the same game. I vaguely think it could have happened.

Beating Northwestern and Minnesota (in '62) were among my fondest team memories. Individually, I remember making a fingertip catch against Iowa. I had broken my hand during the game, and the only way I could catch the

ball was on my fingertips. I still have that picture in my office. You can see I literally caught it on my fingers while fully extended.

I also remember a pass I caught against Illinois. I got into the clear, but I had lost my balance when I had stretched out and I did a gooney bird for about 20 yards. I couldn't pick up my feet, and I stumbled, stumbled and stumbled. Never made it to the end zone.

After leaving school, I didn't get back for another game in Madison until the fall of '71. I had just been cut by Washington. And I didn't really enjoy watching games for a while. Once you've played, there's a tendency to look at the game too closely and pick it apart. You don't take it for what it is. You look at a specific position rather than the overall game.

Right before I took over as the athletic director, if there was one memory that spurred me on, it was the memory of that final game in the 1989 season. Officially, I didn't take over until February of '90. But I remember going to that game. It was snowy and ugly.

And the Badgers couldn't tackle Lorenzo White. They announced 29,000 for the attendance. But there had to be half that number in the stands, if that.

Imagine what it must have felt like for the seniors to run out of the tunnel. It had to be tremendously disappointing. And as we began to consider the offer to come back (as the AD), I remember a number of people who came up to me, parents of players, who said their sons were embarrassed to wear their letter jackets because they didn't have pride in the program.

In this context, I remember that first press conference with Barry Alvarez, and Barry talking about getting your tickets now because you might not be able to get them later. That was the kind of attitude that attracted me to him. That kind of confidence.

There were a lot of games that really stood out at Camp Randall over all those years we were together. But the one game I think I'll always remember will be the Dayne game — when Ron set the rushing record, and we got back to another Rose Bowl.

Looking back, you really feel proud of all the people and the hard work that went into the last 15 or 16 years. It's hard to put into context — what we were in '90 and what we are today. And then, after you come back down to earth, you realize the challenge is to keep it going. You can never forget that. That's the biggest challenge still in front of us.

FOREWORD BARRY ALVAREZ

Living in Burgettstown, Pennsylvania, back in the '60s, I was a big sports fan. I used to go to Steeler and Pirate games in Pittsburgh. And I got a taste of college football by watching the Pitt Panthers or going to West Virginia games. I still remember those Pirate games because I saw how a full house and the electricity in a stadium could motivate the players on the field.

When I got to Nebraska, they were going through some of the things we're doing here right now as far as filling in the seating areas and bowling up the stadium. I can remember the first game I played there — you'd get chills because it's all red and there isn't an empty seat.

In 1966, we played the Badgers at Camp Randall (Alvarez had an interception in a 31-3 Cornhusker win), and I remember the night before the team stayed at the Edgewater Hotel. I remember my uncle coming up to my room and looking out over the lake and the sail boats and it was such a beautiful scene. He said, "I've never seen anything this pretty."

The first time I really took notice of the stadium was my first year on the Iowa coaching staff. Before the game, I remember standing out in the middle of the field, and you could smell beer on the 50-yard line. I sat in the press box that year, and I can also remember the press box moving when the band played or the crowd got into the game.

As assistants, we had to walk from the press box down through the seating areas of the stadium, and I can remember how the fans crowded the aisles. We're wearing Iowa colors, and they made it hard for us to get downstairs. You felt right then that Camp Randall was a very special place and the people were really into their football.

I can remember those Iowa fans being tough, too, those early years. I remember Dan McCarney and I were standing side-by-side and the fans were throwing apples at us. It was probably our second year under Hayden Fry, and we weren't very good, and they were winging those apples. But as we got better, they really got behind us at Kinnick Stadium.

When Pat Richter first talked to me about taking the Wisconsin job, the stadium was part of our discussion. I knew it was big, and I knew people liked football and if you could get things going, you would have a place to accommodate the fans. When I looked at the whole package, and what was offered here, there were a lot of loose ends and fences to mend. As Hayden would say, "We had a lot of snakes to dig up and kill."

That first press conference somebody asked me a question about attendance and building back the fan base. The first thing that came to mind was Nebraska, and I remembered it happening there to the point where everything was sold out. My first thought, then, was something like, "You'd better get (tickets) now because there's going to be a day when you won't be able to get 'em." I was very confident.

Understand, I just had a pretty good run. We had won 24 out of 25 and 23 in a row at Notre Dame, and we should have won back-to-back national championships. I also had gone to eight straight bowls at Iowa, so I thought I had a lot of answers. The one answer that I didn't have — the one I forgot about — was you'd better have some players.

I remember the first game I coached in Camp Randall against a very good team from Cal. I thought we should have won. But we had a split crew, and the Pac-10 officials kept Cal in the game. They called us for motion on the 2-yard-line, wiping out a score. No telling, if we had won the opener, we might have gone on to win a handful of games that season.

In '91, I remember playing Iowa with a lot of young kids, and we had them beat when we got a bad call taking away a touchdown. They called Joe Panos for holding on Bret Bielema (who is now Alvarez's defensive coordinator). That could have been a big win.

In those days, I sent two of my assistants to towns where we had players, and they wound up going around the state. We were just trying to get people to come to our games. They'd set up buses and get entire communities involved, anything to sell tickets.

On campus, I had an assistant coach assigned to every dorm and fraternity and sorority. We were selling football and our program, and trying to get the students back.

Today, when you look around the renovated Camp Randall Stadium and see how far we've come as a program, I'm really proud of what we've been able to accomplish. People who come here for the first time wind up leaving shaking their heads. They're in awe.

Our fans love football, they really do. And it's very gratifying to know that they appreciate what we put out on the field and the effort that our players give and the consistency that we've had in our program. They want to be a part of it.

Selling out this stadium — buying up all the tickets — before the start of the season has been really meaningful to me. I can only speak for 15 years, but this is a very special place and a lot of unique players, coaches and fans have given a little bit of themselves to make it happen, to make it special, to make Camp Randall Stadium what it is today.

On November 3, 1917, Governor Emanuel L. Philipp and University of Wisconsin President Charles Van Hise presided over the dedication ceremonies of the "new" Camp Randall Stadium. Philipp and Van Hise slowly raised American flags at each end of the field while the university band played the "Star Spangled Banner" at halftime of the Minnesota-Wisconsin football game.

The *State Journal* reported, "Adding further to the martial spirit of the occasion, bombs were shot into the air from which burst parachutes suspending flags of the allied nations."

The night before, a campus pep rally drew more than 3,500 students and this disclaimer from Professor Carl Russell: "We are playing fair with the war. The fact that 22 of our football men are already in government service and that others are going is proof of that."

With his back to the fire — a roaring bonfire — Wisconsin football coach J.R. Richards boasted, "There is no science about football. It's only hard work which brings out a team. Dopsters are wrong in not picking Wisconsin as the winner."

(Chris Fowler and Lee Corso were obviously the target of the dopsters reference.)

W.D. Richardson, an alumni member of the athletic board, stirred passions to a far greater degree when he addressed the crowd and promised, "We will bury Minnesota."

Fueled by conviction and confidence, the Badgers pulled off the upset in front of a nearly 12,000. The *State Journal* wrote, "Doc Williams' Gophers, who came here to wipe the earth with Wisconsin, went back home stinging under a 10 to 7 defeat."

A great moment, for sure.

But it didn't make the cut: the Top 25.

Neither did Wisconsin's 22-6 win over Notre Dame, even though the 1928 upset — engineered by Frank "Little Bo" Cuisinier — was achieved at the expense of Irish icon Knute Rockne, who complained afterward that his boys were slowed down by the grass. (Not the kind that would become a campus staple, but the turf, the long grass on the floor of the stadium.)

"Truth to tell," wrote Hank Casserly in the *Capital Times*, "the Notre Dame eleven failed to look like the Fighting Irish of old."

Indeed. That '28 team finished with a subpar 5-4 record, which is noteworthy since Rockne lost only 12 times (105-12-5) during his 13 glorious seasons at Notre Dame. "The Rockne Ramblers failed to ramble," Casserly concluded, "while the battling Badgers ripped, clawed, tore and maimed the fighting Irish...before a throng of 32,000 pop-eyed fans."

That triumph ranked honorable mention, at the very least. Camp Randall moments were evaluated on the basis of individual achievement; team accomplishment; magnitude; atmosphere; or all of the above.

I personally covered 17 of the 25 moments, 15 for the *Capital Times*, and two for the *Daily Cardinal*. As part of the project, I contacted at least two players, coaches and/or observers from each game on the Top 25 list, and solicited their remembrances.

There was one noteworthy technicality. In May, 1992, the Udub administration got clearance to move its 1993 home game against Michigan State to Japan.

Chancellor Donna Shalala wanted to tap into the Far East alumni, and Coach Barry Alvarez felt like the trip could enhance recruiting and the overall image of his program. The Spartans had no objections to the switch; better the Tokyo Dome than Camp Randall.

Wisconsin and Michigan State, thus, became the first Big Ten schools to play in the Coca-Cola Bowl. Each was guaranteed $400,000 and travel expenses.

Harmless fun. A meaningless game. Or so everyone thought.

Who knew the Badgers would be playing for the Rose Bowl?

Hence, the 41-20 victory over the Spartans in Tokyo will officially go down in the books as a Wisconsin home game, and a truly great moment, one of the greatest.

(As the UW players celebrated on the field, I can still see offensive coordinator Brad Childress sandwiched in a bear hug between assistants John Palermo and Jim Hueber. With their arms locked around each other, they danced in small, happy circles.)

That game didn't make the Top 25 list. Nor did another great moment, the pep rally at Camp Randall Stadium following the return trip from Japan.

A noisy crowd of over 10,000 greeted the weary "world" travelers, the Rose Bowl-bound Badgers, as the five team buses — with their lights flashing and the players' noses pressed against the windows — were led onto the field by a police escort.

"Driving in for that pep rally — absolutely — that was my fondest memory," said co-captain Joe Panos, reflecting on the sequence of events, 10-plus years later. "None of us slept that night; people were honking at the buses all the way from Chicago to Madison. It was insane, ridiculous; it was my most memorable moment, my greatest moment."

What's yours?

Let the great debate begin.

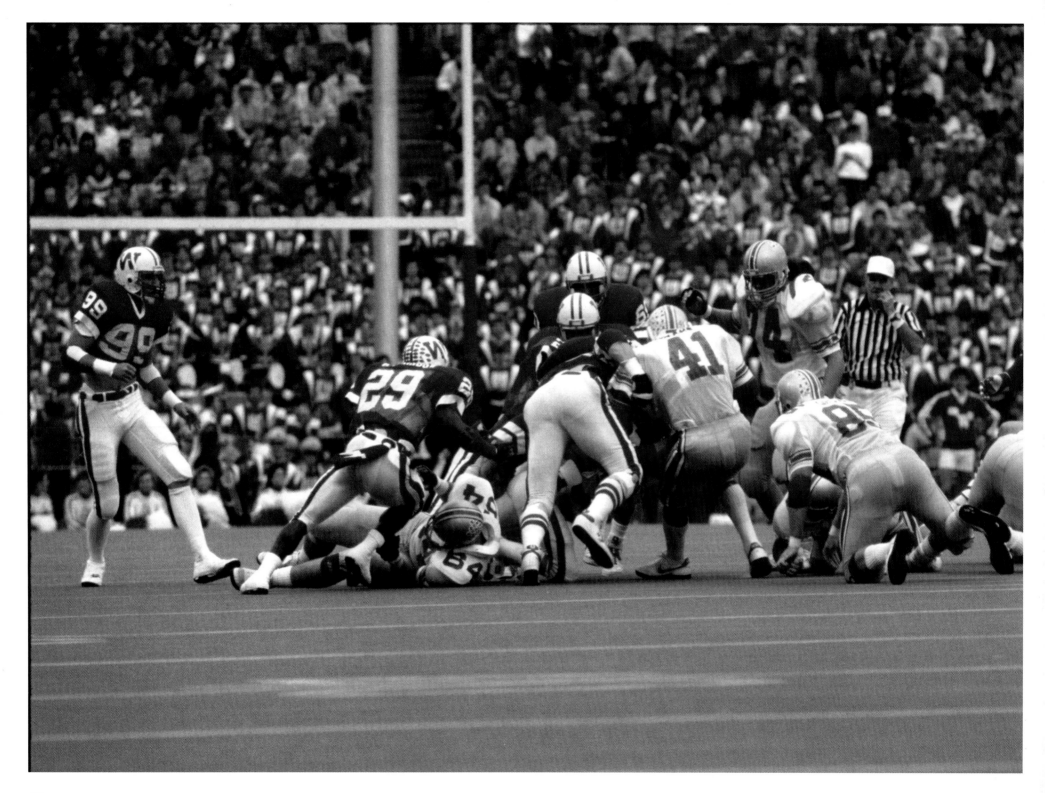

Wisconsin 16 Ohio State 14

October 27, 1984

After a disappointing home loss to Minnesota, the third defeat in four Big Ten games, Wisconsin's superstitious and free-spirited offensive line coach Ron McBride wanted to change the luck of an under-achieving team that was falling woefully short of its own lofty preseason expectations to compete for the conference title.

The raspy-voiced McBride was known for his unbridled passion and unconventional motivational techniques. To this end, McBride began wearing a baseball cap, his "lucky" cap. Mind you, this was not an ordinary "W" cap, but a bright blue Chicago Cubs baseball cap. Not that any such cap on the head of a Cubs player has ever been characterized as a lucky charm in Chicago. Nonetheless, it worked for McBride, who wore the Cubs cap on the Badger sidelines during a 20-16 victory at Indiana that snapped a two-game losing streak.

"My wife had given it to me and the Cubs are kind of my team, and I had a good feeling when it was on," explained McBride, acknowledging that his chapeau had become a curious topic of conversation around the conference. "Some people have asked me, 'What the hell are you doing with a Cubs cap on?' I tell them, 'Hey, it's just a hat.'"

McBride has never made a habit of talking through his. Nor has he ever conformed to one way of thinking or coaching, even when running his own programs at the University of Utah and Weber State. "He was a hybrid, a crossbreed," said UW offensive guard Bob Landsee. "On one hand, he was a throwback to the '60s — mean, tough, pound them into the ground, fight to the end type of coach. On the other hand, he was a '70s guy, West Coast, longer hair, good sense of humor, never let anything get to him."

Opposite page: Linebacker Rick Graf (99) and cornerback Richard Johnson (29) pinch from outside, and linebacker Jim Melka closes the hole on Buckeye tailback Keith Byars (41).

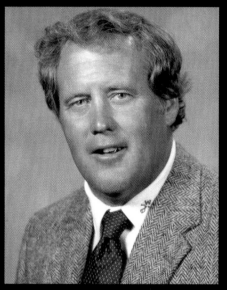

Courtesy of UW Sports Information

Former Wisconsin offensive line coach Ron McBride, a Los Angeles native, is the current head coach at Weber State.

But McBride, the realist, would be the first to admit that luck can carry a football team only so far. While the Badgers were able to slip past the hapless and winless Hoosiers — on the strength of a fake field goal attempt which holder Bob Kobza converted into a touchdown — it was a costly victory for Wisconsin.

Early in the second half, the Badgers ran a "35 Ram" against the Indiana defense. This was an off-tackle play designed for sophomore tailback Larry Emery, the team's leading rusher, who was very adept at cutting back or bouncing the ball outside. On this occasion, the 5-foot-9, 190-pound Emery got caught between two players and took a hit flush on his knee. "My leg went just completely numb," said Emery, a sophomore from Macon, Georgia.

On a gloomy, rainy day in Bloomington, Emery was helped off the field. He later received the game ball from his teammates. He had rushed for 110 yards in the first half before being injured on his fourth carry of the third quarter. Emery's season was over. The following Monday, he had knee surgery to repair a torn anterior cruciate ligament.

This was a cruel blow for the Badgers who now had to get ready for Ohio State without one of their most explosive weapons — Emery had rushed for 185 yards against Michigan and 174 against Northwestern. The injury forced UW coach Dave McClain to juggle his offensive backfield. Marck Harrison, who started the year as a fullback, took over as the No. 1 tailback, while Bobby Taylor moved over from defense to provide some depth at the position.

Just when it seemed like things couldn't get any worse, starting linebacker Michael Reid broke his right thumb on a teammate's helmet during Wednesday's practice and was lost for the remainder of the season. Reid, who had moved into the starting lineup in late September after an injury to Russ Fields, was Wisconsin's

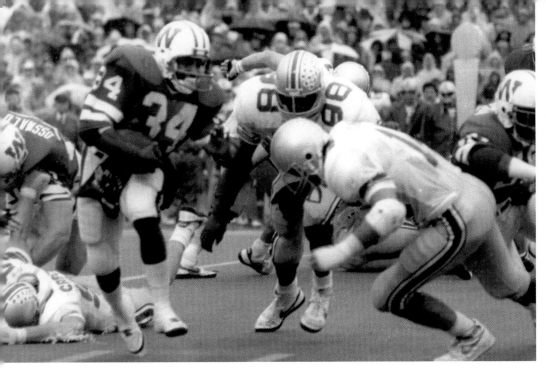

Wisconsin tailback Marck Harrison bursts into the second level of the Ohio State defense and braces for linebacker Pepper Johnson (98) and safety Terry White.

leading tackler.

Craig Raddatz, a sophomore from Cedarburg, replaced Reid on the No. 1 defense, partnering inside with Jim Melka. Charlie Fawley moved up as a backup. When Reid was injured at Illinois in early October, Raddatz got his first career start against Minnesota, boosting his confidence. Still, he was nervous.

Little did anyone know at the time what impact, if any, these two subs — Harrison and Raddatz — would have on the eventual outcome of the Ohio State game. One thing was certain: the Badgers didn't lack confidence against the Buckeyes, due in large part to their recent success in the series—victories in two of their last three meetings, including a rare triumph in Columbus, their first since 1918.

McClain, a former Woody Hayes assistant, had instinctively circled the Ohio State game on the 1984 schedule. McClain also coached under Bo Schembechler at Miami (Ohio). But he was most fond of quoting Hayes, especially when the Badgers were forced to drill in the rain. "If you're going to play in the North Atlantic," he barked, "then you have to practice in the North Atlantic." (Ironically, the school would later build an indoor practice facility on campus and name it after McClain, who died from a heart attack in 1986).

Per his pregame custom, McClain asked one of his assistants to say a few words to the team before the opening kickoff. McBride drew the assignment for Ohio State, and many of the words he used during an emotionally-charged soliloquy matched the color of his blue Cubs cap. (McBride was reknowned for turning off the locker room lights during his presentations — reveling in the yelling and screaming that would pierce the darkness.)

"There were just some things that I had been thinking about," McBride said of his inspirational message. "It had to do with how people were looking at our team, and their attitude toward us. I just found a way to communicate that. I guess you could say that I offered them a challenge. I do things off the wall. I'm an emotional coach. That's the way I am and that's the way I do things. I think about something, and then I express it. It's not something I write down on a piece of paper."

What kind of response was McBride seeking? "You can look into a kid's eyes and you can tell what's inside," he said. "You'll either get a blank look or a real look. When I looked in their eyes before the Ohio State game, I could tell that they were ready to play."

His words hit hard — triggering the desired response.

"That's the first time I've ever seen him (McBride) that emotional," said UW defensive tackle Darryl Sims. "He told us the game would give us an opportunity to show what we really could do." Added Melka, "After he talked to us in the locker room, we just got kind of crazy. You could see it in people's eyes. It was like electricity."

"The difference between the Minnesota (loss) and the Ohio State game was emotion," said UW running back Joe Armentrout. "Against Minnesota, we had none. But Coach McBride's talk fired us up. We knew we were on national TV and had something to prove."

The CBS broadcasting team of Brent Musberger and Ara Parseghian showed up in Madison to call the action between the No. 6 ranked Buckeyes (4-1 in the Big Ten, 6-1 overall) and the Badgers (2-3, 4-3). The network's focal point was Ohio State's powerful tailback Keith Byars, a budding Heisman Trophy candidate. Byars was leading the nation in rushing (1,197 yards and 17 touchdowns) and all-purpose running. Against Illinois, he ran for 274 yards, breaking Archie Griffin's single-game school record. The Badgers were just hoping to slow down or contain Byars, who was averaging 171 rushing yards per game.

Harrison, meanwhile, was an after thought. Not that he didn't have his own story to tell, a darn good one at that. Harrison grew up in Columbus, dreaming of playing for Ohio State. All the Buckeyes had to do was make an offer, and Harrison would have jumped at a chance to play in the fabled Horseshoe. But he never heard from OSU coach Earle Bruce, so the Eastmoor High School product headed to Wisconsin with a bit of a chip on his broad shoulders. As it evolved, the muscular 5-8, 190-pound Harrison had played sparingly for the Badgers. Going into his senior year, he had rushed for 332 yards on 54 carries.

Russ Bellford (37), Tim Jordan (95), Averick Walker (2), Ken Stills (3), and Jim Melka (33) rally to the ball after this Craig Raddatz (53) interception in the third quarter.

Leading up to the Wisconsin game, Bruce was asked about Harrison starting for Emery and whether the Buckeyes considered recruiting him. Bruce jogged his memory and recalled watching some tape of Harrison. Reminded him of Archie's little brother, Bruce said. "We looked at him (Harrison)," Bruce volunteered to the Columbus media, "but we already had three or four running backs that we liked better."

If Bruce's dismissive words weren't motivation enough, Harrison derived even more inspiration from his four-year-old son Marck Jr., who was still dealing with the complications resulting from being born three months premature. Marck Jr. was living with Harrison's grandmother in Columbus and undergoing intensive therapy for an equilibrium problem that had affected his ability to walk. As part of his uniform, Marck Harrison wore a towel dedicated to his son, who attended the Ohio State game in Madison.

"I saw it as the University of Wisconsin Badgers against the Ohio States Buckeyes," Harrison said of the matchup. "That's how I tried to keep it in perspective. I had confidence in myself and my ability to go out and do the job. It was definitely a dream for me."

And a nightmare for Byars and the Buckeyes as the Badgers stormed past Ohio State, 16-14, in front of a rain-drenched crowd of 78,606, which included the ol' curmudgeon himself, Woody Hayes,

who viewed the proceedings from the press box. Hayes spent a lot of time pacing, if not cursing under his breath, whenever Wisconsin's No. 34 broke another tackle. That was the explosive Harrison, who had his number called 31 times. In turn, he responded with 203 rushing yards. His previous high was 60. By contrast, Byars rushed 26 times for 142 yards, his longest run 33 yards. He also had five receptions for 91 yards.

"We all knew that we could do anything we wanted against them," said Wisconsin offensive tackle Jeff Dellenbach after the Badgers generated 461 yards of total offense to Ohio State's 320. "At the end of the first quarter, it seemed like they were afraid to come up to the line against us. They were just standing there with long faces. You would think they would be fired up and flying high. We were, and they weren't."

The Badgers controlled the line of scrimmage, with Dellenbach and Kevin Belcher at the tackles, Landsee and Dave Mielke at the guards and Dan Turk at center. Tight end Bret Pearson and fullback Joe Armentrout also created running seams for Harrison, who was able to square his shoulders and explode upfield. By using new formations, quarterback draws, flat passes and toss sweeps, the Badgers took away some of Ohio State's aggressiveness, particularly in the inexperienced OSU secondary. The game plan was to attack the

Wide receiver Al Toon throws a key block on Ohio State's William White (37), clearing a path on the sidelines for Thad McFadden (20) who scores Wisconsin's first touchdown on a 34-yard pass from Mike Howard in the second quarter.

Fullback Joe Armentrout (23) breaks through Dave Crecelius' arm tackle and lowers his shoulder on Ohio State linebacker Mark Pfister.

Buckeyes' middle linebacker Pepper Johnson, according to Harrison.

"If he (Johnson) comes in there at 100 mph, and if I'm running at 100 mph," Harrison said of his pregame strategy, "and I put my face on his chest I can intimidate him. That sounds ironic, doesn't it? Marck Harrison intimidating 240-pound Pepper Johnson. But I felt if I could stop his penetration on blitzes, I could rob him of some of his confidence."

Wisconsin's defense attacked the Ohio State offense and Byars in the same aggressive manner. (In retrospect, the Buckeyes had trouble absorbing the loss of starting center Kirk Lowdermilk, who broke his leg on the third play of the game.)

"Everybody thought they were the great American team," said UW outside linebacker Tim Jordan. "But we were stopping them early in the game and our confidence was building. I watched Byars on film against Purdue and he knocked out an inside linebacker. But I knew that he was human. He's not Superman. He doesn't wear a big "S" on his chest."

Neither did either quarterback. Wisconsin's Mike Howard completed 17 of 29 passes for 158 yards and one touchdown (34 yards to Thad McFadden). But he was intercepted three times. Ohio State's Mike Tomczak was even less effective, completing just 8 of 21 for 106 yards. Tomczak was also guilty of three picks — one by Melka and two by Raddatz, who finished with a game-high 11 tackles, eight solos.

Raddatz and Melka saved their best (hits) for last. Ohio State's final possession started from its own 20 with 69 seconds left. Three incompletions left the Buckeyes with a fourth-and-10. A desperate Tomczak couldn't find anyone open downfield and checked to Byars

who caught the pass between the hash marks and was immediately tackled — by Raddatz and Melka — one yard short of the first down. End of drive. End of game.

"We just came up and hit him as hard we could," said the 230-pound Raddatz. "Byars was a load for two guys our size. I hit him in the waist and slipped down to his ankles. He started lunging, but Melka hit him and drove him back."

Truth is, the Badgers were lucky to hold on to the lead against Ohio State, given a rash of costly penalties (8 for 99 yards) and blown scoring opportunities (they were inside the 35 nine times and got only four scores). That's why Todd Gregoire's three field goals — from 27, 34 and 35 yards — were crucial to the win. Gregoire and snapper Bill Schick performed admirably under adverse weather conditions.

"I knew I was going to be a part of the game and outcome," Gregoire said. "If I was in high school on a day like this kicking on grass, I would have slipped a couple of times. I wouldn't have had my footing. But the turf in Camp Randall is sticky in the rain."

McClain got a ride on the shoulders of jubilant players after the game, and two backups, Harrison and Raddatz, got plenty of notoriety for their clutch efforts. Harrison was named the Midwest Offensive Player of the Week by the Associated Press and United Press International. Raddatz was honored by the AP and UPI, along with being selected as the national Defensive Player of the Week by *Sports Illustrated.*

"You don't make a career on one game," cautioned Raddatz, who was a physical wreck. On his second interception, he took a helmet on his thigh, just above the knee and below his thigh pad. That hurt

But it was not as painful as his drive to Milwaukee that Saturday night. Raddatz felt like he had swallowed Byars whole.

"I'm not sure on what play it happened," Raddatz related, "but I probably had my voice box closed on a tackle and there was no where for the air to go, so it blew a couple of sacs in my lungs. My throat had really enlarged, and even though we had played all day in the rain, I didn't think it was a cold. That night, I had dinner with my mom and had plans to go out later. Didn't make it. By midnight, I had to go to the hospital because I could hardly breathe. I had an odd feeling in my throat - it was like snap, crackle, and pop. There was a lot of constriction. That's why I had so much trouble breathing at first."

As a precaution, Raddatz returned to Madison in an ambulance Sunday night. But he was back practicing the following week in preparation for Iowa. And, despite playing with that deep thigh bruise, Raddatz had one of four interceptions off Hawkeyes quarterback Chuck Long in a 10-10 tie at Kinnick Stadium memorable for the hitting and intensity on both sides. On successive fourth quarter plays, Ronnie Harmon broke his leg in two places and Long was knocked unconscious in addition to injuring his knee.

Adding insult to those injuries was the fact that Wisconsin took a 10-0 lead on its first two possessions and failed to capitalize on the momentum because of some conservative play-calling. McClain, after all, was a Hayes disciple, and he sat on the lead. As a result, the tie felt like a loss to many Badgers players who had to settle for a consolation prize: a postseason appearance against Kentucky in the Hall of Fame Bowl, which fell well short of their stated preseason goals and the Rose Bowl.

"We never accomplished what we should have accomplished as a team," Landsee lamented. "We never fulfilled our own expectations."

Few Wisconsin teams have fielded so much raw talent. Sims, receiver Al Toon (who became the school's all-time leading receiver in the Ohio State game), and defensive back Richard Johnson were all taken in the first round of the 1985 National Football League draft. Turk, Dellenbach, Belcher, Pearson, Melka, Scott Bergold, Gary Ellerson (who had been ineligible), and Ken Stills were also drafted.

In the end, the Badgers couldn't overcome their own mistakes and slow start — they lost five fumbles during a 20-14 loss at Michigan in the Big Ten opener — but they gave everyone something to remember from their rain-swept 16-14 victory over Ohio State.

"This meant more to me personally than any other game of the season," said Harrison who, along with Raddatz, received a game ball. Harrison didn't keep his. Instead, he had each of his offensive linemen autograph the ball, and then Harrison presented it to the assistant coach that he felt was most responsible for getting the team ready for the Buckeyes.

The coach?
Ron McBride.

Top: Snubbed by his hometown Buckeyes, Marck Harrison, a dynamic 5-foot-8 senior tailback, gets his revenge by outdueling Keith Byars and rushing for 203 yards.

Bottom: Ohio State's Keith Byars has nowhere to run as nose tackle Michael Boykins (63) and inside linebacker Jim Melka help shut down the running game.

"Mickey" McGuire
Right Halfback

Wisconsin 20 Minnesota 13
November 12, 1932

In 1932, people were listening to Cab Calloway's "I've Got the World on a String", Rudy Valle's "Brother, Can You Spare a Dime?", Fred Astaire's "Night and Day" and Bing Crosby's "Please".

In 1932, movie goers were watching the original *Scarface*, produced by the eccentric Howard Hughes and starring Paul Muni; *A Farewell to Arms*, based on the Hemingway novel and featuring Helen Hayes and Gary Cooper; and *Grand Hotel* which won the Oscar.

In 1932, Al Capone went to prison for income tax evasion; Amelia Earhart was the first woman to fly solo across the Atlantic; Jack Benny debuted on radio; the Winter Olympics were held in Lake Placid, NY, and the Summer Olympics in Los Angeles.

In 1932, Iraq gained full independence from Britain; the New York Yankees swept the Chicago Cubs in the World Series; and Wallace Beery (*The Champ*) and Fredric March (*Dr. Jekyll and Mr. Hyde*) shared the Academy Award for best actor.

In 1932, Charles Lindbergh's 19-month-old son was kidnapped and later found dead; Jack Sharkey outfought Max Schmeling for the heavyweight boxing crown; and the Chicago Bears edged the Portsmouth (Ohio) Spartans, 9-0, in the first NFL playoff game.

In 1932, Elizabeth Taylor, Teddy Kennedy, Halston, Chuck Noll, Jayne Mansfield and Donald Rumsfeld were born; the "Mickey Mouse" comic strip was syndicated; and West Liberty State's Joe Kershalla scored 71 points in a college football game.

Courtesy University of Wisconsin-Madison Archives

Opposite page: Walter Francis "Mickey, Himself" McGuire, the team MVP, gave Badger fans something to cheer about in the midst of the Great Depression.

Courtesy UW Sports Information

Clarence Wiley "Doc" Spears replaced Glenn Thistlethwaite on the UW sidelines and posted a 6-1-1 record during the 1932 season.

On November 8, 1932, Franklin Delano Roosevelt and his running mate John W. Garner won a landslide victory over the incumbent, President Herbert Hoover.

On November 12, 1932, Walter Francis "Mickey, Himself" McGuire scored all three touchdowns in Wisconsin's 20-13 win over Minnesota in what the *Capital Times* labeled a "game that will go down in history as one of the greatest played on any gridiron." Happy days were here again. Take the word (oftimes incoherent word) of the *State Journal's* legendary sports columnist Joseph "Roundy" Coughlin.

"The ending of the game was like Armistice Day as far as excitement," Roundy proclaimed, "when hats sailed into the air off men and women. As McGuire scored that last touchdown everybody seemed to rush back of the goal post as if they were going to open up that first keg of that democrat beer. Many a wife who ain't kissed hubby in a long while hung one of them old time kisses right on his lips when Wisconsin-scored . . . ."

That was the backdrop to McGuire's greatest moment at Camp Randall Stadium. What more could be fairer? "There have been performances and performances at Randall field," the *Capital Times* suggested, " but none in history excel the deeds of . . . ."

Mickey, Himself.

Both Madison newspapers, the *Capital Times* and the *State Journal*, got in the routine of referencing the indefatigable McGuire as "Mickey (Himself)" — a spinoff on a character from a Fontaine Fox comic strip "Toonerville Folks" which was also known as "Toonerville Trolley." Mickey (Himself) McGuire was the town bully in the fictional Toonerville. Or the antithesis of Mickey (Himself) at Wisconsin.

Mickey McGuire returns to Madison and celebrates a Homecoming win with UW band director Ray Dvorak, who was credited with getting the students to punctuate the singing of "Varsity" by waving their arms, giving birth to a Wisconsin tradition.

Courtesy UW Sports Information

The strip, which ran from 1908 to 1955, was the source of over 40 silent film shorts which starred a young actor whose given name was Joe Yule, Jr. For a while, the actor adopted the Mickey McGuire name for himself. In 1932, he got it legally changed to Mickey Rooney.

"I was only eight years old when McGuire had that big game against Minnesota, but I remember reading about it," observed Tom Butler, who would become a fixture on the Madison scene for 34 years as a sportswriter and columnist for the *State Journal* (1953-1987). Butler was raised on the east-side. "And as kids," he said, "we used to play sandlot football and all of us wanted to be little Mickey McGuires."

Whereas it might have been more fashionable in other parts of the country to grow up emulating gridiron heroes like Red Grange, Bronko Nagurski or Ernie Nevers, according to Butler, this was clearly the Mickey McGuire era in Badger football. And his three-touchdown performance against arch-rival Minnesota was definitely the capper.

"The Gophers used to beat Wisconsin just about every year when I was growing up," said Butler, referring to a seven game winless streak from 1923 to 1929. "And everybody reflected back on McGuire's great day when the Badgers beat Minnesota at Camp Randall because they didn't beat them again until 1942 (a nine-game losing streak)."

McGuire didn't waste any time establishing the tempo in that 1932 game against the Gophers as the fleet UW halfback returned the opening kickoff 88 yards for a touchdown.

"He caught the ball in the far right corner of the field as the Badger linemen came back to form a flying wedge," wrote *Capital Times* sports editor Hank Casserly. "Behind the wedge he sprinted to the center of the field, sped through the opening of the spearhead and reversed the field to the right. His twinkling feet barely touched the ground as he outdistanced his pursuers and crossed the goal line. The throng in the stands was amazed, only to break forth in a wild roar of acclaim as they realized what had happened."

The game was interrupted briefly during the first quarter when a rabbit strayed on the playing field. The players chased him away, and the rabbit circled the horseshoe of the stadium before reappearing on the field. The *Capital Times* also reported, "A rat, without the rabbit's ambition, tried to see the game from sections E and F. To a chorus of shrieks from the ladies present, he was driven out of sight by Sangree Watrous of Kansas." Eat your heart out, Woodward and Bernstein. Now, that's investigative reporting.

Because of McGuire's speed — he ran like a jackrabbit, after all — Casserly couldn't resist this bit of prose, "A dark gray rabbit gained more yardage than any of the players, racing up and down the field early in the first quarter, but it's a good thing that 'Mickey-Himself McGuire had his mind on the game, else he would have run Br'er Rabbit into the ground."

McGuire's running ability was no laughing matter. On the final play of the 1932 season opener, he made a game-saving tackle on Marquette receiver Richard Quirk, preserving a 7-2 victory over the Hilltoppers at Camp Randall Stadium.

"With only a second or two of play remaining," wrote *State Journal* sports editor Henry J. McCormick, "Gene Ronzani, Marquette's dashing Grenadier, dropped back and threw a long pass to Richard Quirk, substitute halfback; Quirk gathered the ball into his arms on Wisconsin's 45-yard line, managed to hold his feet when 'Buckets' Goldberg made a sorry attempt at tackling him and sprinted down to the five yard line before he was hauled down by McGuire, who caught him from behind. The game was over when McGuire hauled Quirk to earth and the spectators swarmed out onto the field in their excitement, slapping players on the backs indiscriminately."

As a high school athlete in Honolulu, Hawaii, where he was born and raised, McGuire ran track. And that would be his ticket to Wisconsin. "He came here as a trackman," Butler recalled. "Wisconsin track coach Tom Jones saw McGuire with his half-mile relay team in the Penn Relays. And I know he was awfully fast for that era."

Because of his Irish ancestry and Hawaiian upbringing, McGuire made great copy for the local scribes, who wrote about how McGuire saved $300 from a summer job in a pineapple cannery and used the money to book passage on a steamer to San Francisco. From there, he took a train to Madison, where he became a household name — Mickey (Himself) — at least in the Butler household on Lakeland Avenue.

"Mickey had a lot of charisma and he was a big hero to the kids," remembered Butler, who, as a kid, used to pay 25-cents on Knothole Day to watch the Badgers play in Camp Randall. "Mickey loved Wisconsin and he would try to come back as often as possible. He was big buddies with Moon Molinaro and Moose Tobias. They owned a bar on State Street — Tobey's and Moon — and Mickey would work the cash register when he came back and give half the profits away to his old buddies from the university."

McGuire was not the only Hawaiian-bred player in college football during the early '30s. He shared that distinction with Navy halfback Cordon Chung Hoon. An Associated Press story noted, "From the land of dusky, shimmy-shaking maidens do these two football players hail. Both are from Hawaii, where football is taught and played in bare feet."

The Gophers surely had no answer for McGuire's quick feet. Besides returning the opening kick for a score, McGuire accounted for another first quarter touchdown on an 18-yard pass from quarterback Joe Linfor. Not that he was completely a one-man gang.

The *Capital Times* singled out Clair Strain, who replaced the injured Hal Smith at fullback, along with Linfor, Molinaro, Bill Koenig, Greg Kabat, John Schneller, Nello Pacetti, and Marvin Peterson. But it was Mickey (Himself) who stole the show.

"Came the closing moments of the game with the score tied at 13-all," Casserly wrote, "who but McGuire came to the rescue, this time taking a pass from Linfor for 15 yards and battling his way across for the winning touchdown with nine seconds left to play."

Another dispatch had McGuire taking the ball away from a Minnesota defender on a decisive play and fighting "his way the remaining three yards for a touchdown with Gophers hanging onto his legs and riding his back."

That made a loser out of the Gophers whose starting left guard, Milt Bruhn, would later return to Madison as Wisconsin's coach and lead the Badgers to a Rose Bowl. The '32 Gophers had another Cheesehead connection: All-American halfback Francis "Pug" Lund, who played the final month of the season with a fractured rib.

"Crippled by a bad knee from which water was removed at 11 o'clock Saturday morning," the *Capital Times* reported, "the Rice Lake, Wisconsin Boy (Lund) did most of Minnesota's ball carrying, all the punting and passing, and he took enough punishment to ruin several star players. Lund is a great gridder and he has a lion heart. He might have come to Wisconsin and played on a winning eleven."

Such was the competitiveness of the Wisconsin-Minnesota rivalry, even in the fishwraps. The locals ripped Gopher coach Bernie Bierman after he was critical of the officiating, especially on UW's game-winning final possession. Editorialized one writer, "Minnesota cried before the game, during the game and after the game, and the 'Wailing Wall of China" would fit in well as a shrine for the disappointed Minnesota coaches, players and fans." That was followed by this jab, "Minnesota cried for interference on passes all during the game and then when the same penalty was invoked against them, they wept copious tears."

Wisconsin coach Dr. Clarence Wiley (Doc) Spears was unwilling to get into a verbal joust with Bierman. Mickey (Himself) stayed clear of controversy, too. Not that there weren't some issues sandwiched around the game itself. For example, the *Capital Times* reported, "In

Courtesy University of Minnesota Sports Information   Courtesy University of Minnesota Sports Information

Left: Minnesota's coach Bernie Bierman,— a Hall of Famer nicknamed "The Silver Fox" and "The Grey Eagle"— ripped the officials after the Wisconsin loss. Bierman won five national championships and seven Big Ten titles during his 16 seasons with the Gophers.

Right: The One That Got Away— Rice Lake's Francis "Pug" Lund— had water drained from his knee hours before kickoff but still carried the Minnesota attack against Wisconsin. "Our opponents might break him in two, but they couldn't stop him," Gopher coach Bernie Bierman said of Lund.

a surprise, pre-football game raid Friday afternoon and night, local federal prohibition agents swooped down on nine well-known student speakeasies, arresting 14 persons, and seizing quantities of beer, whiskey and alcohol. Stocked up with spirits for the football crowds today, the proprietors were totally unprepared for the dry squad."

After the game, UW's business manager George W. Levis announced that football receipts had fallen $40,000 below estimates on which the year's athletic budget was based. Thus, there was little or no chance of reviving some minor sports. Hockey, wrestling, swimming, water polo, gymnastics, crew and golf were eliminated in May.

Hence, by single-handedly dominating Minnesota, Mickey (Himself) lifted spirits.

"McGuire's offensive play was worthy of All-American consideration," the *Capital Times* concluded, "but while his ball carrying and receiving of passes, plus his passing, was sensational and caught the eye, his defensive play was equally brilliant although probably not so recognized by those present.

"McGuire has played excellent football all season, but he rose to new heights in the defeat of the ponderous Gophers. It was his final home appearance in a Badger uniform and he painted a picture that will live long in the memory of the 30,000 fans present."

Wisconsin 29 Penn State 16

October 3, 1970

His jaw was taut, his scowl was menacing, his resolve was being tested and John Jardine was only midway through his first game as Wisconsin's head coach. Like his players, the 34-year-old Jardine was feeling the heat — the stifling heat in the cramped visitors' locker room at Owen Field, shielded from whatever wind comes sweepin' down the plain.

The Badgers had just taken a shocking 7-0 halftime lead over heavily-favored Oklahoma, and while Jardine was trying to figure out a way to hold on to the momentum, a stunned crowd of 58,100 sat in silence, knowing it could have been worse had a UW running back not lost a fumble inside the Sooners' 10-yard line just before the end of the half.

So much for moral victories.

The Badgers wilted in the second half, falling prey to Oklahoma's depth and the oppressive 84-degree heat and 90-percent humidity that radiated off the Tartan Turf griddle. The Sooners scored twice in the third quarter to take control of the game while limiting Wisconsin to just one first down over the final 30 minutes.

Despite the meltdown, Jardine, a product of the hard core Chicago Catholic League, was proud of his defense. And rightly so. Sparked by the inspired play of linebacker Chuck Winfrey and end Bill Gregory, the Badgers hounded Oklahoma quarterback Jack Mildren and picked off five passes, two by Neovia Greyer.

The Wisconsin offense was far less effective, especially without fullback Alan (A-Train) Thompson who was sidelined with a leg injury. How much was Thompson missed? A year earlier,

Courtesy of UW Sports Information

Top: Head Coach John Jardine
Bottom: Alan (A-Train) Thompson

Courtesy of UW Sports Information

Courtesy of UW Sports Information

Opposite page: Wisconsin's Neil Graff was not only a passing threat (3,699 career yards), also rushed for the second most yards (580) on the team during the 1970 season. His net total was only 248 because of 332 yards in losses, mostly the result of sacks.

he rushed 33 times for 220-yards in a 48-21 loss to the Sooners in Madison, outdueling Steve Owens, who had 189 yards on 40 carries. (Owens won the 1969 Heisman.)

Jardine regained Thompson's services the following week for the home opener against Texas Christian, and 61,539 showed up at Camp Randall Stadium to see how much progress the Badgers had made from the Dark Ages (three wins the previous three years).

The turnout was the largest since 1967, and the largest opening day audience in school history, underlining renewed faith in the program and the people in charge.

There was the no-nonsense approach of Jardine, the former Purdue nose guard and Tommy Prothro assistant at UCLA. And there was the non-stop hustle of athletic director Elroy (Crazy Legs) Hirsch, who had stumped all regions of the state, winning back the confidence of long-suffering Wisconsin fans.

Alas, they suffered some more against TCU. The Badgers fumbled away the opening kickoff and the Horned Frogs led 7-0 before many had closed the trunks on their tailgating. In the end, Wisconsin would have to settle for a 14-14 tie.

The best player on the field was TCU's Ray Rhodes, who split time between flanker and running back, while also returning punts and kickoffs, one for 62 yards. (This was the same Ray Rhodes who coached the Packers to an 8-8 record in 1999.)

The most electrifying play of the game was produced by a couple of roommates — an odd couple, at that — Wisconsin quarterback Neil Graff, a soft-spoken junior from Sioux Falls, South Dakota, and tight end Larry Mialik, a gregarious junior from Clifton, New Jersey. Graff hooked up with Mialik, a converted fullback, on a 50-yard

Larry Mialik had the ability to stretch a defense, and his 21.3 yards per reception average still ranks No. 1 in the Wisconsin record book.

Anyone seen the Penn State defensive backs? Tight end Larry Mialik, a converted fullback, scores on one of his two touchdown passes from quarterback Neil Graff.

touchdown pass. Mialik's burst off the line caught the TCU secondary napping.

"You get off the ball as if you were running the 100-yard dash," said the 6-foot-2, 220-pound Mialik, who ran sprints as a prep. "And if the quarterback throws the ball as well as Neil did — laying it up there like that — you just go and get it."

Decades later, Mialik admitted that the scoring catch had been a turning point in his career (which spanned six years in the NFL). "A light went on for me," he said. "It was like, 'Hmmm, I guess I can run faster than I thought I could.' And I think (the UW's offensive coordinator) Paul Roach said, 'Hmmm, I think he can run faster than I think he can, too.'"

With his confidence bolstered, Mialik was looking forward to Wisconsin's final 1970 non-conference tune-up, a home date with Penn State and JoePa. Following a 16-year apprenticeship as an assistant, Joe Paterno had fashioned a 36-8-1 record during his first four-plus seasons as the head coach in State College.

"I was always really aware of Penn State when I was growing up," said Mialik who caused double-takes in Madison with his Joe Namath-like facial features. "Being an East Coast guy in those days,

if you didn't go to Penn State, you went to Syracuse. And if you didn't go to either, you went away to school."

Jardine was convinced that the Badgers were catching the Nittany Lions at the worst possible time — coming off an embarrassing 41-13 trouncing at Colorado, which ended Penn State's 23-game winning streak and 31 game unbeaten streak.

"It was the worst thing that could have happened to us — I wanted them to come in here unbeaten," said Jardine in his trademark whiskey baritone voice. "Before that loss there might have been a chance to sneak up on them. We won't be able to sneak up on them now. I guess it all depends on how they feel about that (Colorado) loss. That might just stoke 'em up to run the ball right down somebody's throat."

Wisconsin's senior captain, the hulking 6-6 Bill Gregory, welcomed the challenge. "We've got a good chance to knock off Penn State," he predicted in the *State Journal*. "When we play each other, they're just another team. They've got the same number of players on the field at the same time and they put their pants on the same way we do."

Penn State's pants just didn't have any adornments. Nor did its helmets. And because of graduation losses, these vanilla-uniformed Nittany Lions didn't look like any of the Paterno teams that strung together that long unbeaten streak. Coming to Madison, the avuncular Paterno confided, "I think we're going to be ready to play, but beyond that I don't know."

Both teams confronted an unexpected challenge the morning of the game: the unsettling news that a chartered airplane, carrying half of the Wichita State University football team, had crashed and burned the day before in the Colorado Rockies. A second plane, carrying the rest of the team, landed safely an hour after the crash.

The worst disaster in American sports history had claimed the lives of 29 people, including 13 players, the team's head coach and wife, and the school's athletic director and wife. Wichita State was en route to its game at Utah State when the plane went down.

Datelined Silver Plume, Colorado, the UPI story on the front page of the *State Journal* detailed the tragedy. "Battered black and gold football helmets littered the wreckage site. There were smoldering shirts and ties, shoulder pads, a pair of shoes with No. 63 written inside, and a charred book of Wichita State football plays."

In a lower corner of the front page was a box alerting local readers to the football game at Camp Randall Stadium: "Badgers, Lions tangle today, kickoff 1 p.m."

If you didn't have a ticket for the game — and only 55,204 were sold — you had to listen to the play-by-play on radio because the intersectional match-up wasn't televised. Wisconsin had won the only previous meeting between the schools, 20-0, in 1953. And they made it 2-0 over the Nittany Lions by pulling off the upset, 29-16.

On paper, it was a mismatch.

Behind the tandem of tailback Lydell Mitchell and fullback Franco Harris, Penn State dominated the statistics: 23 first downs to 12 (14 rushing to 4) and 392 total yards to 215. But the Badgers still managed to knock off the No. 17-ranked Nittany Lions behind an opportunistic defense which forced six turnovers (four picks) and three big plays on offense.

Despite getting sacked a Big Ten record 14 times (minus-99 yards), Graff completed touchdown passes of 68 and 52 yards to Mialik and 26 yards to Terry Whittaker. "I was either getting sacked or throwing touchdowns passes," Graff acknowledged. "Afterward in the locker room my back and ribs were so sore. The next day I could hardly get out of bed."

Jardine chuckled and said, "I'm glad he got out alive. We ought to award him the Purple Heart." Instead, the Associated Press honored Graff as the Midwest Back of the Week.

"One of the things he did real well was to stand in there as someone was coming in on his face," Jardine went on. "With that 5-3-3 defensive alignment they could bring a lot of people, and we didn't expect them to rush their linebackers as much as they did."

Jardine snickered, again. "Paul Roach played a heck of a game," he said of his chain-smoking offensive coordinator. "He called 'em and Mialik caught 'em."

Roach was a character and a brilliant offensive strategist. "When I was in the NFL, I played one season in San Diego and Bill Walsh was on that staff," Mialik said. "Roach was a Walsh-type guy. Maybe it was out of necessity at the time because we didn't have as many weapons. But he was a guy who looked for opportunities against specific opponents.

"Our playbook wasn't that thick when the season got started, but plays were added each week, specials, and that's how Walsh was working in those days when he had Dan Fouts and Charlie Joiner with the Chargers."

It helped that Graff and Mialik were on the same wave length, the same page. "Neil came out and spent time with me that summer and all we did was play catch," Mialik remembered. "At that stage of the game, he was figuring I might be his go-to guy."

Graff got the most out of his eight completions — 8 of 14 for 220 yards — against Penn State's defense, anchored by All-American linebacker Jack Ham. With the Nittany Lions committing so many players to the pass rush, there were some windows in the three-deep secondary for Mialik, especially when Penn State doubled Al Hannah.

"Both of my touchdown catches were on crossing patterns, kind of like dig patterns, they turned into almost skinny posts," Mialik said. "In reading the coverage, I got inside the free safety and turned the routes into posts. When I was setting it up, Neil always seemed to know the way I was going because we had spent so much time together."

With the game tied 16-all in the fourth quarter, the Badgers faced a third-and-goal from the Penn State 27 after a couple of minus-yardage plays and a penalty. With the defense shaded to Mialik, the heady Graff found Whittaker for the go-ahead score.

Whittaker finished with six receptions, Mialik had three. (UW backup quarterback Tim Healy completed the only pass that he attempted in a cameo appearance.)

"We just made too many mistakes," grumbled Paterno after losing

Neil Graff had full command of the huddle: tackle Elbert Walker (71), guard Dennis Stephenson (60), center Jim Fedenia (51), guard Keith Nosbusch (61), tight end Larry Mialik (88), fullback Alan "A-Train" Thompson (37), and wide receiver Terry Whittaker (82).

back-to-back games for the first time since 1966, his rookie season as head coach. He sighed and ended his press conference by rationalizing, "At least the world hasn't come to an end."

After a 2-3 start, Paterno installed sophomore John Hufnagel as his No. 1 quarterback and Hufnagel guided the Nittany Lions to five straight wins and a 7-3 record.

Years later, Paterno reflected on his 1970 Madison trip and told the *State Journal*, "When we went out to Wisconsin, and me being a young coach, I had the kids so fired up with so much blood in their eyes they couldn't see anything. Wisconsin was all over us, around us, and by us, the whole bit. They gave us a real good licking."

Mialik had one keepsake from that game — the memory of going up to Paterno and shaking his hand. "And I remember JoePa saying to me, 'You're suppose to be a fullback,'" Mialik related. "That was all he said."

Jardine had plenty to talk about after his first victory as Wisconsin's head coach. He lauded the stellar defensive play of Winfrey, Gregory, Jim DeLisle, Bob Storck and the ball-hawking of Greyer, Danny Crooks, Gary Buss, and Ron Buss.

UW offensive coordinator Paul Roach went on to become one of the greatest head coaches and athletic directors in University of Wyoming history.

And then Jardine broke into a wry Irish grin, perhaps remembering being carried off the field on the shoulders of exuberant fans — many of whom would stop traffic on University Ave. as the happy processional followed the marching band through campus. The celebration continued into the early morning hours.

"I think now we have shown 'em that we are a football team," Jardine said. "People better take notice that Wisconsin is here. I'm not saying we're a contender yet. But we've come a long way and I think we can go farther."

More than a half century later, and Kenton Peters still has a bitter-sweet recollection of the 1952 regular season finale against Minnesota. Bitter might be too strong of a word. Disappointed would be a more accurate description for how the Badgers felt after a 21-21 tie with the Gophers prevented them from winning an outright Big Ten championship. "There was a real low after the game," recalled Peters, a starting end.

But as depressed as the UW players may have felt at the time, nothing could match the euphoria that followed on Monday when the conference athletic directors voted to send Wisconsin, not Purdue, to the Rose Bowl — marking the Badgers' first bowl trip. "State Street was just wild that whole night," remembered Peters, a prominent Madison architect.

In retrospect, then, a tie was like kissing Leah Feland, who may or may not have been somebody's sister. But she was the Rose Queen and presided over the 1953 game in Pasadena. Although the Badgers lost 7-0 to Southern California — despite outrushing the Trojans, 211-48 — just getting to Pasadena was one of the great moments in school history.

And it wouldn't have been possible without gaining at least a draw with the Gophers, which not only earned the Badgers a slice of the Big Ten championship — ending a 40-year title drought — but the 21-21 tie dropped the Rose Bowl selection into the laps of the athletic directors, who gave Wisconsin the nod over Purdue by a 7-3 vote.

Sweet.

"Monday was magnificent," said Peters, relishing the memory. "The announcement was at noon and when they let classes out, the students poured in front of the union."

As news leaked out, parading revelers brought traffic to a standstill

Opposite page: When healthy, Harland Carl, a 5-11, 185-pound speedster from tiny Greenwood, was one of the most exciting and explosive running backs in the Big Ten. During an injury-plagued career, he scored once every 10 times that he carried or caught the football.

on State Street. The *State Journal* reported that many stopped in flower shops and staged a "run on the roses." Most of the long-stemmed roses were purchased, some were given away. Upon reaching the steps of the state capitol, the group chanted, "We want Kohler, we want Kohler."

Gov. Walter Kohler summarily left a budget meeting and greeted the students from a first floor balcony with a "V" for Victory salute. "We all have great reason to be proud," Kohler told the gathering. "I want to say that I think the election of this team to go to the Rose Bowl is richly deserved by a Badger team that fought hard and fought cleanly, and won."

Or tied — 21-21 — which turned out to be just as rewarding for Wisconsin. Whereas sports teams have forever adopted the "Winning Ugly" phrase, the Badgers and Gophers came up with their own unique definition for "Tying Ugly" by combining for 14 turnovers.

Not that a tie wasn't compelling drama.

"This will go down as one of the great spectator games of all time," wrote Lloyd Larson in the *Milwaukee Sentinel*. "Certainly the greatest for sustained suspense and entertainment dollar value ever staged at historic old Camp Randall.

"From the moment Harland Carl lugged the opening kickoff back to his 32 yard line and Alan (The Horse) Ameche got the Badgers rolling against the wind for 16 yards — until Burt Hable intercepted Paul Giel's pass to snuff out Minnesota's final threat on the last play of the game — this climax and battle had the 52,131 eye witnesses gasping for breath."

So did that long-winded paragraph. But he made his point. And so did Charles Johnson upon offering the Gophers' perspective in the *Minneapolis Star-Tribune*.

"One of the most sensational football games of all time was played here Saturday afternoon," Johnson wrote. "Seldom in the history of

Kenton Peters was never afraid to mix it up along the line of scrimmage for the Badgers, an aggressive and confident mind-set that he would carry into a controversial and successful career as a Madison architect.

Wisconsin safety Burt Hable, a 6-foot-3, 172-pound senior from Bloomer, intercepted Paul Giel twice in the frenetic closing seconds, including this desperation heave to the end zone on the final play. Hable picked off three passes in the game and wound up as the leading interceptor in the Big Ten during the 1952 season.

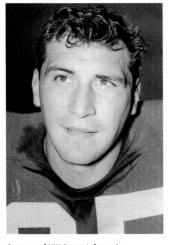

Alan Ameche rushed for 125 yards against the Gophers.

this grand old college sport have two ancient rivals put on a gridiron drama that equaled this remarkable exhibition of fight, courage, spectacular plays and heart throbs."

Not to mention turnovers. *State Journal* sports editor Henry J. McCormick observed that the sell-out crowd "witnessed as wild a finish as any football game ever has produced on that historic field. The ball changed hands four times in the last 65 seconds as each team strove desperately to break the deadlock, and there wasn't a spectator who wasn't on his feet in those dramatic final seconds."

Here's how it played out.

Minnesota had a first down on the UW 41 with 94 seconds left. After two incompletions, Paul Giel's pass was intercepted by Hable.

Wisconsin had a first down on its own 26. A Jim Haluska pass completion to Carl moved the ball to the Gopher 47. Haluska then completed a 5-yard pass to Jerry Witt. But his next throw was intercepted by Geno Cappelletti and returned 25 yards.

Minnesota had a first down on the UW 48 with 65 seconds left. Giel ran for eight yards before a jarring Don Voss tackle knocked the ball loose. Voss recovered the fumble.

Wisconsin had a first down on its own 45 with 31 seconds left. But Haluska's pass was picked off by Clinton Andrus and returned 11 yards.

Minnesota had a first down on the UW 28 with 14 seconds left. On the final play, Giel's pass was intercepted by Hable in the end zone and returned to the 16 as time expired.

"As the final gun sounded to end one of the most heart-pulling games in the long rivalry between the Gophers and Badgers," Dick Gordon wrote in the Minneapolis Star-Tribune, "the Wisconsin warriors walked off the field as if they'd suffered one of the prime disappointments in life."

Gordon went on to quote UW freshman coach George Lanphear, who summarized the mood. "It was really funny going into the locker room. Here we finally win a Big Ten title and there's nothing but gloom. The boys were really disappointed."

So were the football purists. Wisconsin was guilty of three lost fumbles and three interceptions and rallied from a 14-7 deficit. Minnesota was guilty of three lost fumbles and five interceptions and rallied from 7-0 and 21-14 deficits.

"Everyone was disappointed that we didn't win," Peters confirmed, "but it was really an exciting game and the one person who comes to mind was Paul Giel. We just could not keep him contained. He moved the ball all over the field and really controlled the action."

Giel, a multi-sport jock, touched all bases for the Gophers. He rushed 29 times for 85 yards. He completed 9 of 19 passes for 167 yards. He caught a couple of passes and averaged 42 yards punting. Overall, he accounted for 271 of Minnesota's 322 total yards.

"If he's not the best, I don't want to play against anyone better," responded Wisconsin coach Ivy Williamson when asked if Giel was the best offensive player the Badgers had seen. "He's awfully hard to protect against. If you rush him, he'll break your back by running; if you don't rush him, he'll hit someone with a pass."

Giel was the runner-up to Notre Dame's Johnny Lattner in the 1953 Heisman voting. Giel was also an All-American baseball player at Minnesota, and went on to pitch for four Major League teams. In football, he was a combination halfback-quarterback, who would later become the Gophers athletic director. Giel had his own personal motivation for Wisconsin.

"I'm not kidding you a bit, I was really scared to death before the game," Giel told Ted Randolph of the *St. Paul Pioneer-Press*. "I was more scared than I've ever been in all my life. I knew everyone was depending on me to do a lot, and I was just worried that I wouldn't be able to come through. I wanted so bad to have a good day against Wisconsin and close the season with a win. I just worried myself sick."

By rushing for 125 yards, Ameche didn't necessarily take a backseat to Giel. Neither did the fleet-footed Carl, who totaled 109 yards on nine carries. Carl had seen limited playing time over the previous four games while nursing some nagging injuries.

"Wisconsin certainly wasn't a better team than we were," Giel groused to Sid Hartman in the *Minneapolis Star Tribune*. "In my book, we deserved to win the game. Right now, I think we have the best team in the Big Ten...but I'd vote for Wisconsin as the best all-around team we have met."

Minnesota head coach Wes Fesler shared those sentiments. And, according to the *State Journal*, he challenged the press corps to tell it like it is.

Left to Right: Burt Hable, Kenton Peters, Harland Carl, Jim Haluska

"Any person leaving the stands today who was not tremendously proud of his team should have his head examined," Fesler opined. "I never saw two teams that wanted to win so badly; neither one wanted a tie or played for it. I never saw a harder fought game."

And it was not without controversy. With the Badgers holding a 21-14 lead in the third quarter, they were moving closer to another score that might have sealed a victory. Haluska completed a pass to Erv Andrykowski and Wisconsin appeared to have a first-and-goal on the Minnesota 4-yard line. But a 15-yard penalty wiped out the play, taking the ball back to the 43, and the Badgers failed to score on the possession.

Capital Times sports writer Harry Golden intimated the flag was thrown by "an official who has done little or nothing good for the Badgers all season — in fact, at Rice, they thought he was from the Southwestern Conference — and found one of our little gentlemen out of order...that changed the entire picture."

Added Williamson, "No question, it was disastrous to us." That no doubt contributed to his somber post-game mood. "Naturally, we'd hoped to win," Williamson told the *Capital Times*, "and a tie now just leaves everybody kind of flat."

Not for long.

Wisconsin and Purdue tied for the Big Ten championship with 4-1-1 records. But since the Badgers and the Boilermakers didn't play each other, a number of other factors had to be evaluated in determining the conference representative for the Rose Bowl.

"One thing is certain," McCormick wrote in the *State Journal*, "this is the most difficult selection the Big Ten has been called upon to make since the modern Rose Bowl pact with the Pacific Coast Conference went into effect with the 1946 campaign."

Seemed like such a no-brainer, based on the team's overall records: Wisconsin was 6-2-1, and Purdue was 4-3-2. The Big Ten athletic directors agreed and selected the Badgers.

"I feel great about the whole thing," Ameche told the *State Journal*. And well he should. Not only were the Badgers going bowling for the first time, but Ameche could now use the West Coast trip for his honeymoon.

All along, Ameche had planned on getting married on Thanksgiving Day. And he was not alone in those plans. His UW teammate, Terry Durkin, was getting the married the same day. In both cases, the Rose Bowl was the ultimate wedding gift.

Top Right: Going into the regular season finale against Minnesota, Wisconsin sophomore quarterback Jim Haluska— whose teammates nicknamed him "Bumbles"- led the Big Ten in pass completion percentage (.614).

Bottom Right: Minnesota halfback-quarterback Paul Giel was the Big Ten's MVP in back-to-back seasons (1952-53) and a threat to score from anywhere on the field. During his illustrious career, Giel, who later served as the Gopher athletic director (1971-1988), rushed for 2,148 yards and passed for 3,165 yards. He also punted and returned all kicks.

Wisconsin 20 Ohio State 16
October 3, 1992

The seeds to beat a ranked team were planted during a loss to a ranked team—a 27-10 loss to the No. 2-ranked University of Washington Huskies, the defending co-national champions. The Badgers, a 33-point underdog, learned something valuable about themselves during the 1992 opener at picturesque Husky Stadium in Seattle.

"Our kids competed and played hard," said Barry Alvarez, entering his third season as Wisconsin's head coach, "and we can build on that."

In winning their 16th straight game overall and 13th straight over a Big Ten opponent, the Huskies exhibited their strength and talent against the Badgers. Washington had a huge edge in total offense (455-218), first downs (26-9) and plays (93-54).

Still, the Badgers, two years removed from a 1-10 season, left a good impression.

"I kind of misjudged these guys," said Washington defensive back Walter Bailey, who had his hands full with wideout Lee DeRamus. "I give Wisconsin credit. They really played their butts off. I think we were kind of deceived by the stuff we saw on film of them from last year. They were able to do some things to us that we didn't expect."

Like score 10 points in Husky Stadium. During the 1992 season, Washington beat Kansas State, Arizona, Toledo and Oregon by a combined total of 207-10.

Like not turn the ball over. This marked the first time in three seasons that the Huskies didn't produce at least one turnover against an opponent.

Like limit the Huskies to just seven points in the second half.

"When you're matched against someone better than you are," said UW offensive center Cory Raymer, a voluble sophomore from Fond du Lac (Goodrich), "you have to

Opposite page: Quarterback Darrell Bevell, then a 22-year-old freshman, gets ready to unload a pass over Ohio State's Derrick Foster. Bevell, a transfer from Northern Arizona, had spent the last two years on a Mormon mission in Cleveland.

Wisconsin's pugnacious offensive line made a "Smash-Mouth" statement against Ohio State: tight end Mike Roan (81); right tackle Joe Panos (58); right guard Mike Bryan (65), subbing for the injured Joe Rudolph; center Cory Raymer (52); and left guard Chuck Belin (75). Not pictured is left tackle Mike Verstegen (67).

look at it as an opportunity to get better. And I think we did. We wanted to play hard and not give up, and we didn't give up. That's what this is all about."

As the final seconds ticked off, a contingent of about 3,000 Wisconsin fans, who dutifully went sleepless in Seattle, chanted "We beat the spread, we beat the spread."

The seeds to beat a ranked team were planted during a win over an unranked team—a come-from-behind 18-17 win over spunky Northern Illinois at Camp Randall Stadium. In the final 1992 non-conference tune-up, the turnover-prone Badgers fell behind 17-3 with 12:41 to play. A disenchanted audience of 50,688 had seen this movie before.

"We shot ourselves in the foot so many times," Alvarez told the *State Journal*, "we may not have any feet left." Added UW quarterback Darrell Bevell, "There were times when we went over to the sidelines and we were really down."

With reason. The Badgers were careless and the result was five turnovers, including two lost fumbles inside the NIU 5-yard line. But in the fourth quarter they rallied around Bevell, who drove the offense 90 yards in 16 plays to pull Wisconsin within one possession.

After Terrell Fletcher left the game with 124 yards and an ankle injury, Brent Moss shifted from fullback — where he had been subbing for the injured Mark Montgomery — to his favorite position, tailback, and responded with 88 tough yards and two scores. "I took it upon myself when I got the chance to make it happen," said Moss, whose second touchdown on an 11-yard run set up a two-point conversion for the win.

Bevell punctuated the comeback by rolling to his right and lunging into the end zone, pushing Wisconsin into the lead, 18-17, with 2 minutes and 9 seconds remaining. Northern Illinois coach Charlie Sadler later complained that Bevell had not broken the plane of the goal line with his body or the football when his knee hit the turf.

Inside linebacker Gary Casper, a senior from Chicago Mt. Carmel, chases down Ohio State tailback Butler By'not'e. Casper had 142 tackles (17 for losses) during the 1992 season.

Cliché but true, the outcome was determined along the line of scrimmage where Wisconsin's interior threesome— Carlos Fowler, Lamark Shackerford and Mike Thompson— won most of the battles. The Buckeyes were held to 80 rushing yards on 25 carries, and their 3.2 yards per carry was well under their season average (4.4) coming into the game.

"I didn't even know what the call was until the pile started getting heavier and that's when I figured I must have been in," Bevell said to the *State Journal*. "I didn't know if I was going to make it or not. But it seemed like an eternity while I was running."

Thus, the Badgers avoided a disaster; an upset loss to the Huskies.

"In my five years here," said UW linebacker Gary Casper, a battled-toughened senior from Chicago Mt. Carmel, "we have never come back to win a game like that."

Moss agreed. "Wisconsin hasn't been known to come back like that," he chimed in. "But this is a new ball club, and a different attitude. This win is going to help us build more confidence and give us the strength to go against Ohio State."

Leading up to the Big Ten opener against the Buckeyes, who swept their first three games and loomed as a 10-point favorite, Alvarez invited Rev. Jesse Jackson to speak to the team after Tuesday's practice. Jackson was in Madison to give a speech that night at the UW Field House, and he was accompanied by his son, Yusef, a former linebacker at Virginia.

According to folklore, spun by Alvarez, at the end of Jackson's presentation to the football team he took questions, one of which was, "How did it feel to hit those three homers in the World Series and who named you Mr. October?" That would be

Reggie, not Jesse Jackson. And that would be Alvarez' story, and he was sticking to it.

Seriously, though, Jackson, a prep quarterback, delivered a serious message, stressing the importance of athletes using their gifts and seizing the moment. Jackson told the players they would be cheating themselves if "they don't use the same amount of time to develop their mind" as they do their bodies, challenging them "to be as smart as you are tough."

UW wide receiver Aaron Brown, a senior from Newark, Ohio, was visibly moved by Jackson's presence. "I'm about to call home and tell them that I shook hands with Jesse Jackson," he said afterward. "This is a big week for me. I just met Jesse. I'm about to play Ohio State. And my parents are coming to the game."

The Buckeyes were coming off their most impressive performance of the young season, a 35-12 trouncing of No. 8-ranked Syracuse in the Carrier Dome. Plus, they had an extra week to prepare for Wisconsin. That also gave them some extra time to ponder the fickleness of their home fans, who had booed them in a win over Bowling Green.

"It's unfortunate you're in your own stadium and getting booed," Ohio State quarterback Kirk Herbstreit told the Associated Press. "I don't know if they're booing me or if they're booing the offense or if they're booing coach (John) Cooper."

Most were booing Cooper. Some were booing Herbstreit, a fifth-year senior.

"I realize the fans want results, just like the media and everyone else wants results," said Herbstreit, who had sprained his ankle the second week of the season. "If we can meet some of the challenges and our expectations, this is the most talented team as far as athletic ability, since I've been at Ohio State."

Yet, the Badgers came into the game with a psychological edge as the seeds to beat a ranked team had already been planted. "After the things we did at Washington," said UW nose guard Lamark Shackerford, "we knew we could beat them (the Buckeyes)."

And they were prepared to beat them up, too. "I don't know if they thought they were coming in here and it was going to be some kind of a joke or what," said UW offensive guard Chuck Belin. "We came ready to play, ready to be physical."

Along with a national cable audience (ESPN), a sun-splashed gathering of 72,203 watched history in the making as Wisconsin upset the No. 12-ranked Buckeyes, 20-16.

For openers, this was the first time since 1981 (and an upset of No. 1 ranked Michigan) that the Badgers had won their Big Ten opener; this was also their first victory over a ranked team since 1985 (when the Buckeyes were the victims in Columbus).

"It's way too early to say we've turned the corner," said Alvarez, who finally collected his first triumph over a ranked opponent, "but obviously this was a huge step."

Trailing 10-3 at halftime, the Badgers scored on three of their first four possessions of the second half — scoring drives of 78, 58 and 66 yards — and held on to the ball for 21 of the final 30 minutes. "We wanted to keep pounding and pounding them and keep scratching and biting," Raymer said. "We knew what we had to do, and we went out and did it."

The Wisconsin offensive coaches were confident that they could take advantage of Ohio State's defensive schemes. The Buckeyes utilize their four down linemen to get penetration by charging aggressively upfield. The philosophy to attack and disrupt is partly born out of the conviction that nobody can physically knock them off the line of scrimmage.

Or, so they thought.

In the secondary, the Buckeyes like to play a two-deep zone, discouraging any deep passes because the safeties are nearly 14 yards downfield. The Badgers went to school on what they saw on film. Many of the running plays were designed to cut inside of the aggressive, attacking linemen. And a shovel pass was added for the same reason.

Bevell concentrated on hitting the corner throws and intermediate passes. In the second half, he was 12 of 16 for 140 yards. "I got in the groove," he said. "Every time you throw a pass and it's complete, you start thinking you're kind of invincible."

That thought never crossed Herbstreit's mind. Not after getting sacked five times. Wisconsin outside linebacker Chad Yocum was most responsible for hastening Herbstreit's transition from the playing field to the broadcast booth.

Yocum, a rangy sophomore from Windsor, had three sacks (for losses of 8, 10 and 11 yards) and three quarterback hurries. "He (Herbstreit) was very tentative, I thought," said Yocum, who took over for the injured Curt Maternowski in the second quarter. "He didn't want to hold on to the ball. He didn't feel very safe in the pocket."

The Badgers weren't afraid of Herbstreit's arm strength. And since the Buckeyes hadn't run any option all season — because of Herbstreit's tender ankle — the UW defense focused on stopping the tailbacks. The task became easier when Robert Smith went out early with an ankle injury. Smith was averaging nearly 180 rushing yards per game.

Without him, the Buckeyes couldn't run (45 net yards on 35 attempts) but they were still a tough out. And with 4 minutes and 29 seconds remaining, Herbstreit completed a short touchdown pass to Brian Stablein, making it 20-17. Check that. Korey Manley was flagged for roughing the kicker on the successful conversion.

Cooper took the extra point off the board and Ohio State lined up for a two point conversion. "If you can't make it from 1½ yards out, you don't deserve it," Cooper said.

The Buckeyes didn't make it. Stumbling away from his center, Herbstreit barely got the handoff to Raymond Harris, who was met in the hole by

Courtesy of Ohio State Sports Information

Ohio St. quarterback and current ESPN college football commentator Kirk Herbstreit.

Courtesy of University of Wisconsin Archives

Long-suffering fans charge the field after the Badgers shock the Buckeyes for their first win over a ranked team since 1985 and first win in a Big Ten opener since the 1981 upset of Michigan. While the students were tearing down the goal posts, Ohio State's John Cooper was grumbling, "I'm about as low as you can be. How else would you expect me to feel?"

Casper, who went high, and Aaron Norvell, who drilled him low. Manley finished off Harris, short of the goal line.

"All we talked about was finding a way to win," Manley said. "The defense is a close-knit group and we brought ourselves together on the sidelines and said, 'If it comes down to us, we're going out there and doing it.'"

It came down to one final play for the Buckeyes: a fourth-and-6 from the UW 26 with 2:24 left. Instead of having the option to potentially kick a game-tying field goal — which would have been the scenario if Cooper hadn't erased the PAT and gone for two — Ohio State was forced to try and keep the drive alive by picking up a first down.

The Buckeyes came up short, again.

Herbstreit scrambled out of the pocket and was dropped by UW safety Reggie Holt, who confessed, "I was expecting a sprintout, they had been running that all season."

While the Buckeyes were crestfallen ("We're in shock," said fullback Jeff Cothran), the Badgers basked in the victory. Especially senior place kicker Rich Thompson, who regaled the quote-starved media with horror stories from the Don Morton era.

"I remember going to class," Thompson said, "and sitting in an auditorium with 350 people and hearing the professor say, 'Our football team sucks.' I remember going to class and making sure that I would take off my football shirt and letter jacket because it was a shame to be on the football team here. It was ridiculous. We've been through the valleys."

And this was the first peak, and peek ahead, so to speak.

"This was a win for the fans who have been backing us for all those years the program was downhill," Raymer said. "Now, it's going uphill and we ain't going back down."

Nobody was more thrilled than Aaron Brown, who went 3-for-3. He shook hands with Jesse Jackson, he played in a victory over his home state team, Ohio State, and his parents were on hand to celebrate with him. "I'll never forget this week," he said.

(On December 14, 2003, Brown was killed in a car accident near Columbus. Also killed was his wife, Nedra. Their 7-month-old infant son, Aaron, Jr., was thrown from the car and survived the crash. Aaron Brown, Sr. was 32.)

Wisconsin 25 Iowa 16
October 17, 1959

When it rained, it poured. And then it rained some more, and Purdue poured it on — ending a 14-year slump against Wisconsin with an overwhelming 21-0 skunking on a muddy turf in dreary Lafayette, Indiana. More dreary than normal, that is.

Obviously, this was not the way the Badgers had envisioned opening the 1959 Big Ten season — as footwipes for the Boilermakers, who had gone winless in their last 10 games (0-9-1) against Wisconsin, dating to 1945.

Th█ung.

Among the casualties was co-captain Bob Zeman, who suffered bruised ribs. But it was nothing compared to the team's overall bruised ego. Quarterback Dale Hackbart, the spiritual leader, called the loss devastating and a real blow to Wisconsin's title aspirations. "We were mad with how we played," said tackle Jim Heineke. "We just couldn't get anything started."

How bad were the Badgers? Four lost fumbles bad. Three interceptions bad. Never once getting inside the Purdue 20 bad. And last, but certainly not least, zero-points bad. This was the first time in 23 games that Wisconsin had been shutout.

The Boilermakers made an early statement, scoring on their first two possessions. Both were set up by Badger turnovers. Quarterback Bernie Allen, making his first career start, passed 5 and 22 yards to Len Jardine for the scores. (Jardine was the brother of former Purdue nose guard John Jardine, who would coach Wisconsin in the '70s).

How bad were the Badgers? The *Milwaukee Sentinel's* Tony Ingrassia weighed in, "Purdue threw off 14 years of domination by Wisconsin with a couple of aerial haymakers in the first seven minutes then rubbed the conservative Badgers' noses in the mud of gale-swept Ross-Ade Stadium. This was the game the Boilermakers were pointing for all fall and they wasted no time showing the Badgers who was boss."

Courtesy of UW Sports Information

Opposite page: Whenever quarterback Dale Hackbart (28) got outside of the pocket, he put a lot of pressure on the edge of a defense because of his running ability. During the 1959 season, Hackbart completed 51 of 108 passes for 734 yards and two touchdowns. He was also the UW's leading rusher with 387 yards.

Who knows how many they would have scored on a dry field? Clearly, the Boilermakers were superior — before and after the clouds opened up. "The deluge which rolled in from the west in the second quarter was something to see," wrote the *Milwaukee Journal's* Oliver E. Kuechle. "It has rained on Wisconsin teams before, but never like this. The rain came down in sheets that obliterated the other side of the stands. At the finish, no more than 10,000 of the 41,542 who saw the kickoff in sunshine were still in the stands."

While the Badgers were getting humbled in Lafayette, the Iowa Hawkeyes, the defending Big Ten champs, were crushing Michigan State, 37-8, in front of a record crowd of 59,300 in Iowa City. The Hawks led 23-0 at halftime.

In evening its conference record at 1-1, Iowa got a strong game from quarterback Olen Treadway, who completed 14 of 24 passes for 154 yards. Treadway, a first-year starter, had served his apprenticeship under the incomparable Randy Duncan.

Iowa ran for 247 yards against Michigan State, making Treadway's job that much easier. Halfbacks Ray Jauch and Bob Jeter and fullback Don Horn could hold their own with any other backfield combination in the conference. (Jeter would go on to star in the defensive secondary of the Green Bay Packers.)

As expected, then, Iowa was the heavy betting favorite to beat Wisconsin on Dad's Day at Camp Randall Stadium. It was rare for the Badgers to be cast in the role of the underdog (though they had lost the last three games in the series to the Hawks). The stakes were high, because the loser would likely be eliminated from the Big Ten title chase.

On the eve of the game, UW coach Milt Bruhn, who was 0-for-3 against Iowa's Forest Evashevski, gave his players a pep talk and told the *State Journal*, "We really haven't sacked anybody this year, and it's about time we do something about it."

During the 1958 season, the Badgers had taken a 9-0 halftime lead Iowa in front of a giddy and record crowd of 65, 241 at Camp Randall. Among the spectators was tackle Dan Lanphear who was sidelined with an injury. The happiness was short-lived.

The Hawkeyes stormed back and scored 20 unanswered points,

Courtesy of UW Sports Information

Dale Hackbart, who grew up on Madison's eastside idolizing Yankee centerfielder Mickey Mantle, had pro baseball aspirations. As a senior, he batted over .300 for the Badgers and that led to a minor league contract with the Pittsburgh Pirates. When Hackbart joined the Packers, though, Vince Lombardi convinced him to focus on one sport. "Lombardi said baseball players were wimps and football players were real men," Hackbart told writer Robert Janis. Hackbart went on to a 14-year career in the NFL as a defensive back and linebacker.

outgaining the Badgers, 205-91, in the second half. The shocking meltdown saddled Wisconsin with its only loss - the Badgers wound up 7-1-1 - and helped catapult Iowa to the title.

"The stadium usually empties fast," wrote the *State Journal's* Monte McCormick, "but fans remained quite awhile after the game watching Iowa rooters try to tear down Wisconsin's goal posts. They didn't succeed."

A year later, Wisconsin was determined to finish what it had started the previous year against Iowa. And there was no hesitation on the part of the Badgers, who scored 17 points in the first 21 minutes and then delivered the knockout punch on the first series of the third quarter, marching 70 yards on 12 plays for a touchdown that made it 25-0.

The Hawkeyes eventually made it competitive, but it was too little too late. Much to the delight of another record-setting Camp Randall crowd of 65,256, the Badgers got a field goal from Karl Holzwarth and touchdowns from Hackbart, Tom Wiesner and Eddie Hart to keep their Rose Bowl hopes alive with the 25-16 win.

A great moment? *State Journal* sports editor Henry J. McCormick thought so. "This was a deliriously happy Wisconsin crowd," he reported, "and some of them tore down the north goal posts while the big crowd took its time about leaving."

The Hawkeyes were the perfect guests, contributing to their own demise by losing five fumbles. "You can't give the ball away that often and win," Evashevski commented to the *Capital Times*. "We lost scoring opportunities too often."

Treadway, a 5-10, 159-pound senior, did his best to rally the Hawkeyes, breaking two Big Ten and three school records in the process. Treadway completed 26 of 41 passes for 304 yards. But most of the damage was done after the Badgers had mounted the big lead.

"We played loose on pass defense on purpose," Bruhn explained to Bonnie Ryan of the *Capital Times*. "Our boys did tend to be over cautious, but that's because we have been playing on muddy turf for so long and they developed some bad habits.

"We did try to rush the passer (Treadway) but he usually got the ball away in a hurry because of those short passes...better to have them complete than long ...they just ate up the clock and that is what we wanted with the lead that we had.

"We didn't red dog because we were afraid of that long one with Jeter back there. Remember last year when they pulled the screen on us and Jeter went all the way? Well, they tried that again this year, but Jim Heineke was there ready for it and broke it up."

Wisconsin's offensive line dominated the Hawkeyes, creating holes for Billy Hobbs, who led both teams in rushing with 83 yards, and Wiesner, who had 51 yards running behind Heineke, Lanphear, Ron

Perkins, Jerry Stalcup and Bob Nelson.

"I wouldn't trade Wisconsin's pair of starting tackles for any pair on any other college team in the country," McCormick wrote. "Danny Lanphear and Jim Heineke are big, fast, mobile, hard-hitting tackles who take a lot out of the opposing team.

"Furthermore, I would not be prepared to trade Perkins and Stalcup for any other pair of guards. They were expected to be top-notchers and that they are."

Bruhn placed the same value on his backfield rotation. The Badgers were eight deep with Hackbart, Hobbs, Zeman, Wiesner, Hart, Jim Bakken, Ron Steiner, and Bob Altmann. The Hawkeyes had given up just 102 total rushing yards in their first two Big Ten outings against Northwestern and Michigan State. Wisconsin rushed for 214.

Give credit to Bruhn who tweaked the offense. "It's the first time since I have been head coach that we have ever used the man-in-motion the way we did," Bruhn told the *Capital Times*. "We had him running in front of the deep backs instead of behind them. (As a result) they can't overshift on us and it gives us a more balanced defense to run against."

By motioning either Zeman or Bob Altmann, the Badgers were able to get one of their best blockers at the point of attack. And it paid off right away as Hobbs broke free for a 46-yard run on Wisconsin's second offensive play.

"That run may have been the turning point of the game — Billy did a great job and played one of his best games ever," Bruhn said. "Stalcup had another great game; the last two games he has been out of this world. And Dale Hackbart had his best game of the year."

The 6-3, 200-pound Hackbart, a Madison East product, was still getting into a comfortable playing rhythm after suffering an injury during a scrimmage two weeks before the opener. Against Iowa, he made the plays that he had to make — characteristic of his career — completing five of seven passes for 75 yards. He also rushed for 29 yards.

Hackbart was a catalyst and a character. As the cliché goes, he played hard, on and off the field, and never shied away from that colorful reputation. Although he got more praise for his savvy than his smarts, he was a first time Academic All-American in '59.

A mult-tasker, Hackbart set the example on so many different levels for the Badgers---offense, defense and special teams. During his junior year, he established a school record with seven interceptions. As a senior, he led the Big Ten in total offense.

"Leadership is sometimes difficult to explain," said Bakken, who alternated at quarterback with Hackbart. "When I played in St. Louis (with the NFL Cardinals), Larry Wilson was our leader. But Larry wasn't that good in the locker room. Some guys are really good both ways. They can put the word out and they can back it up on the playing field.

"Hack obviously backed it up. And he was such a likeable, charismatic guy. Even today, when he comes back for charity golf outings,

Courtesy of UW Sports Information

Top & Bottom: Dan Lanphear was a 6-foot-3, 222-pound tackle from Madison West who led the Regents to a Big Eight football title and a state championship in track. He won individual crowns in the discus and shot put. At Wisconsin, he was a three-year starter and consensus All-American in 1959. Lanphear went on to play for the Houston Oilers of the American Football League. One of his AFL teammates was Billy Cannon, who won the 1959 Heisman. Lanphear's former UW teammate, Dale Hackbart, was seventh in the voting.

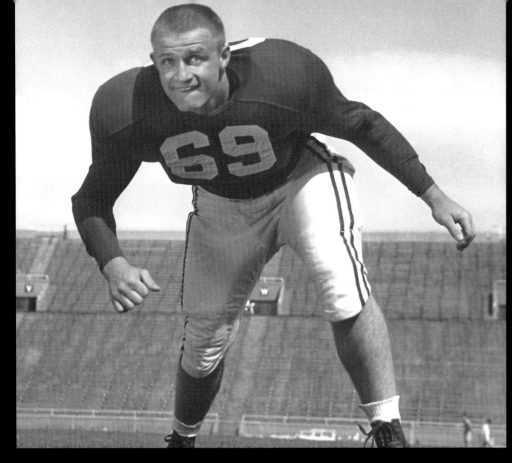

Courtesy of UW Sports Information

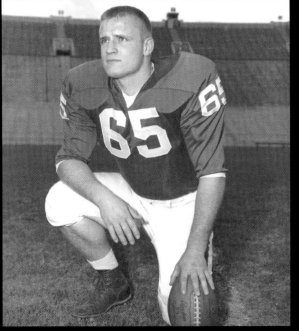

Top & Bottom: Jim Heineke was a 6-foot, 227-pound tackle from Wisconsin Dells, who went on to play in the Hula Bowl after Wisconsin's 44-8 loss in the Rose Bowl to Washington and quarterback Bob Schloredt, who had impaired vision in one eye. "We had a good team," Heineke said, "but Washington just had a spectacular team." Heineke's older brother, John, also lettered in 1957 for the Badgers and enjoyed a long and successful coaching career at Beloit Memorial High School.

still gravitate to him. In my opinion, he's as fine an athlete in the modern era to ever play at Wisconsin."

Heineke agreed, noting that Hackbart and Stalcup "were the guys who usually got us going — they got us all revved up." The strength of the '59 team, according to Heineke, was the sum of its parts. "No one guy really stood out," he said. "We were all about on the same level, and one game it might be one guy and the next game it would be somebody else."

Wisconsin's starting defensive ends, Jim Holmes and Henry Derleth, were injured against Iowa. Was depth a question? "We didn't have many reserves," Heineke conceded. "Each of us was averaging about 56 minutes a game, and that was an awful lot. I don't think anyone today could play 56 minutes. They wouldn't weigh 300 pounds, that's for sure."

Beating Iowa was the turning point in the season, Heineke recounted. Not only did it erase the awful memory from Purdue, but it put the Badgers in the proper frame of mind for their next opponent, the Ohio State Buckeyes, at Camp Randall Stadium.

History was not on Bucky's side. Ohio State had a stranglehold on the series, 18-6-4. In addition, the Badgers were winless over the last 11 meetings (0-9-2), dating to 1946.

The *State Journal* singled out Hackbart "as the key to the Wisconsin attack. He's a talented runner and passer, and he can be an excellent defensive player because of his speed and range. Wisconsin has no other backs who are in (Bob) White's class."

White, a senior, was the workhorse at Ohio State. A year earlier, he had 36 carries for 153 yards against Wisconsin in Columbus. A week earlier, he had 31 rushes against Purdue. Complementing the dependable White was the strapping 217-pound Bob Ferguson.

White and Ferguson liked to run "power" behind right guard Ernie Wright (6-3, 242), right tackle Jim Tyrer (6-5, 244) and right end Jim Houston (6-2, 218).

The Buckeyes also featured two running quarterbacks, Jerry Fields and Tom Mattie, and a speedy little 5-8 flanker, Jimmy Herbstreit (the father of ESPN analyst Kirk Herbstreit).

The Badgers went into the game without the injured Holmes, who was replaced in the starting lineup by Allan Schoonover. Both teams were coming off impressive victories the week before — Wisconsin over Iowa and Ohio Sate over Purdue, 15-0.

So, whose momentum would carry over?

Lanphear supplied the answer — jump-starting the Badgers by blocking Ohio State's second punt out of the end zone for a safety. "And that was just a prelude for what Lanphear did most of the afternoon," McCormick wrote, "as he played one of the greatest games at tackle this historic old field has ever seen."

In sparking Wisconsin to a 12-3 win over the Buckeyes, Lanphear was a one-man wrecking crew in front of 55,440 who were rewarded for braving the rain and raging hawk (27 miles per hour out of the

36

northwest with gusts up to 40).

In the second quarter, McCormick detailed how Lanphear "wracked up fullback Bob White with a savage tackle that put the brawny Buckeye out of action for the day and maybe for some future games, too." White had only five rushes for 14 yards.

In the fourth quarter, Lanphear belted Ferguson on a punt return and knocked him out of the game. "As I recall," Bakken said, "Dan hit Ferguson with a left forearm. Ferguson got up, went back to the huddle and when the huddle broke slumped to the ground."

Lanphear went on to earn All-American honors and a few kind words from Ohio State's cantankerous Woody Hayes. A gracious Hayes — yes, that's right, a gracious Hayes — had nothing but good things to say afterward.

"If I have to lose to any single team — and I don't like to lose — I'd rather lose to Wisconsin than any other team," Hayes told the *State Journal*. "We squeaked by the last two years and they (the Badgers) were perfect gentlemen in losing and they are when they win, too. I have never met a more sporting department than Wisconsin.

"There is no belly-aching when they lose and they play good, clean, hard football. Milt Bruhn is a fine football coach, and he deserved to win this one. I'm not saying I want Wisconsin to win the championship, but I do say it couldn't happen to a finer bunch of players and coaches. We just got beat by a better team."

To underscore how much he really didn't like to lose football games — especially to Wisconsin — Hayes never again lost to Wisconsin. (In fact, the Buckeyes won 21 straight in the series before losing again to the Badgers).

As the crowd counted off the final seconds, the *State Journal* reported, "A segment in the northwest section of the stadium boomed, 'We want the goal posts.' However, riotous upheaval was not to mark the heralded triumph...in contrast to the Iowa game a week ago."

In retrospect, the Iowa win had been the springboard to a great moment against Ohio State and the school's first outright Big Ten championship since 1912.

"To be honest with you, we were probably lucky to win the title," admitted Heineke, citing a 9-6 loss to Illinois in the home finale. But the Badgers were able to overcome that disappointment — Bill Brown scored on the final play of the game — to bounce back with an 11-7 win at Minnesota. "We took care of business when it had to be taken care of," Heineke said. "And we knew that we could do something big after beating Iowa."

A great moment, Heineke assured, for the blue collar Badgers, who capitalized on their chances (scoring every time they landed inside the red zone during the '59 regular season). Years later, Zeman related to the *State Journal*, "We had a lot of hard-nosed, rough players who would go out and battle with any team in the country, or each other. We won our games by out-hitting rather than outsmarting people." And that was their curse, and charm.

Courtesy of UW Sports Information

Top & Bottom: Jerry "Sparky" Stalcup was a 6-foot, 217-pound guard and the Most Valuable Player on the 1959 Badgers. He was All-Big Ten and a co-captain with Bob Zeman. "We had a lot of players who mirrored Dale Hackbart's personality that season," recalled longtime UW sports information director Jim Mott. "But Jerry Stalcup, Bob Zeman, Danny Lanphear, Ron Perkins and Jim Heineke were all tough like him."

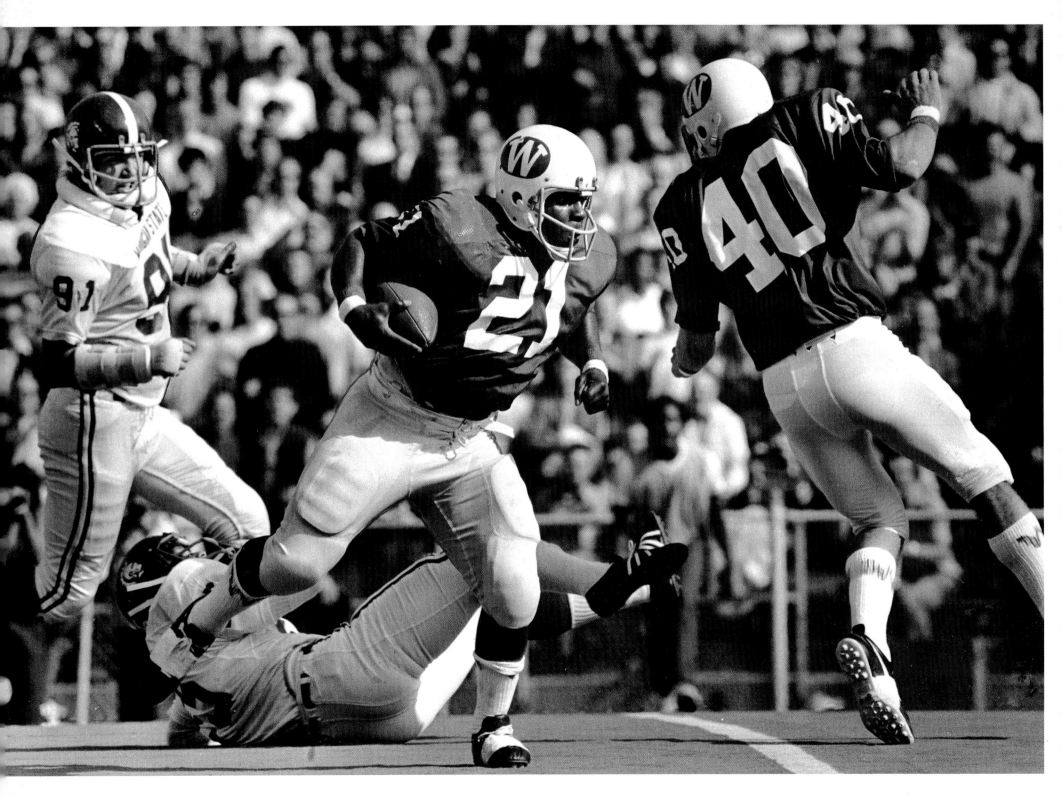

Wisconsin 31 Michigan State 28
October 16, 1971

Rufus Ferguson sat quietly in front of his locker, stripped down to a gray T-shirt and gym shorts. His sprained right ankle was wrapped with white tape. The sprain had kept him out of action for two games. His practice jersey, No. 21, hung from a hook.

"I've been happy with my last four years here, very happy," said Ferguson, reflecting on the distance that he had traveled as a collegian. In yards, it was 2,702 — with one last hurrah remaining at Camp Randall Stadium. "I'm not a number anymore. Wherever I go people know me. They say, 'Hey, there's Rufus' and I like that."

Ferguson's senior year had not gone as planned. The Badgers had not been very good. Mired once again among the Big Ten's also-rans, they had won just two conference games and were bringing a 4-6 overall record into the 1972 season finale against Minnesota.

Ferguson's personal expectations had fallen short, too, because of injuries. Against Northwestern, he rushed for 197 yards. But he also took a damaging shot to his brawny upper torso, and his shoulder went numb. He played hurt the next three weeks.

When he finally got back up to speed, he sprained his ankle in the eighth game of the season against Iowa. That injury forced him to miss the Purdue and Illinois games and left him questionable for the Gophers, though he vowed that he'd play.

"I was always prepared in case something like this (injuries) happened," Ferguson said to the *State Journal*. "Life is like this. You have your ups and downs. When it's down, you have to take it in stride. When the sun is out, prepare for rain. Right now it's raining for me. It was sunny all those early ball games."

Opposite page: Rufus Ferguson spins away from traffic and heads for the goal line after getting a crunching block from flanker Tim Klosek (40), a junior from Whiting, Indiana.

Ferguson rushed for 149 yards in a 20-20 tie versus Syracuse.

In rushing for 1,222 yards and 13 touchdowns during an expanded 11-game 1971 season (previously schools played 10 games), Ferguson shattered Alan Ameche's single-season rushing mark of 946 yards. He also raised the bar for the Badgers.

"As a senior, I want to go out a winner," he had said. "I'm tired of being called respectable. For two years now, we've proved that we've got the foundation for a winning team. And, right now, I'm thinking roses; there's no other way to be."

Still seated pensively in front of his locker, Ferguson right now was thinking about going out with a bang and not a whimper against Minnesota. Either way, he would be leaving Wisconsin the following spring with his degree in business. "Worked hard for it," Ferguson asserted proudly. "Can't survive without it."

Prodded to list his greatest moments as a UW running back, Ferguson had a flashback to a 1969 game against Northern Michigan. That was the year when he was selected as the Most Valuable Player on the freshman team. He rushed for 380 yards in two games.

"I can still remember that first touchdown I scored as a sophomore," he said of an 11-yard run that gave the Badgers a 7-0 lead at Oklahoma in the 1970 opener. They went on to lose the game, 22-7. But he finished with a 5.2 average (11 rushes for 57 yards).

"I've had quite a few memories," stressed Ferguson, who rushed for over 100 yards twice as a sophomore and six times as a junior, including 211 yards at Minnesota.

Among his 1971 highlights was a trip to Syracuse, where he rushed for 149 yards — 127 in the first half — in a 20-20 tie with the Orangemen. He also scored twice.

"Rufus had the best day I've ever seen him have," UW coach John Jardine said afterward. "He ran with complete abandon. The way he

The first sellout at Camp Randall-September 25, 1971 against LSU.

Head Coach John Jardine looks on as the Badgers drive for a score against Michigan State.

gives himself in a football game is something. He just gives 100 per cent every play."

All of a sudden the Badgers had a drawing card in the 5-foot-6, 190-pound Ferguson, who enthusiastically answered to the nickname of "Roadrunner," bestowed upon him as an American Legion baseball player after having stolen 42 bases in 19 games.

John Coatta, who was fired after the '69 season, had recruited Ferguson out of South Florida — Miami Killian High School — and predicted that he would put fannies in the seats at Camp Randall with his engaging personality and unique running style.

Physically, Ferguson conjured up memories of Buddy Young, a diminutive 5-5, 163-pound speedster who earned 1944 All-American honors at the University of Illinois. Young, a member of the College Football Hall of Fame, went on to a splendid pro career.

Ferguson's flamboyance and emerging presence as a player had an impact on ticket buyers. On September 25, 1971, the Badgers attracted a record crowd of 78,535 for a non-conference game against LSU. This was the first time all the seats had been filled since the construction of the upper deck in 1966. The largest previous crowd had been 72,758.

"I think this actually marks the turning point of Operation Turnaround in that it shows complete acceptance of our new football program," Wisconsin athletic director Elroy Hirsch told the *State Journal*. "It opens unlimited opportunities for the athletic department.

"And this is the time for me to thank all those loyal people who stuck with us for two years when things weren't so good — the people who had faith that better days were ahead. Nothing could please me more than to see that stadium filled. Nothing...except to win."

The Badgers lost to LSU, 38-28. They were entertaining, even if they couldn't slow anybody down. The teams combined for 991 yards of total offense — 586 for the Tigers and 405 for the Badgers. Fullback Alan (A-Train) Thompson was the leading rusher with 109 yards on 13 carries. Ferguson picked up 97 yards and scored twice.

"I'll tell ya what, Rufus is a showman — he puts life into football," drawled LSU head coach Charlie McClendon. "But, more importantly, he's a true player. He's big-time. He runs so low slung that our ball players couldn't get their arms around him."

By now, Ferguson had danced his way into the hearts of Badger fans. Literally. As part of the show, he danced — choreographing his own routine, the Roadrunner Shuffle. With arms held high, he would nimbly shuffle his feet and shake his ample caboose.

(In today's stodgy game, such a display, or even the slightest hint of premeditated joy on the part of a player, would draw an excessive celebration penalty.)

Some liked it more than others.

"We had watched him do his dance on films all week, and we were laughing at it," LSU middle linebacker Warren Capone said before the '72 rematch in Baton Rouge. "But by Friday we didn't think it was too funny. We certainly didn't want him doing it against us."

Mike Passini, the backup center to Mike Webster, remembered sitting in a film meeting with the offensive line when position coach Chuck McBride replayed the Roadrunner Shuffle. "McBride had noticed it on film and we all laughed, too," said Passini. "Rufus got pushed out of bounds (at Syracuse) and he did this little dance, and it grew from there."

That growth reached dizzying heights in Wisconsin's 35-29 win over Indiana on October 9, 1971. Welcome to the Dance Fever Era. Ferguson rushed for 152 yards and three touchdowns and humored the home crowd with his Shuffle after each score.

When the straight-laced Jardine was asked about Ferguson's end zone routine, he did his own song and dance and contended, "I didn't even look." What got into Rufus? Ferguson explained, "It's to get the team together. It's for unity — to give 'em pep."

State Journal sports editor Glenn Miller, a mushy and unabashed cheerleader, wrote, "I hope John Jardine doesn't make Rufus Ferguson stop doing that little kick-dance in the end zone. Rufus and the rest of us get such a lift from it...The dance is flagrantly doggy, and if anybody but lovable and effervescent Rufus did it, he'd be run out of town."

Indiana coach John Pont had a different take on Ferguson, the runner. "Rufus is a great player," Pont said. "He's so squat you have to go down to meet him. But it's his great second effort that makes him go. He's a great runner. I'm not so sure he isn't the best in the Big Ten."

Was he the best? Pont's claim was put to the test the following Saturday in Madison in what amounted to the Battle of Little Big Men: Wisconsin's Rufus (Roadrunner) Ferguson versus Michigan State's Eric (The Flea) Allen, a 165-pound mighty mite.

Ferguson had rushed for 537 yards and nine touchdowns in five games. He led the Big Ten in rushing and scoring. On the other hand, Allen had accounted for 67 percent of the Spartans' rushing yardage with 350 yards on 90 carries.

Jardine on Allen: "A great daylight runner."

MSU's Duffy Daugherty on Ferguson: "He runs like a tank."

Jardine on MSU's offense: "I'm worried about stopping them. Especially their option attack. They run it out of three or four different formations and really attack a defense."

Daugherty on UW's offense: "Nobody has really contained them yet. Their offense has great balance, the best of any team in the conference, or equal to the best."

What transpired was one of the great moments — from an offensive standpoint. Although the Flea bested the Roadrunner (247 rushing yards to 103), the Badgers outlasted Michigan State, 31-28, snapping a six-game losing streak to the Spartans, dating to 1961.

The game was tied four times before Roger Jaeger settled the lively gridiron debate by kicking a 30-yard field goal with 5 minutes and 12 seconds left.

Rufus Ferguson shuffled his way into the hearts of Badger fans with his productivity as a running back and flair as an entertainer. John Coatta recruited Ferguson out of Miami and predicted Ferguson would sell tickets with skills and showmanship. UW assistant LaVern Van Dyke tells the story of picking up Ferguson at the airport on his official recruiting visit. It was a typical winter day in Madison— windy and below freezing — when Ferguson stepped off the plane dressed for South Beach, not central Wisconsin. Van Dyke easily picked Ferguson out of the crowd and shouted out his name, whereupon an innocent and puzzled Ferguson inquired, "How'd ya know it was me?" Four years later, no introductions were needed.

Courtesy of UW Sports Information

Courtesy of UW Sports Information

Top: Fullback Alan "A-Train" Thompson, a 213-pound senior from Dallas, and tailback Rufus "Roadrunner" Ferguson, a 186-pound junior from Miami, celebrate a score. Thompson rushed for 907 yards and nine touchdowns as a sophomore in 1969 before being derailed by a knee injury that greatly impacted his career. Who knows how good he could have been? Thompson finished with 462 career rushes for 2,005 yards (4.3) and 19 scores. Thompson was the owner of the single most productive debut as a Badger - 220 yards against Oklahoma - until Brian Calhoun came along and rushed 43 times for 258 yards and five touchdowns in the 2005 opener against Bowling Green.

Bottom: The Roadrunner Shuffle, and the Center of Attention. Everything on the offensive line revolved around the inspired play of center Mike Webster (51), an undersized 6-1, 218-pounder from Rhinelander, who helped get Rufus Ferguson into the end zone. Webster, who was born in Tomahawk, went on to a Hall of Fame career with the Pittsburgh Steelers. He played in four Super Bowls and was named to nine Pro Bowl rosters.

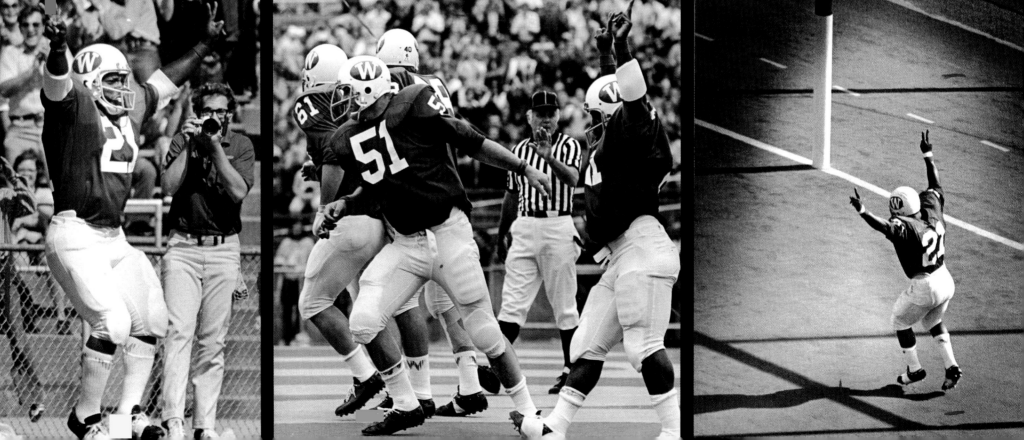

"It felt good when I hit it," Jaeger said. "Earlier in the year, I was watching the ball come back form the center instead of watching the placement area. Consequently, I wasn't always hitting the ball in the middle. With the adjustments I've made, I'm more confident."

Besides his placement duties, Jaeger was also a starting offensive guard opposite Bob Braun. The tackles were Elbert Walker and Keith Nosbusch, and the center was Mike Webster, who wasn't even expected to play against Michigan State.

Webster, a sophomore, had torn cartilage in his right knee. "He actually played on only one sound leg out there," McBride said. "He was all guts and heart." Added Jardine, "Webster played a helluva game. The kid has got a lot of courage."

Jardine used Lance Moon as a wingback in a full-house backfield against Michigan State, and the Badgers wound up running for 182 yards. Moon and the powerful Thompson helped clear a path for Ferguson, whose only score came on a memorable 34-yard run.

And the memory of his subsequent end zone dance, the Roadrunner Shuffle, was preserved for the ages when a poster was made from an Edwin Stein photo that appeared in the Sunday edition of the State Journal.

Courtesy of UW Sports Information

Mike Webster, who went on to a 17-year NFL career, anchored the offensive line along with guards Roger Jaeger and Bob Braun, and tackles Elbert Walker and Keith Nosbusch.

"You know when I knew for sure we were going to win this ball game," the sappy Miller posed in his Sunday column. "I knew it when Rufus Ferguson's dad gave that flamboyant wave to the crowd when he was introduced just before the game. But let's not give all the glory to Rufus this week. Let's even give a big, sweet bite of glory to the defense"

Defensively, the Badgers gave up 403 yards on the ground and had no answer for Allen. Few defenses did in 1971. "Eric Allen is the best running back I've seen in my 18 years in the Big Ten," said Minnesota's Murray Warmath. "I haven't seen all the backs in the nation, but I don't believe there's a running back in the country who can touch Allen."

After Jaeger's field goal, the Spartans put together a sustained march that ended when Wisconsin safety Ron Buss picked off a tipped pass on the UW 16 with 55 seconds left. In the first quarter, Buss had returned an interception 29 yards for a touchdown. "The defense was there when the chips were down," Jardine said.

So was Tim Klosek, a junior wide receiver from Whiting, Indiana. Klosek caught five passes for 135 yards, including a 75-yard touchdown strike from quarterback Neil Graff.

"I lined up a yard behind (Larry) Mialik and I ran straight down the field," said Klosek, describing his route. "I was really surprised when no one picked me up. I think Neil was too because he lofted the ball a little and I didn't think it was ever going to come down."

Klosek and Graff hooked up on a 38-yard completion that set up Jaeger's game-winning kick. Klosek lined up as a slot back, ran into the flat and down the right sidelines, while Terry Whitaker occupied the corner and safety with a skinny post. "The defensive end was supposed to pick me up and I knew I could outrun him," Klosek said, laughing.

Nobody smiled, laughed or horsed around more than Klosek, one of the most popular members of the team. And nobody cried more than his UW teammates the following summer when Klosek was struck and killed by a car in a freak accident on the South Beltline.

Klosek, who was returning to Madison after attending a wedding in Indiana, was standing in the roadway changing a tire on his vehicle when he was struck by another UW student in the early morning hours of July 4, 1972. Klosek was 21.

"He was the greatest guy and tight with everybody on the team," Passini related. "When we all learned about what had happened, I think it wrecked our whole (1972) season. In all honesty, I don't think we recovered from that."

Wisconsin won just one more Big Ten game in 1971 and it represented another great Camp Randall moment. With nine seconds remaining, A-Train (Thompson) barreled into the end zone from three yards out to give the Badgers a 14-10 Homecoming win over Purdue.

Who knows how great Thompson could have been with two good knees? And who knows how good the Badgers could have been in 1972 if Klosek had been around to liven things up and Ferguson had stayed healthy?

Ferguson climaxed his career by rushing 36 times for 112 yards in a 14-6 loss to Minnesota. That put him over the top — 1,004 yards — for the second consecutive year. And it was no coincidence that Wisconsin set attendance records in each of those two seasons, averaging 68,131 in 1971 and 70, 454 in 1972.

Prior to the Dance Fever Era — the Roadrunner and his Shuffle — the Badgers averaged 56,223 in 1970 and 48,898 in 1969. "I don't believe football has to be hardship," Ferguson rationalized on his exit. "I love the game and that's the way it should be played."

Wisconsin 49 Minnesota 31
November 23, 2002

Wisconsin offensive coordinator Brian White didn't mince words with his marquee players, Brooks Bollinger and Anthony Davis. White pulled them aside after practice and told them the facts of life — as they related to the game plan for Minnesota.

"Anthony," White said, addressing the 5-8, 190-pound sophomore tailback from Plainfield, New York, "we're going to give you the ball 30 to 40 times."

"Brooks," White said, addressing the 6-2, 205-pound senior quarterback from Grand Forks, North Dakota, "you're going to carry the ball on draws and options, maybe 20 carries."

These were no little White lies, either.

"We wanted to do a combination of things on offense," White elaborated. "We wanted to run the toss sweep and then run counter to the backside and have a couple of rhythm throws in the package, too. And we told our players all week that the tailback and the quarterback were going to win the game for us. The emphasis was on the run.

"A bowl was on the line. So, we were going back to basics. We just felt like we had to go with our strengths and we thought we were a bigger team and a more physical team than Minnesota. And before we did anything else in our offensive package, we wanted to make sure they could stop us from running the ball."

There was no sugar-coating what was riding on the outcome of the 2002 regular season finale against the Gophers in Camp Randall Stadium. Win, and the Badgers would qualify for a bowl. Lose, and they would be home for the holidays for a second straight year.

Nothing personal but ....

Nobody wanted to spend another Christmas with their families, according to offensive tackle Jason Jowers, a fifth-year senior from Libertyville, Illinois, who had experienced back-to-back Rose Bowls and a Sun Bowl before drawing a lump of coal. "We just couldn't end this season like we ended last season," he said. "Especially the seniors."

Courtesy of John Maniaci, Wisconsin State Journal

Opposite page: Minnesota safety Eli Ward (27) is among the leading tacklers in the Big Ten, twice leading the Gophers in stops. But he's no match for Anthony Davis' power and speed.

The 2001 season had ended in mind-numbing frustration — back-to-back losses to Michigan (knocking the Badgers out of a bowl for the first time since 1995), and Minnesota (snapping a six-game winning streak against the Gophers).

That added up to a very unfulfilling 5-7 record. So, while the Paul Bunyan Axe was changing hands in the Metrodome, the UW players were trying to get a handle on their own personal disappointment brought on by their bowl-less reality.

"I can't imagine how much this is hurting the seniors because it's hurting me a lot," said cornerback Scott Starks, a true freshman from St. Louis, who had started the final 10 games. "These seniors have accomplished so much in the years they've been here, and they should have gone out with at least a bowl, and we couldn't get them that."

The 42-31 Minnesota loss was a microcosm of the 2001 season, which had hit rock bottom in a hurry against Indiana with an embarrassing 63-32 home loss. The Hoosiers, who got six rushing touchdowns from Levron Williams, led 32-0 in the first quarter.

As a whole, the Badgers had more scoring power than staying power, especially on a defense that ranked No. 82 in the nation in average points allowed (28.8).

To wit: they scored over 30 points three times and lost all three games. They broke the school record for passing and became the first team in Big Ten history to have a 1,000-yard rusher (Davis), a 1,000-yard receiver (Lee Evans) and two 1,000-yard passers (Bollinger and Jim Sorgi). And still lost more than they won.

So, even after the Badgers rallied to take the lead in the third quarter at Minnesota, there was no assurance the defense would stop the Gophers. And it didn't. There was no stopping quarterback Asad Abdul-Khaliq who completed 17 of 25 passes for 265 yards. And there was no stopping running back Tellis Redmon who rushed for 128 yards.

For that matter, there was no stopping Wisconsin's "two-man" game. Davis ran for a career-high 208 yards before complaining of dizziness. He didn't play in the fourth quarter. (Davis broke the

NCAA freshman rushing mark with his 10th game over 100 yards).

Evans also did his part, catching nine passes for 151 yards. (Overall, the gifted Evans broke the Big Ten's single-season receiving record with 75 receptions for 1,545 yards. He caught nine touchdown passes and went over 100 yards receiving eight times.)

Still, it wasn't enough. The Badgers gave up four plays of 39-plus yards to the Gophers, including three touchdowns. A beat-up Bollinger — who took a physical pounding throughout the season and was now having trouble breathing through a broken nose — stayed in character and beat himself up for not doing more to offset the sieve-like defense.

"We've got a long way to go as a football team," Bollinger told the *State Journal*, "but it's something where I feel the character of this program and the foundation it has won't crumble. I've got to learn from it and try to make myself a better player."

Ditto from Starks. "I probably got two years of experience in 12 games," he said. "And I want to make sure every player who's coming back next year is going to go out his senior year with a bowl, and I'll do everything within my power to help make it happen,"

That was the mindset in November. But everything changed dramatically the following spring when Evans tragically blew out his knee during the intrasquad game. Undaunted, Evans pledged to rehab aggressively after undergoing surgery on May 22. He was confident enough to target the Big Ten opener against Penn State as his return date.

The Badgers may have been playing with that faint hope in mind — the hope of regaining their very special playmaker — when they opened the 2002 season with five straight non-conference victories, peaking with a near flawless 31-10 rout of Arizona.

But the Badgers couldn't sustain the momentum from their fast start and lost their first three Big Ten games by a combined total of 11 points. Evans never made it back and required a second surgery on November 22 and Wisconsin went on life support (losing six of seven).

Lifeless would be the best way to categorize a 37-20 home loss to Illinois in early November. Neither Bollinger nor Davis played. The former was still woozy from a blow to the head in the Iowa game. The latter was recovering from a stab wound to his thigh.

Davis was hospitalized for a couple of days after getting into a domestic dispute and nasty altercation at his apartment with his ex-girlfriend. Davis was placed in a first offender program after pleading guilty to misdemeanor battery.

Following the Illinois debacle, things didn't get much better for Davis or the Badgers in the early going at Michigan. On the UW's first play from scrimmage, Davis coughed up the ball after being tackled by Marlin Jackson, and the Wolverines sprinted to a 14-0 lead.

Davis summarily got off the canvas and threw some haymakers,

picking up 154 tough, hard-earned yards on 26 carries. "That's the best I've seen him run since he's been here," White told the *State Journal.* "He was reckless, he was running with conviction, he was breaking tackles and he had great acceleration."

Davis became the first back to rush for over 100 yards against the Michigan defense in 2002. He had six runs of 10 or more yards. There was some life, after all, and a sense of urgency, but the Badgers still came home a 21-14 loser. They were down to their final out, their final swings against Minnesota, with a bowl riding on the outcome.

In addition to becoming bowl eligible, there were other sources of motivation for the Badgers. Nobody wanted to lose back-to-back games to the Gophers. And none of the seniors wanted to feel the same pain and emptiness that the seniors before them had felt after losing to Michigan in their final Camp Randall Stadium appearance.

This was not just any loss to Michigan, this was an industrial-strength heart-breaker. After Wisconsin placekicker Mark Neuser missed a chip-shot field goal with 1:26 remaining that would have broken a 17-17 tie, the Wolverines got a break for the ages — recovering a punted ball which had bounced off the leg of an unsuspecting freshman, Brett Bell.

Michigan kicked a 31-yard field goal on the next play and escaped with a 20-17 decision which understandably left most of the Wisconsin players in shock — and searching for words and answers after the gut-wrenching turn of events.

"It just tears my heart out," Bollinger said. "A bunch of these seniors came in my (recruiting) class and I love them to death. They gave so much to the program, and they didn't deserve this type of ending for their final game in Camp Randall."

That was the devastating memory that Bollinger carried into his final home game, and he was determined to make sure his teammates recognized what was at stake. In fact, he got so worked up, so emotional about the potential consequences that he broke down in tears.

"He broke down crying a couple of times," pointed out Wisconsin coach Barry Alvarez. "It took him a long time to say what he wanted to say because he kept breaking down. But it was really meaningful, and he tried to get across to the kids how important this game was to him, and how important it was for the program."

Message received.

"Brooks had the utmost respect of his offensive line — we would have done anything for him — plus, he was really the leader of all 125 guys," Jowers said. "I think back to how fired up and emotional Brooks was before that Minnesota game — he refused to lose. I

Opposite page: The game plan for Minnesota was predicated on getting Anthony Davis on the edge or corner of the defense. Mission accomplished.

remember him saying that our last memory from Camp Randall was not going to be a loss, and we were not leaving here with nothing, we were not leaving without a bowl."

Mission accomplished. But it wasn't easy. The Gophers took leads of 24-21 in the third quarter and 31-28 in the fourth quarter before the Badgers pulled away to a 49-31 win, registering the most points that they had scored since a 59-0 rout of Indiana in 1999.

The Badgers had a season-high 550 total yards and minimized lapses in the kicking game with opportunistic defense, sparked by Jim Leonhard, a gritty sophomore walk-on from Flambeau High in the tiny northern Wisconsin village of Tony.

Playing with a broken wrist, Leonhard still intercepted his ninth and 10th passes of the season, breaking Neovia Greyer's school record. Both picks ended Minnesota scoring threats in the end zone late in the game. Wisconsin coach Barry Alvarez allowed, "That one

(the first interception) was as good of one as I've seen, maybe ever."

Asked if Leonhard, whose No. 18 became a hot seller, could develop into the same type of leader as No. 5 (Bollinger), Alvarez said, "I don't think he's as vocal as Brooks, he's not the same personality as Brooks. But he will lead by example."

That's what Bollinger and Davis did against the Gophers — they led by example, while following the running script that White had written for them.

Bollinger rushed 18 times for 112 yards (6.2) and one score. (He also completed 6 of 12 passes for 134 yards). Davis rushed 45 times for 301 yards and five touchdowns, joining Ron Dayne (339) and Billy Marek (304) in the exclusive 300 Club at Wisconsin.

Minnesota coach Glen Mason could do the math, and he didn't like the end result. "I'm going to state the obvious," he said, charitably giving everyone fair warning. "We got beat. When you give up over

400 yards rushing, you are going to get beat."

Thanks for the insight, Glen. The Badgers rushed for 420 yards, the most since 1999. With time running out, Davis put his signature on the performance with a career-long 71-yard touchdown. Center Al Johnson was the first to reach Davis in the end zone, and Johnson hoisted Davis straight-up in the air, well-above his shoulders, like he was symbolically making a toast to the heavens. On this day, Davis must have felt like he was walking on air.

"I definitely wanted to try and play my best game," Davis said. Well, he didn't really come out and say it. Thinking that nobody had requested his presence at the post-game media interrogation, Davis bolted the locker room. Unlike anyone on the Minnesota defense, a member of the UW public relations staff caught up with him — he was eating dinner in a local restaurant — and relayed his thoughts via a telephone.

"It was the last home game for our seniors, and I wanted to give as much effort as I possibly could," the Davis release read. "Our offensive line dominated the line of scrimmage and that let us keep the running game going."

Weeks later, in advance of Wisconsin's match-up against Colorado in the Alamo Bowl, Davis admitted to the Associated Press that his off the field issues had inspired him.

"When something like that happens to you, it's just human nature to get discouraged, to get down on yourself," Davis said. "I had so much support...and it just made me want to play harder and do everything better."

Few had better freshman years than Anthony Davis. Remember what they were saying then? The streak was in serious jeopardy. For eight straight years, the Wisconsin offense had generated a 1,000-yard rusher. But the Badgers had reached the end of the production line, they said. With the sudden departure of Michael Bennett, who skipped his final year of eligibility for a pro contract, there was nobody to continue the tradition.

Davis proved otherwise during the 2001 season, rushing for 1,466 yards, the sixth highest total by a freshman in NCAA history. "There were some comments made that this was going to be the year where the streak was supposedly going to end," Davis said. "That really stuck in the back of my head and definitely helped motivate me."

The 1,000-yard streak began in 1993 with Brent Moss and reached its peak during Ron Dayne's four record-breaking seasons, culminating in 1999 when Dayne broke the NCAA career rushing mark and won the Heisman Trophy. That same year, Davis won his high school's equivalent of the Heisman in New Jersey.

"I had heard of Dayne because he was from Jersey," Davis said. "And I was aware of the streak of 1,000-yard rushers and it influenced my decision to come to Wisconsin. I looked at their history of

tailbacks and how important that position is to the offense and I saw a school that relies heavily on the running back, and I liked that."

All Davis needed was a chance to establish his own football identity, separate from Dayne and Bennett. All he needed was a chance to show what he could do. Yet there was a stretch during his first year on campus when he was buried on the depth chart, and he wondered if he would ever get that opportunity.

"Those were some rough times for me," Davis said. "I never thought I was going to have a chance to play here. I'd call my family and tell them, 'I'm never going to play, the coaches don't like me, this and that, and that and this.' And they just told me to be patient and the cream will rise to the top."

After Davis rushed for 147 yards in his college debut against Virginia, there was never any doubt about his ability. In breaking Tony Dorsett's freshman record for 100-yard games, he showed off his speed with a 69-yard run at Oregon and a 61-yard gallop at Minnesota. And, a year later, he was still running wild against the Gophers in Camp Randall.

"Anthony's consistent productivity — when healthy — was pretty remarkable," White said. "His standard of performance really never deviated regardless of who we were playing, whether it was Ohio State, Penn State or even Michigan. Playing against those 'elite' teams, Anthony's record was as impressive as anybody's."

When healthy.

The caveat.

Davis rushed for more yardage (3,021) than anybody in the nation during the 2001 and 2002 seasons, carrying the ball 591 times and missing just one game each year.

Watching Davis explode for 247 yards against Akron in the 2003 home opener, Alvarez said, "We've been around a lot of good backs, but I don't know if we've ever had one playing as good as Anthony is playing right now. Ron played at a pretty high level for four years, and I'm just saying Anthony is every bit in that category. He's truly special."

After getting off to the fastest start of his career with 414 rushing yards in the first two games of the '03 season, Davis injured his ankle on his second carry of the UNLV game. And the high ankle sprain had a lingering effect. The 1,000-yard streak ended at 10.

Outside of one great moment his senior year against Illinois — 27 rushes for 213 yards and three scores — Davis never again came close to dominating like he did against the Gophers at the end of the 2002 regular season.

At the very least, Davis and his teammates had an Axe to grind again, and the 11 seniors had a fitting sendoff and lasting memory from their final home game.

"You kind of envision how you want it to all end," Bollinger said contentedly, "and fortunately today it was pretty much exactly how I envisioned it ending."

Opposite page: The victorious Badgers reclaim the Paul Bunyan Axe, a symbol of the border rivalry between Minnesota and Wisconsin, at 114 games, the longest series in Division I-A football. The W-Club instituted the Axe in 1948. Prior to that (circa 1930), the schools played for the "Slab of Bacon" trophy.

Wisconsin 22 Oregon 19

On the Monday before the 1978 season opener, Wisconsin's first-year head coach Dave McClain revealed that John Josten, a true freshman and prep All-American from St. Viator in Arlington Heights, Illinois, would be his starting quarterback against Richmond.

Three days earlier, Josten had turned 18. But he had been preparing for this challenge ever since he became one of McClain's first recruits and building blocks.

"When I reported to training camp, I had the dream and hope that I would be starting," said Josten, who picked Wisconsin over Michigan. "There was pressure to get the (No. 1) job but now the pressure is to perform and do a good job."

Josten, who patterned his option skills after Wolverines quarterback Rick Leach, beat out three John Jardine-recruited players for the starting assignment: senior Charles Green and juniors Jeff Buss and Mike Kalasmiki.

Leach was also a freshman starter — his college debut coming against Wisconsin in the 1975 opener at Camp Randall Stadium. Despite throwing three interceptions, Leach led the Wolverines to a 23-6 victory. Leach tried to recruit Josten to Michigan.

"Leach has the ability to wait until the last second to make the pitch, and that's something a good option quarterback has to do," said the 6-foot, 190-pound Josten. "A lot of people have said I'm too small. I don't think so. I know Leach is not much bigger than I

Opposite page: There was never any question about Mike Kalasmiki's arm strength. Dubbed the "Polish Rifle," he used to play around before and after practices by standing in front of the lower row of seats and winging the ball out of the stadium.

The Portage Plumber (aka Terry Westegard) was a fixture at home games with his unusual dress and dance routine. "People are getting to the point where they expect me to do it good," Westegard said of his pom-pon skit. "Before, when I messed up, they got a kick out of it. But now when I do, they start booing and asking themselves, 'What's wrong with this guy? Is he slipping?' I just need a little more practice, that's all."

am."

The last freshman "quarterback" to start an opening game for Wisconsin was Allen Shafer, Jr., in the 1944 opener against Northwestern. The distinction? When the Badgers shifted their formation, it was usually halfback Earl (Jug) Girard, also a freshman, who handled the ball from center with Shafer utilized as a blocking back.

(Shafer was fatally injured in the Iowa game that season and his No. 83 is one of four retired numbers. Shafer was one of two UW players to die from a football related injury. The other was Jay Seiler, a freshman on McClain's 1978 team.)

"After a few guys found out I was starting, Dave Crossen came over to my locker and told me everyone would have faith in me," Josten said. Crossen, a senior linebacker, was the team's leading tackler and reigning MVP. "He told me to relax, take it easy, and do the best job I could. For him to say that to me meant a lot."

Although McClain had run power football at Ball State, he was in the midst of converting to a much different system with the Badgers. "I went to Michigan and I picked up the option from them," McClain said. "We try to do the same things."

And that was to Josten's advantage. He ran the veer option in high school for two years and was best suited to handle McClain's playbook. One of the holdovers, Kalasmiki, was more of a pure dropback passer and the odd-man out. Temporarily.

Josten completed just one pass —he was 1-of-5 — in his debut against Richmond. But it was a thing of beauty, an 80-yard touchdown pass to David Charles, equaling, at the time, the longest

Quarterback Mike Kalasmiki barks out the signals and awaits the snap from center Jim Moore, a senior from Rhinelander and three-year starter.

Courtesy of UW Sports Information

Courtesy of UW Sports Information

Bottom left: Starting quarterback John Josten, a true freshman, was chased out of the pocket and dropped for a loss on this play. Josten injured his knee on the second series against Oregon and was sidelined for the remainder of the game.

Bottom right: Wisconsin quarterback Mike Kalasmiki was named the Big Ten's Player of the Week on offense after rallying the Badgers to a victory over Oregon. Observed UW coach Dave McClain, "That was the most unbelievable game I think I've ever coached in."

pass-and-catch in school history, dating to 1919 (Wally Barr to Paul Meyers).

So much for the scoring highlights. The Badgers barely hung on to nip the Spiders, 7-6, as a walk-on, John Kiltz, worked overtime. Kiltz was the UW punter, and he made 11 appearances. The Wisconsin offense was on the field for 52 plays, the defense for 82. Josten played little more than a half, by design, before giving way to Green.

Ohio State also started a freshman quarterback in the '78 opener, and the Buckeyes paid for the choice. Art Schlichter threw five picks and lost a fumble in a 19-0 loss to Penn State. You can bet Schlichter's struggles didn't make McClain feel any better about his sputtering offense and rookie starter. And he wasn't the only restless soul in Camp Randall.

"The fans must really get bored with a game like that," said center Jim Moore after the Badgers collected just seven first downs against Richmond. "Three plays, and punt. Three plays, and punt. Heck, we didn't give them anything to cheer about all day. The only time I heard the crowd was when the pom-pom girls were out there."

And over 70,000 spectators weren't reacting to them — or the drummers or the tuba-players — as much as they were reacting to the fabled Portage Plumber.

Terry Westegard was not actually a plumber but a portly 5-foot-11, 235-pound steamfitter in Portage. During a lull in a 1976 home game, he morphed into the Plumber. "I was just sitting there by myself," he said, "and things were so lopsided in the game that I decided to go down and stir up some action."

His routine was basic. During the fourth quarter, he would pop out of his seat — seat 13, row 48, Section X — and join the Badger pom-pom squad on the cement runway circling the artificial playing surface at Camp Randall.

His attire was outlandish. He wore a furry red cap, pulled down over his ears; a white T-shirt with "The Pride" emblazoned on his chest; and a furry skirt over a pair of white Levis. His choreography was simple. Positioning himself at the end of the dance line, he tried to follow the lead of the girls who twirled their pom-poms to the beat of the drums.

UW band director Michael Leckrone was not initially amused. "We had always had trouble with kids following and pestering the tubas," Leckrone recalled. "And the first time I heard this roar go up from the crowd, I just thought it was another drunk."

But The Plumber's act grew on Leckrone, who confessed, "The first time I met him I was expecting to find a real nut. But he was so nice and gracious and he had fun intentions."

Still, there were attempts to get rid of The Plumber by some university officials who feared that he was taking away from the "game atmosphere." The previous season, a security guard was instructed to yank Westegard from the pom-pom line.

UW athletic director Elroy Hirsch, sensing a student revolt and potentially dangerous situation, called down to the field from the press box, and waved off the security goon. "Elroy later thanked me for helping them through the lean years," said Westegard, who retired his pom-poms in the early '80's, once the Badgers started making noise on the field.

Of his routine, he said, "I'm limited in what I can do. I'm not like that chicken in San Diego (Ted Giannoulas, whose act was hatched in 1974). I don't run all over the stadium and get nuts. But as long as people are having fun, I want to continue. Every place I go, someone will recognize me and bring his wife over for my autograph. I like the notoriety."

As you might expect, McClain didn't like the distraction and his immediate goal was to get everyone talking about his team, not The Plumber. The Badgers took a step in that direction with a 28-7 road win at Northwestern in Week 2 of the '78 season.

Ira Matthews rushed for 125 yards and scored on a 78-yard punt return, and fullback Tom Stauss ran for 123 yards and two scores. Despite playing in front of family and friends, who made the short trip from Palatine to Evanston, Josten managed the offense with more poise than he had shown in the opener. Plus, he completed 7-of-7 passes for 79 yards.

Nonetheless, McClain wasn't yet ready to completely abandon his tag-team rotation of Josten and Green. And Kalasmiki, another Chicago area product (Addison Trail), wasn't yet ready to make a serious move on the depth chart. Or hadn't to that point. Truth is, Kalasmiki couldn't get out of his own way, a troubling predicament.

As a freshman, with limited experience in anything but a dropback scheme, he wasn't ready to compete for playing time, physically or mentally. Instead, he worked on improving his mobility for Jardine's sprint-out offense. As a sophomore, he was still No. 3 behind Green and Anthony Dudley, though some players favored his arm over the others.

Kalasmiki finally got his break to start a game — by default. Dudley, who had been holding down the No. 1 spot, was out with a

Courtesy of UW Sports Information

Dave McClain discusses strategy with quarterback Mike Kalasmiki, a 6-4, 206-pound junior from Addison Trail, Illinois.

wrist injury, while Green was nursing a sore ankle. Jardine had nowhere else to turn, no other options.

Thus, the rangy 6-foot-4, 206-pound Kalasmiki got his first career start against none other than the Ohio State Buckeyes in front of the 55th consecutive sell-out crowd (87, 837) to watch a game in Columbus. Thanks for the memories. The Buckeyes won 42-0.

Kalasmiki completed 7 of 14 passes for 54 yards. He was intercepted twice and knocked down multiple times. "I don't remember much about the first half," he said. And it would get much worse for him before it would get better.

The following Monday, Kalasmiki and Buss were playing a friendly game of catch on the practice field when Kalasmiki ran a deep pattern, went up in the air, caught the ball, and came down hard on the turf. His left knee buckled and he had surgery that week.

Some feared it might be a career-ending injury. When McClain and the new staff arrived, Kalasmiki was damaged goods, the great unknown. "But I knew that I could throw the ball," he said. "And I had confidence in myself. I just had to wait for my shot."

The week of the Oregon game, it got even more bizarre for Kalasmiki who had entered his junior season with a swollen knee and more than his fair share of question marks.

After Tuesday's practice, he slipped and fell on the fire escape outside his State Street apartment. "I tried to grab the rail when I fell," he told the *State Journal.* "But I missed."

Kalasmiki needed 11 stitches to close the wound across the bridge of his nose, while his blackened left eye was so swollen that he had to ice it down each morning just to see out of it. He couldn't even get his helmet on the day after the freak accident.

Could anyone make this up? It gets better. "Mike has been saying he wants to throw a football out of the stadium," UW offensive coordinator Bill Dudley said. "I mean throw it completely out of it; stand on the field and throw it over the stands. Well, the other day, he did

In a jubilant post-game celebration, Dave McClain gets carried off the field and exchanges a heartfelt victory handshake with UW band director Michael Leckrone.

it for the first time." A legend in waiting.

On the morning of the Oregon game, Kalasmiki was still icing down his bruises; not that it mattered if he had both eyes closed since he wasn't in the plans. Then fate intervened. On the UW's first offensive series against the Ducks, the Badgers lost their starting fullback, Stauss, with a knee injury. On their second series, they lost Josten to another knee injury. Early in the second quarter, Matthews had to be helped off the field with a shoulder injury.

Green took over for Josten but when he couldn't move the offense, Kalasmiki inherited the controls, ready or not. Mike who? "I never even heard of him before," admitted Oregon's second-year head coach Rich Brooks. "He didn't show up on any of the film we had. He didn't even show up on the depth chart."

Through three quarters, the Badgers were still an ugly rumor. Wrote Tom Butler in the *State Journal*, "By this time, the natives in the $8 seats were getting restless. After the Badgers executed 14 straight running plays without a pass in the second half, the boo's rang out."

The winless Ducks (0-3) led 13-0 before Kalasmiki connected with David Charles on a 26-yard touchdown pass in the fourth quarter. But Oregon quickly answered with a 70-yard scoring march, making it 19-7 with just 7 minutes and 7 seconds left.

Wisconsin appeared to inch closer on a 49-yard touchdown pass from Kalasmiki to Sugar Ray Sydnor. But the 6-7 Sydnor was flagged for offensive pass interference. The Badgers failed to score on that series but caught a huge break moments later.

With 3:04 remaining, Brooks had to make a play-calling decision: a third-and-5 call from the Oregon 30. He could have — should have — kept the clock moving with a run. But he opted to put the ball in

Instructed by athletic department officials to only play the "Bud Song" after the game, the UW Marching Band began a new tradition—the Fifth Quarter.

the air. Wrong choice. UW linebacker Dave Levenick intercepted Mike Kennedy's errant throw and returned it to the 24. The Badgers had new life.

"I was unbelievably surprised when he did that," said McClain, noting that he had made a similar clock management mistake earlier in his career. "And I wound up getting my tail beat and I vowed I wouldn't do it again. I imagine he (Brooks) would do it over, if he could. But it was definitely the turning point in the game, and it got us back into it."

The Badgers converted the turnover into another score: a 12-yard pass from Kalasmiki to Tim Stracka, the former Madison West star. That made it 19-14. On the ensuing kickoff, McClain substituted Steve Veith, who handled the placements, for Mike Brhely, the regular kickoff specialist. Veith was inserted to lift the ball over the wedge.

The strategy worked. Mickey Casey recovered Veith's pooch kick on the Oregon 25 and Kalasmiki was back in business. The drive stalled at the 15 when Kalasmiki misfired on a third down pass. But the Ducks were guilty of another mistake: roughing the passer.

Two plays later, with 1:32 still showing on the clock, Kevin Cohee, subbing for Matthews, scored the game-winning touchdown on a five-yard run. And that completed one of the most improbable comebacks in Camp Randall history — 22 points in the final 10 minutes and 29 seconds (with the last two scores coming less than a minute apart.)

The architect of the rally, of course, was Kalasmiki, who finally lived up to his nickname "The Polish Rifle" by completing 16 of 35 passes for 232 yards. What he needed was the time to throw, and he got it from his offensive line: Moore, tackles Dave Krall and Ray Snell, and guards Jim Martine and Patrick Kelly. He was sacked just once.

"I've never been in a game like this — never," Kalasmiki said. "The crowd was great, and it was the most emotional moment I've ever experienced in football."

Later in the season, Kalasmiki rallied Wisconsin from a 24-6 fourth quarter deficit against Mark Herrmann and Purdue. The Badgers scored with 25 seconds left in the game and Kalasmiki successfully executed the two-point conversion with a pass to Wayne Souza who caught the ball on his knees in the end zone. That produced a memorable 24-24 tie.

Still, it couldn't top the Oregon rally for sheer drama or theatrics. Kalasmiki and some of his teammates joined over 200 students on the field about 30 minutes after the 22-19 thriller over the Ducks to dance and revel in their amazing comeback. Adding to the fourth quarter emotion and the atmosphere that day was Leckrone and the UW band.

"We had played 'On Wisconsin' to the point of ad nauseam," Leckrone said. "I was looking for something else and there was a tune that we had started playing at hockey games in 1973 that had worked. The kids knew it and I remember saying, 'Well, let's play it.'"

The tune was the "Bud Song" — known for "When you say WISCONSIN you've said it all." Leckrone kept playing it and playing it throughout the fourth quarter. The good news was that the fans loved it, clapping and stomping their feet to the music. The bad news was the fans loved it—the clapping and stomping caused the upper deck to sway.

The school got complaints from Nervous Nellies, and Hirsch instructed Leckrone to stop playing the "Bud Song" during games. Hence, the popular ditty was relegated to the post-game, and the Fifth Quarter evolved from there.

Wisconsin 16 Penn 7
November 10, 1951

Age has not mellowed Pat O'Donahue. Thankfully.

Once a rock, always a rock, forever a Hard Rock.

Ask the still ornery O'Donahue about the 1950 Ohio State game in Columbus, and he will grumble, "We lost the ballgame, but we kicked the hell out of them actually."

Ask the still competitive O'Donahue about the 1950 Penn game in Philadelphia, and he will concede, "We were nothing, and they knew it and beat the hell out of us."

Ask the still feisty O'Donahue about the 1951 Illinois game in Champaign, and he will growl, "This sounds like sour grapes, but it can be proven — the officials who worked that game never worked another Big Ten game. That's how bad we had it stuck to us."

In the Big Ten opener, Illinois handed Wisconsin a 14-10 loss in front of 56,207 at Memorial Stadium. "And an idea of the savagery with which it was contested," wrote State Journal sports editor Henry J. McCormick, "can be gleaned from the fact that two players from each team were ejected for unsuual roughness."

The turning point occurred in the third quarter. Clinging to a 10-7 lead, Wisconsin had a first-and-goal on the Illinois 1-yard line. And a second of a score here would have made it fully tough for the Illini to rally against the Hard Rocks' defense.

Opposite page: In 1949, Ivy Williamson (far right) replaced Harry Stuhldreher as Wisconsin's head coach, and Williamson quickly assembled a formidable staff. From far left: George Lanphear, Paul Shaw, Fred Marsh, Bob O'Dell and Milt Bruhn.

Pat O'Donahue, No. 88, a 6-0, 190-pound senior end from Eau Claire. All-Big Ten in 1951.

But a costly backfield-in-motion penalty disrupted the series for the Badgers, who managed to pick up just two yards on four plays. Illinois took over on the 4. You will never convince O'Donahue that the officials didn't conspire against Wisconsin, either.

Motion? What motion?

McCormick saw it differently, crediting Illinois linebackers Chuck Boerio and Elie Popa: "They were mad men in blue jerseys as they fought off the Badger touchdown bid."

Wisconsin coach Ivy Williamson agreed with that assessment. "The Illinois line was strong and plenty tough when the going was tough," he told the State Journal. "They just made one of those goal-line stands and we couldn't draw them out.

"We were pretty well keyed up for this one. Now our boys are feeling a bit low. They wanted this game, and they played hard for it. What was the trouble? Well, we just couldn't score the points when they counted. It's the points that count, not the first downs."

True enough, the Badgers had more first downs (20-8), more plays (77-46), and more total yardage (274-142) than Illinois. Unlike Wisconsin, though, the Illini converted on a first-and-goal situation from the Badger 7 in the fourth quarter when halfback Johnny Karras scored his second rushing touchdown, and that spelled the difference in the game.

Summarizing the loss, McCormick wrote, "You can look at it any way you wish. That Illinois' offense rose to the heights when needed.

Courtesy of UW Sports Information

Bob Kennedy, No. 79, a 5-10, 195-pound junior guard from Rhinelander.

Courtesy of UW Sports Information

Jerome Smith, No. 73, a 5-11, 208-pound senior tackle from Dayton, Ohio.

That Illinois' defense put on a stand out of all proportion to its average for the day. That Wisconsin's attack bogged down at the wrong time. That Wisconsin's defense sagged for the brief but fatal seconds. Whatever you choose, Illinois had the winning combination for this day."

The disappointed Badgers couldn't afford to dwell on the defeat because they returned home to play Ohio State, led by consensus All-American halfback Vic Janowicz, the 1950 Heisman Trophy winner. "He could do everything we asked him to do," said Buckeye assistant coach Gene Feteke at a 2000 halftime ceremony retiring Janowicz's No. 31 jersey. "And he could do it in a masterful-type situation."

Many believed Janowicz was Ohio State's greatest player, greater than even tailback Archie Griffin, who won two Heismans. At the core of the Janowicz lore was a game-winning 27-yard field goal that he kicked in blizzard-like conditions to beat Michigan in 1950.

But the Hard Rocks had his number the following season in Madison. Janowicz was held to a scant 11 net yards on 11 carries in a 6-6 draw with the Badgers. He also missed the extra point that could have broken the tie in the fourth quarter as a record crowd of 51,000 in Camp Randall Stadium breathed a collective sigh of relief when his kick went wide.

The fans were treated to something new—cardinal jerseys and pants and plenty of the same old, same old — the same old Badgers who dominated the statistics like they had against Illinois: first downs (19-7) and total yardage (346-106). But it was Janowicz's punting that consistently bailed out the Buckeyes. He averaged 43.8 yards.

"There will be few games any place in the country this year that will be played as brutally as this one between the Badgers and the Buckeyes," McCormick wrote the next day. "As the game ended, the players walked slowly from the field, stopping now and then to shake hands with each other. They had earned each other's respect and the respect of the largest and most enthusiastic crowd ever to see a Wisconsin home game."

After a two game road trip produced victories at Purdue (31-7) and Northwestern (41-0), the Badgers returned to Camp Randall in early November, and they were greeted by a raging snow storm when they took the field against Indiana.

"The driving snow kept coming down throughout the four quarters," Charles Johnson observed in the *Minneapolis Tribune*. "It was impossible to see the yard lines most of the day, but all but 1,000 of the 51,000 tickets sold were used. That's quite a tribute to Wisconsin loyalty for the weather was so bad that before the game, officials didn't expect more than half the stadium, which had been sold out, to be filled."

The temperature was 25 degrees at kickoff, and a 25-mile-per-hour wind blew out of the southeast. But those who came, and stayed, were treated to some last-second heroics by Wisconsin quarterback John Coatta who connected on a 36-yard touchdown pass to Bill Hutchinson with 58 seconds left in the game. And that's how it ended, 6-0.

"I suppose you would call that a shot in the dark," Williamson acknowledged of the TD reception to the *Capital Times*. Hutchinson was subbing for the injured Rollie Strehlow, and it was his first catch of the season. "I thought we played fine ball throughout, considering the conditions," Williamson went on. "When you can't pass the ball, it's hard to operate."

When you can't hold on to the ball, it's hard to score. Wisconsin fumbled 10 times, and lost five. Indiana had just two turnovers. But its offense was simply no match for the Hard Rocks. The Hoosiers crossed midfield just three times, never deeper than the 42. The Badgers finished with a huge edge in confidence and total yards (331-91).

And, in part, they can thank Indiana coach Clyde Smith, who had made the mistake of giving Wisconsin some bulletin board material. The week before, Smith called out the Hard Rocks by insinuating that Illinois had a better defense. "Wisconsin MAY be a better team defensively," Smith was quoted as saying in a Champaign newspaper, "but I doubt it."

Never doubt the Hard Rocks, who carried a grudge into their rematch with the Penn Quakers the following Saturday at Camp Randall Stadium. Big grudge. "We had vowed that we would get even with them," O'Donahue emphasized. Laughingly, he recalled the 1950 trip to Philadelphia. "It was SUPPOSED to be the City of Brotherly Love."

It was not. Penn showed little respect or love for Wisconsin, crushing the Badgers, 20-0, at Franklin Field. A crowd of 60,000 loved every second of the rout, though. "I won't say anything about last week or next week," Penn coach George Munger said to the Associated Press. "But nobody could have taken us today."

Williamson concurred. "All I know is that we would have had to be at the top of our game to stay with Penn, and we simply weren't," he said to the AP. Although the Badgers played without Bill Albright and Roy Burks, and O'Donahue was limited to a few snaps, Williamson refused to use injuries as an alibi. "Penn just beat us," he said.

Others had more to say.

"Those thuds you heard between 12:30 and 2:45 o'clock Saturday afternoon, those loud, disturbing thuds," Oliver Kuechle wrote in the *Milwaukee Journal*, "that was Wisconsin's football team being bounced around Franklin Field."

The *Chicago Tribune's* Irving Vaughn labeled the Badgers as "those doughty boys from the shores of Lake Mendota" and declared them "simply outclassed."

Wrote Joe Hendrickson in the *Minneapolis Tribune*, "Pennslvania was magnificent and Wisconsin sputtered feebly. Back in his famous days of experimentation with electricity, Benjamin Franklin saw no more lightning than Francis (Reds) Bagnell..."

Bagnell was a terror, running and passing for 229 yards. And the Badgers didn't have the energy to contain him. Emotionally, they were a shell of the team that had lost, 19-14, at Ohio State the previous Saturday in a hard-fought, bruising game that was surprisingly free of penalties and took just one hour and 59 minutes to complete.

Coatta, sharper than ever, hit on 12 of 16 passes, including his first 10 attempts, and the Badgers held a 7-6 halftime lead before the Janowicz-led Buckeyes rallied for the victory. "We figured that we were going to win that Ohio State game," O'Donahue said.

And when they didn't win, they played with a hangover at Penn. As the Badgers walked out of Franklin Field, O'Donahue remembered everyone setting their sights on the '51 rematch. Especially since 27 of the 38 players who saw action in Philly were returning.

"When they (the Quakers) came to Madison, they were not aware of what was going to happen because we didn't say much during the week — we just practiced that way (with revenge in mind)," O'Donahue said. "Once the ballgame started, it was like, 'Ok, let's get 'em.' And we did, we absolutely annihilated them. And they had a good ball club, too."

Just not good enough, or tough enough, to handle a buzz saw. That's what the Quakers ran into. And what made this Camp Randall moment so great from O'Donahue's perspective was the fact that the Hard Rocks accounted for nearly all the points in a 16-7 victory.

"This was a savagely played game," McCormick wrote in the *State Journal*, "that developed into a bitter feud at the finish, with the officials stepping off four penalties on Wisconsin in the last few minutes for unnecessary roughness."

The Hard Rocks would define unnecessary roughness as an oxymoron. "It wasn't a dirty ballgame, really," O'Donahue claimed. "But

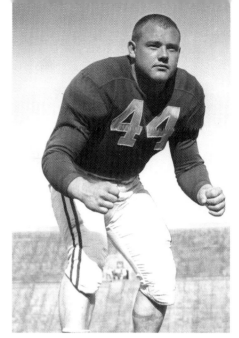

Deral Teteak, No. 44, a 5-9, 185-pound senior linebacker from Oshkosh.

Courtesy of UW Sports Information

when they (the Quakers) left the field, they hadn't even got to the locker room yet, and Penn broke off relations with Wisconsin."

Must have taken a vote of the offense. Penn crossed midfield just twice: driving to the UW 40 in the first half, and the 29 in the second half. Overall, the Quakers rushed 44 times for a net 13 yards. Most of their total yardage came on one pass play: a Jerry Robinson pass to Tom Hanlon in the flat. Hanlon broke a tackle and raced 68 yards for a touchdown.

"Penn's single wing was well contained except for this one brief moment in the third quarter," Kuechle wrote. "They never even came close the rest of the time."

Injuries took a toll on the UW offense. Freshman fullback Alan Ameche left the game early in the second quarter with a shoulder separation. His replacement, Jimmy Hammond, suffered a concussion just before intermission and didn't play in the second half. Coatta, meanwhile, was out of sync, completing just 5 of 22 passes. He had three picks.

Not to fear. The Hard Rocks are here.

In the first quarter, Penn center John Evans' snap flew over the head of Chester Cornog and Wisconsin linebacker Deral (The Little Bull) Teteak caught up with the rolling ball in the end zone for a touchdown. Coatta kicked the extra point, making it 7-0.

Courtesy of UW Sports Information

Don Voss, No. 90, a 6-3, 185-pound freshman end from Milwaukee. Freshmen were eligible due to the Korean War and filled a big void after an injury to Gene Felker. Helped lead the Badgers to the 1952 Big Ten title and first bowl appearance, a 7-0 loss to USC in the 1953 Rose Bowl. Named All-American that season. Also a track All-American. Suffered career-ending knee injury in second quarter of Rose Bowl.

Ed Withers, No. 11, a 5-11, 185-pound senior half-back from Madison Central High School. All-Big Ten in 1951. Eight career interceptions. First African-American athlete to earn All-American recognition at Wisconsin.

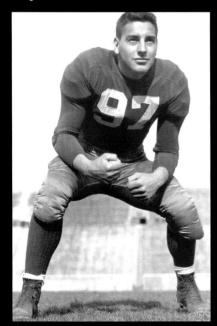

Gene Felker, No. 97, a 6-0, 189-pound senior end from Milwaukee.

O'Donahue and Jerry Smith were also in position to fall on the fumble, but Teteak flew past them. And with good reason. Seems that Williamson had his own scoring system, whereby he would award points and/or bonuses ($$$) for big plays.

"Ivan would score off the film and me and Deral were running one-two in points," O'Donahue said. "Well, their center (Evans) got so sick and tired of Bob Kennedy hitting him in the head when he snapped the ball, he snapped one very poorly into the end zone.

"Teteak and I were going after it, and, of course, I was in front of Deral, when all of a sudden I was on my stomach rolling on the ground. I didn't know what hit me. But in the film you could see Deral tripped me absolutely on purpose because he wanted the points."

Late in the quarter, freshman defensive end Don Voss, subbing for the injured Gene Felker, deflected a pass at the line of scrimmage and defensive tackle Bob Leu picked it out of the air and lumbered 39 yards for a touchdown. With another Coatta extra point, it was 14-0.

In the second half, O'Donahue got into the act, tackling Robinson in the end zone for a safety. That made it Hard Rocks 14, Coatta 2, Penn 7.

"The best defensive team in the country beat Pennsylvania all by itself," Kuechle wrote, "and the best defensive team, of course, is Wisconsin."

The Hard Rocks nearly had another score when Eddie Withers intercepted a pass and returned it 60 yards before getting caught from behind on the Penn 19. Through seven games, the UW defense had four touchdowns and four safeties.

Counting extra points and field goals, the Hard Rocks finished the 1951 season by outscoring all opponents, 58-53. (Eight of the nine seniors scored during their careers.) What made this defense so unique, so special? Was it team chemistry?

"Oh, sure," O'Donahue said. "You might say we were interwoven. We had a great nucleus. We all lived together for four years. When we came here, Wisconsin was nothing and we were told that we were dummies for going there."

The Cheeseheads rallied around each other. O'Donahue (6-0, 190) was from Eau Claire, Teteak (5-9, 185) from Oshkosh, Withers (5-11, 185) from Madison, Hammond (6-0, 188) from Appleton, Lane (5-11, 176) from Edgerton, Leu (6-2, 220) from Ripon, Felker (6-0, 190) and Voss (6-3, 185) from Milwaukee, and Kennedy (5-10, 195) from Rhinelander.

"Most of us had played in a north-south high school all-star game," O'Donahue said. "And that's where the crew first met. We got a little smart-alecky and sassy — we were a cocky bunch — and we all decided that we'd go to Wisconsin and bail them out."

Felker and Hal Faverty, who was selected as the team's Most Valuable Player in 1951, played on offense and defense. As freshmen, they had lived in the stadium with O'Donahue, Teteak, Smith and Coatta. Later, they shared a notorious State Street apartment. "We had fun all the time," O'Donahue said, "and we played after the game, too."

Who was the best player (on the field) among the Hard Rocks?

"That's really impossible to say," O'Donahue pleaded. "We were the sum of our parts. And I can say this in all sincerity, I don't think there was one truly outstanding player — like an Ameche — on the defense. They were all damn good."

In sum, the Hard Rocks were O'Donahue, Felker and Voss at defensive end; Smith and Leu at tackle, Kennedy at nose, Faverty, Teteak and Roger Dornburg at linebacker, Withers and Hammond at corner, and Lane at safety.

"George Lanphear had a great eye for horse flesh," O'Donahue said of the UW assistant coach who recruited many of the players. "You might say Ivan designed the defense. It was physical. But there was a lot of slanting and looping, a lot of game-playing, which was unheard of in those days. And it made a big difference."

Penn brought the best out of them. And then some. But the boys had to share the spotlight with the girls: Margie Terrill (Mineral Point), Ly Anne Fleming (Milwaukee), Sharyn Chessen (Duluth) and Virginia Lee Kehl (Madison). As a group, they were the first women cheerleaders at a Wisconsin football game. There was a lot more to cheer about, too.

The Badgers ended the 1951 season with a flourish, whipping Iowa (34-7) and Minnesota (30-6). Ameche was unstoppable against the Gophers, rushing for 200 yards. "It made no difference where the Horse hurled himself into the line," Kuechle wrote in the *Milwaukee Journal*. "It bent or cracked or was split wide open, and Ameche not infrequently tore on with Minnesota men draped all over him."

Courtesy of UW Sports Information

Left to Right: Hal Faverty, a 6-2, 198-pound senior end from Evanston, Illinois and the team MVP; Jim Hammond, a 6-0, 188-pound senior halfback from Appleton; Billy Lane, a 5-11, 176-pound senior safety from Edgerton; Roger Dornburg, a 5-8, 185-pound sophomore linebacker from Naperville, Illinois; John Coatta, a 5-11, 172-pound senior from Dearborn, Michigan; and Bob Leu, a 6-2, 220-pound senior tackle from Ripon.

Over 1,000 fans were waiting at the railroad station in Madison that Sunday night when the Badgers returned from Minneapolis. According to the *State Journal*, the crowd broke out into a chant for Ameche, who rushed for 824 yards as a freshman.

"If there was a better football team in the country, I don't know about it," Williamson volunteered. "They are wonderful boys. It's by far the best team I've ever coached."

Coatta was first team All-Big Ten and the first quarterback to throw for over 1,000 yards in conference history, completing 64 percent. Jerry Witt was the leading receiver and scorer in the Big Ten. O'Donahue, Teteak, Kennedy and Smith were first-team on defense.

The offense finally caught up with the Hard Rocks during the second half of the year, and Wisconsin wound up leading the conference statistically on both sides of the ball.

The Badgers averaged 379.3 yards of total offense, 155.4 yards passing, 19.3 first downs and 11.9 completions. All were Big Ten records.

The Hard Rocks led the country in total defense (154.8 yards per game), and they were second in rushing defense (66.8). They allowed just 5.9 points per game.

Impressive numbers, except Illinois still went to the Rose Bowl on the strength of its 5-0-1 Big Ten record. (And the Illini represented the Big Ten well, whipping Stanford in Pasadena). In the conference standings, Purdue was second, and Wisconsin was third.

"Sentimentally, you could pull for Wisconsin because it has never enjoyed the glorious California trip," Paul Hornung wrote in the *Columbus Dispatch*. He added that there were more valid reasons to make an argument for the Badgers over the Illini.

"After watching both teams I'd vote for Wisconsin as the most representative...Coach Woody Hayes and his staff probably wouldn't go on the record publicly. But I'd be willing to bet they'd rather meet Illinois again than Wisconsin."

Minneapolis Tribune sportswriter Dick Cullum also jumped on the bandwagon. "No team in the country was better through the second half of the season than Wisconsin."

What kind of team would the Badgers have today if they could put the Hard Rocks on the field every game? "Wisconsin would be undefeated," said O'Donahue, singling out Tom Burke (a starting defensive end on the 1998 Badgers) as Hard Rocks timber.

McCormick was responsible for coming up with the nickname. He also authored a poem — *An Ode to the Hard Rocks* — which O'Donahue still has hanging on the wall.

We thrill to halfbacks swinging wide to fullbacks smashing through.
We dote on passers throwing strikes to ends with hands like glue;
We like the whole offensive show, we cheer each sterling play;
But, best of all, we like that gang that holds the foe at bay.

It picks up later...

Hard Rocks they call this bristling crew of heavy-handed boys;
They play with joyous savagery and wreck opponent's poise.
They crack down halfbacks swinging wide, no fullbacks can smash through;
And passers often find themselves well-marked in black and blue.
They make Wisconsin's goal a thing which foes seldom cross;
They take the field and lose no time in showing who is boss.
They have left their marks on foes and records bear this out;
They'll leave some more I'll bet you, in case, there is any doubt.
They have won high praise on merit, they've earned a solid fame
By digging in and playing a savage, rugged game.

Once a rock, always a rock, forever a Hard Rock.

Wisconsin 27 Oregon 23
September 9, 2000

The first shoe fell, if you will, shortly after the players reported for the opening of the 2000 training camp at the O'Connor Catholic Center on Madison's far west side. During a non-contact drill, Wisconsin's prize receiver Chris Chambers, a senior captain from Bedford, Ohio, was injured while making a routine cut on a grass practice field.

On August 15, Chambers had surgery on his right foot and a pin was inserted to stabilize a stress fracture. Estimated recovery time was four to six weeks. That cast the first cloud over this star-crossed team. Chambers was one of the more valued pieces to the offensive puzzle because of his silky athleticism and ability to stretch a defense.

"I'm just happy that it happened now rather than the middle of the season because I would have been so crushed then," said Chambers, who had posted modest but respectable career numbers (75 catches for 1,191 yards and 11 scores) as a complementary player in a ground-hugging offense that revolved around Ron Dayne.

Chambers felt like the timing of the injury was a "blessing" in that he would still be able to salvage most, if not all, of the Big Ten sea-

Courtesy Craig Schreiner, Wisconsin State Journal

Jamar Fletcher (2), a former high school quarterback, makes a quick transition from defense to offense after picking off Oregon quarterback Joey Harrington for a third time ending the Ducks final threat. UW middle linebacker Nick Greisen (45) is trying to get a blocking angle on split end Marschaun Tucker (5).

son if the rehab went according to plan. He also felt that his absence would accelerate the development of two promising young receivers: split end Nick Davis and flanker Lee Evans, who also prepped in Bedford.

Losing Chambers was a jolt, but the No. 4-ranked Badgers still had two weeks to make the necessary adjustments before the August 31 season opener against Western Michigan. "We can't go around slouching because another person is down," said Evans. "They say, 'One man's adversity is another man's opportunity.' So we have to make the best of it."

To this end, Jamar Fletcher, a Playboy All-American cornerback, began taking a few more snaps at wide receiver. The intent all along was to slowly integrate Fletcher into the offense to improve the depth and take advantage of his explosiveness in the open field (14 interceptions and five touchdown returns in two seasons).

Fletcher has always felt comfortable with the football in his hands. As a prep, he was an option quarterback and kick return specialist. Asked how he planned to utilize Fletcher in the game plan, UW coach Barry Alvarez said, "Receiver is not going to be his top priority and we're not going to base our offense around him. We're going to piecemeal it."

At least until Chambers returned.

Opposite page: Among the 11 players suspended for the 2000 opener were five starters, including Nick Davis (left) who's seated next to Jamar Fletcher on the UW bench. "You hear me talk about adversity," said UW coach Barry Alvarez. "You hear me talk about leadership and guys pulling together. That's what we saw here tonight. This was a huge win."

Courtesy Craig Schreiner, Wisconsin State Journal

Josh Hunt, an obscure walk-on from Thiensville, lives out a dream by returning a punt 89 yards for a touchdown in the second quarter against Western Michigan.

"It always affects you when you lose a great football player, particularly someone who has been as productive as Chris," pointed out offensive coordinator Brian White. "With that said, this program has been built on guys stepping up when guys have gone down."

In 1997, for example, Dayne was injured on the first offensive series, but Eddie Faulkner came off the bench to rush for 119 yards in a 13-10 win over Iowa. In 1998, Dayne and Faulkner were both on the sidelines with injuries when Carlos Daniels filled the void by rushing for 113 yards in a 26-14 victory over San Diego State.

And the beat goes on. "That's football, you have to deal with it, and move on," White said. "We talked about that in our first meeting on offense — the standard of performance doesn't change regardless of who's playing. We still expect to win."

In the wake of Chambers' injury, the players bought into that mindset, too. "The rest of the teams in the Big Ten aren't going to be looking at this and feeling sorry for us," said sophomore wideout David Braun, a former walk-on from Madison Edgewood. "We just have to rally the troops together and everybody has to rely on each other."

Little did they know, at the time, what calamity awaited them and what they were each foreshadowing—Evans' "One man's adversity is another man's opportunity," or Alvarez' "We're going to piecemeal it," or White's "The standard of performance doesn't change," or Braun's "We just have to rally the troops."

And then, the other shoe dropped.

"All the work you did as a team, all the plans you made to be cohesive, all the attempts you made to find a group of guys who could play together without a lot of disruption," sighed UW offensive line coach Jim Hueber, "and, boom, you get hit right in the face."

Shoegate '00 (oh-oh).

Hours before the Badgers were scheduled to take the field against Western Michigan, they were slapped with penalties from the NCAA for players accepting extra benefits and credit arrangements not offered to other non-student athletes at the Shoe Box in Black Earth. In retrospect, they would have been better off accepting the keys to SUVs or pocketing cash payments and negotiating a court settlement (i.e., the Ohio State justice system).

The final count was staggering: 26 football players were under suspension; 11 for three games, and 15 for one game each. The window? All the suspensions had to be served in the first four games, with the Badgers having some flexibility to mix and match and stagger the suspensions. (Chambers, Davis and Fletcher were among those suspended for three games.) In addition, 21 players were obligated to perform 24 hours of community service.

"That's got to be unprecedented for anybody to go through what we just went through," said Alvarez after telling 11 players, including five starters (the injured Chambers, Davis, Fletcher, offensive tackle Ben Johnson and linebacker Bryson Thompson) that they would not be suiting up for the opener. "We always talk about not having any distractions and I don't know how you could be any more distracted than this...

"We will live by it. Those are the cards dealt us and we have no other choice...guys need to bow their necks and not feel sorry for themselves."

On a sweltering Thursday night in Camp Randall Stadium — the temperature reached 90 with a heat index of over 100 degrees — the Badgers avoided further indignity by escaping with a 19-7 win over a stubborn MAC opponent that was hellbent on pulling off the upset. "This may be the longest day I've ever had to go through in coaching," said an emotionally drained Alvarez. "But I'm telling you, I'm thrilled with this win."

Western Michigan capitalized on the day's turmoil with an aggressive defense (12 tackles behind the line of scrimmage) and limited Wisconsin to a couple of touchdowns. One was scored on special teams by an unlikely source: the infamous "player to be named later."

Josh Hunt, a backup receiver, was pressed into action as a punt returner, replacing Davis, who was sitting out the first game of his suspension. Hunt was No. 23 in the program, a duplicate number he shared with cornerback B.J. Tucker. Since both were on special teams, Hunt switched to No. 20 (also worn by kicker Vitaly Pisetsky and tailback Jerone Pettus).

The real kicker? Hunt had to wait until halftime to get his name stitched on the back of his home jersey. By then, everyone knew his identity. Late in the second quarter, Hunt electrified the crowd by returning a punt 89 yards for a touchdown, the second longest return in school history (behind Troy Vincent's 90-yard return against Western Illinois in 1991).

"I think for tonight and the next few days people will know who I am," said Hunt, a junior walk-on, who returned two punts for scores during his senior year at Homestead High School in Mequon. "Personally, it was a great feeling to finally be out there playing."

After backpedaling to field Matt Steffan's booming 57-yard punt — Steffen out-kicked his coverage — Hunt broke an arm tackle by Western Michigan's Garrett Soldano on the UW 25 and made a nice cut behind an Evans block to spring into the open field.

"Once I got past my last blocker (Evans), I just tried to kick it in," Hunt said. "My legs were tired. And I was like, 'Please, God, don't let anyone catch me, I'm almost there.' When I crossed the goal line, I turned and saw my teammates running toward me. It was such a

Courtesy Craig Schreiner, Wisconsin State Journal

Going, going, gone. Tailback Michael Bennett turns on his 4.3 speed (in the 40) and scores on a 59-yard touchdown sprint in the third quarter. Beep, beep. A dumbfounded Joey Harrington (3) is looking on helplessly from the Oregon bench.

great feeling, because they deserve it as much as I do."

Hunt gave Wisconsin a 10-0 lead with 4:23 remaining in the first half. "You always look for a silver lining," Alvarez offered. "So, how can you ask any more out of a Josh Hunt? It's satisfying to know that he stepped up with the biggest play of the game."

But Alvarez was far from satisfied with the final results. The Badgers managed just 252 yards of total offense, the lowest output in 16 games. Quarterback Brooks Bollinger didn't have a lot of time (five sacks) or open receivers (six completions for 96 yards). "I took a couple of shots, a couple of big hits," a fatigued Bollinger conceded afterward. "One more question, guys," he commanded to a small group of reporters. "I'm about to pass out."

Michael Bennett was one of the last players to enter the post-game interview room in the McClain Facility. It may have finally dawned on the exhausted Bennett what Dayne was saying about running backs and the toll of all those carries and collisions. "Now I know what Ron was going through after 30 to 40 carries a game," said Bennett, still perspiring. "It was so humid out there, I thought I was seeing smoke at times."

Bennett rushed for 128 yards on 30 carries, or 17 more carries than his previous high (13 rushes against Murray State in the 1999 opener). "I think I did okay," said Bennett when quizzed on what kind of grade he would give himself. "It was real hot and sweaty and muggy. I'll give it a C-plus. But we're going to need some A's and B's around here real soon."

Hueber's class room is a darkened film room where the front row seating is reserved for the starters on the UW's offensive line. Teased Hueber, "We always used to say, "Mac (Chris McIntosh) sat at the left hand of God and Gibby (Aaron Gibson) sat at the right hand of God and Casey (Rabach) sat in the middle and the guards fit in."

Jamar Fletcher (2) and Ryan Marks (30) converge on Oregon running back and kickoff return specialist Allan Amundson. Marks, a senior from Wisconsin Rapids, blocked a punt and recovered the loose ball in the end zone for a third quarter touchdown.

The left tackle takes the far left seat and sits to the left of the left guard, who sits to the left of the center, who sits to the left of the right guard, who sits to the left of the right tackle, who's sitting in the far right seat of the front row.

"We've always done it that way," Hueber explained, "because they're watching film and they're talking about line calls with the guys they're playing next to. I can remember (Jerry) Wunsch sitting in that right chair while Mac sat in that left chair for so long."

McIntosh started 50 games at left tackle, tying a Big Ten record. After the '99 season, McIntosh was a first round draft choice of the Seattle Seahawks, while Wisconsin's starting right tackle, Mark Tauscher, went in the seventh round to the Green Bay Packers. So even before the Shoegate suspensions, Hueber was dealing with new combinations.

Brian Lamont and Josh Jakubowski made their first career starts at tackle against Western Michigan. "Those young offensive tackles," Alvarez noted, "saw some things they hadn't seen before and weren't experienced enough to adjust."

Hueber gave some serious thought to moving Dave Costa from right guard to left tackle when he first learned of Ben Johnson's suspension. But he wanted to avoid further disruption. At least Jakubowski had practiced at tackle; Costa had not.

But since Jakubowski, like Ben Johnson, also had to serve a three-game suspension, Hueber was forced to draw up another seating chart for the Oregon game. Costa had been groomed as an emergency tackle, so he made the move to starting left tackle, flanking Bill Ferrario, the left guard, and Rabach. That created an opening at right guard.

Hueber juggled some more by installing Al Johnson as the starting center for Oregon and moving Rabach, who had started 37 games at center, to right guard next to Lamont. "It was strictly a maturity deal," Hueber said. "The best alternative for us was to play Al Johnson at a position where he would be the most comfortable and move somebody else (Rabach)."

Rabach had his own ideas, kiddingly suggesting to Costa, "Dave, this week maybe you should move to center, have Al bump out to guard and I'll play tackle to see how good we really are — to see if we really are the utility group."

Idea rejected, though Hueber's mission was to get the five best "available" players on the field. "I don't think we went into the Oregon game thinking it was an experiment," Hueber said. "Rather, this is what we were going to try and win with. There was no desperation involved."

Not even after a terribly inept first half offensively against the Ducks. The Badgers picked up just 24 rushing yards on 20 carries and trailed 6-0. "We made the corrections," Hueber said of the halftime skull session. "We put some things on the board and we talked to them about straining, making something happen and finishing blocks. It wasn't a situation where we thought there was a miracle out there. We needed to revert back to techniques."

And a heavy dose of Michael Bennett, whose blazing speed rates as a miracle cure for any slumbering offense. Just dial "29" for long distance. Bennett broke off runs of 59, 75 and 83 yards, leading the Badgers to a spirited 27-23 win over the Ducks.

Quicker than you can say "Fletcher picked off Harrington again" the dynamic Bennett had rushed for 258 of his 290 yards in a wild and quacky, er, wacky second half.

Bennett felt like he was being guided by the Spirit of Ron Dayne Past. "Actually, I really feel his presence out there with me sometimes," Bennett said. "Just like a ghost. Certain reads, I read my blocks so well, I just felt he was there with me, guiding me along."

Just the same, Mike was trying to be like Mike, not Ron. "Ron has deadly eyes and Ron's a more powerful back," Bennett said. "I just feel we've got a different style of running. But if I get in the open field, I don't feel that anybody can catch me."

Bennett has taken to heart the advice of UW offensive coordinator and running backs coach Brian White. "Coach White says we've got to run like a scolded dog," Bennett said, "so I'm always ready to release that scolded dog."

Just follow the vapor trail.

"It's up to the blockers up front to give him the hole that he needs," Rabach said of Bennett, who set state records in the 100 (10.33) and 200 meters (20.68) at Milwaukee Tech, "and seeing him streak down the field is like a dream come true for an offensive lineman."

"If he gets through a hole, and if he squirts out the other side, he's gone," Costa chimed in. "Ronny did it, too. But when Michael gets in the open field, and it's a foot race, there are not many people in the country who are going to catch him."

One did actually catch him from behind, a Duck, no less, Rashad Bauman. But not before Bennett had carried the ball 83 yards to the Oregon 1, setting up the game-winning score. That was a game-changing run because a Bollinger pass had just been intercepted — his first pick in 150 pass attempts — by Matt Smith and returned 47 yards for a touchdown. Bennett, of course, has the type of speed that can erase mistakes, his and others.

"You don't see that kind of speed very often. Michael's got God-given talent," said UW tight end Mark Anelli. "I knew that he could be special after that Indiana game."

That was during the 1999 season when Bennett gave everyone a sneak preview of his 4.3 speed by racing for 114 yards on just six carries against the Hoosiers. That included a 73-yard lightning bolt for a score after which Bennett couldn't wait to replay the highlights on the phone with his uncle, Tony Bennett, the former Packer linebacker.

These would be the Mississippi Bennetts — Tony and Michael — born and raised in Alligator, MS (population: 300), which sits just

down U.S. 61 apiece from Clarksdale, east of the Arkansas state line. "My dad was a great runner and my mom played basketball and ran track," said Michael. "I've always loved to run."

A year later, he put his passion on display against Oregon. But the Badgers had a handful of worthy players who gave Bennett a run for Player of the Game honors.

There was senior Ryan Marks, a former walk-on and reserve linebacker from Wisconsin Rapids, who blocked a Kurtis Doerr punt and fell on the loose ball in the end zone for a third quarter touchdown that increased the UW's lead to 14-6.

Another senior, Kevin Stemke, averaged 49.1 yards on eight punts, including a critical 72-yarder in the fourth quarter that pinned the Ducks deep in their own territory.

Yet another senior, free safety Jason Doering, had 18 tackles against Oregon. "He probably played as well at that position as anyone I've ever coached," Alvarez said.

Doering has always been known as a head-banger, the Big Bopper. "What's the first thing that comes to mind when I think of Jason Doering?" Bennett posed. "As a running back, I think of stitches — stitches, concussions, and headaches. He really unloads."

Oregon's receivers were guilty of 11 drops, reflecting the intimidation factor. As it turned out, Jamar Fletcher was the only player on the turf who didn't flub one of Joey Harrington's passes. Fletcher caught three of them — three picks. "It's sure nice to have No. 2 (Fletcher) out there," Alvarez said, deadpanning, "You do notice him out there, don't you?

Did Harrington? After throwing for 362 yards, he wasn't convinced that the better team had won. "We wasted a lot of opportunities in the end zone, three times we had to kick field goals," he griped. As for Fletcher's hat trick, he said, "The first one he earned. That's a great play. The second one was tipped and the last one was a desperation throw."

Alvarez decided to play Fletcher against Oregon - with Mike Echols sitting out his one-game suspension — because the Ducks' sprint—out offense is frequently directed to Fletcher's side of the field. But it didn't take the wily Harrington long to figure out that he had a much better match-up against B. J. Tucker, subbing for Echols.

Tucker was no match for Marshaun Tucker, who had six catches for 196 yards. But whenever Harrington got careless, Fletcher made him pay, full price, no discounts.

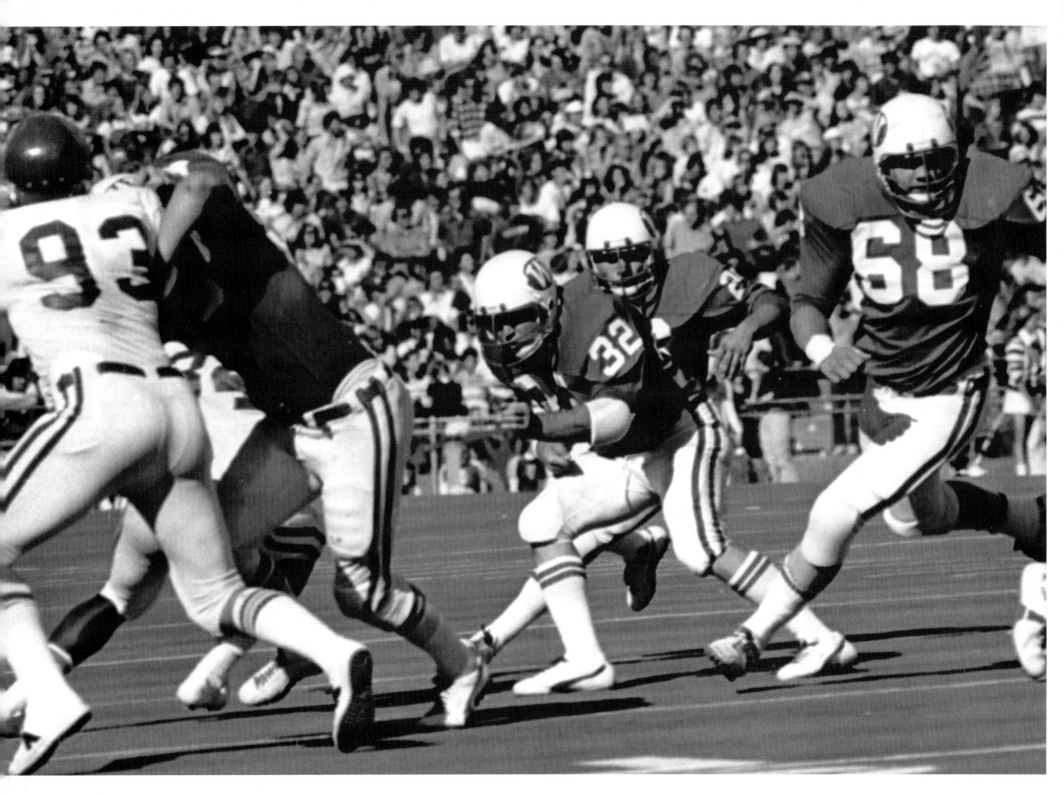

Terry Stieve took a seat next to Billy Marek on the charter bus and initiated the conversation with the 5-foot-8, 185-pound All-Big Ten tailback. The Badgers were headed to Iowa City for a Saturday game against the Hawkeyes. And this was a good time to talk, Stieve figured. Maybe even a better time for a pep talk.

Stieve, a junior guard from Baraboo, was the unofficial spokesman of the Wisconsin offensive line (i.e., the "Blocking Grunts" or "Marek's Marauders"). In general, he felt like he had the pulse of the team. And he could sense that Marek was down.

The Badgers had lost three of their first four Big Ten games, and they were coming off a sloppy 28-21 defeat to Michigan State the week before in Madison. Marek, who lost a fumble against the Spartans, was still trying to get into a rhythm.

After sacrificing nearly three full games to injuries, Marek seemed to be losing some of his patience, if not his confidence. Not that the stoic Marek was easy to read. But he may have been frustrated. At least that was the impression that he had left on Stieve.

"I realized Billy was having a rough year with injuries and everything, so I just sat down on the bus and we talked," Stieve said, adding that Marek reassured him that everything was still okay and a 1,000-yard season wasn't completely out of the question.

Not yet. But it would take a Herculean effort on the part of Marek and his offensive line to reach that plateau, and the odds were against them. Going into the ninth game of the 1974 season, Marek wasn't even leading the Badgers in rushing.

That honor belonged to fullback Ken Starch who had rushed 79

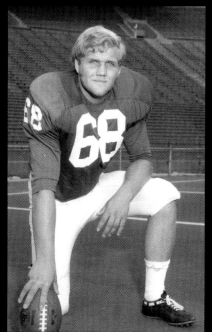

Courtesy of UW Sports Information

Terry Stieve was one of the leaders of the offensive line affectionately known as Marek's Marauders.

times for 523 yards. Marek had 99 carries for 475 yards. Stieve didn't need any help with the math. Marek would have to average 175 yards over the last three games to get 1,000.

"Our whole line got together and decided we would help get it for him," Stieve said, underlining the respect the linemen had for Marek as a player and person. "Our original goal was an 8-3 season, but after Michigan State we had to set another goal for ourselves."

The loss to the Spartans left the demoralized Badgers with a 4-4 record overall. Although Marek led all rushers with 107 yards, he also fumbled with five minutes left in the third quarter and the game tied, 14-14. Two plays later, Michigan State converted the turnover into points.

Another fumble, this one by Marek's understudy — Mike Morgan, a true freshman from Chicago Lane Tech (who would grow up to be the state Revenue Secretary in Gov. Jim Doyle's cabinet) — stopped another UW drive with 11:46 left in a 21-21 game. The opportunistic Spartans cashed that turnover into the winning score.

In addition, the Badgers lost two starting offensive linemen against Michigan State. Center Joe Norwick sprained his ankle in the first quarter, while right tackle Dennis Lick injured his knee on the first running play of the second half.

Art Zeimetz, a senior from Chicago, replaced Norwick and graded out well. So did John Reimer, a junior from Wisconsin Rapids, who took over for Lick. That was the good news. Monday, it was learned that Lick needed surgery and was done for the year.

Lick, a junior All-American candidate from Chicago St. Rita — the same school that turned out Norwick and Marek — had been a starter since his freshman season (28 consecutive starts). He was a second team All-Big Ten selection as a sophomore.

Courtesy of UW Sports Information

Opposite page: Terry Stieve (68) and fullback Ken Starch (32) lead the way for running back Billy Marek.

UW offensive line coach Chuck McBride was philosophical about Lick's loss. "The way I look at it, the defense has been sucking it up," said McBride, referring to season-ending injuries to linebacker Mark Zakula and tackle Bob Czechowicz, "and now that's what we have to do. We'll find out what we're made of, and what some of our kids are made of."

Reimer was an interesting study. He spent his first two years as an offensive tackle on the varsity reserves before moving to defense during spring drills. Over the summer, he injured his back unloading a box car of pulp logs at a paper mill. So, when he reported for training camp, he was shifted back to offense to ease the strain on his back.

"There's no doubt that Dennis Lick is a helluva ballplayer and a bona fide All-American," Reimer said after moving into the starting lineup. "But I don't look at it as a step down for me to be playing. The incentive now is to prove myself to people."

Lick and Reimer offered contrasting styles. "Dennis has excellent balance, and when he hits someone he stays with him," said Reimer. "I like the one-on-one situation where I blow off the line and hope to obliterate the guy. Then you hope he falls out of your way so you can keep going. I'm not a rah-rah guy, but when the time comes to get tough, I'm there."

Not much fazed Reimer, a likeable galoot from Baron, just outside of Wisconsin Rapids. In high school, he used to skip practice to go bear hunting.

"When I go home, I hunt bears to bobcats," he said. "But I'm not psychotic about it. It's simply a way to relax, to unwind. I really used to get my high school coaches (Gene Noonan and Dick Basham) mad because I would take off in the middle of week to go bear hunting. Wasn't bad, either. We had as many as 15 bears strung up at one time."

The Badgers had built some depth on the interior line with Lick (6-4, 255), Reimer (6-3, 262), and Bob Johnson (6-3, 239) at tackle; Stieve (6-2, 240) and Rick Koeck (6-1, 225) at guard; and Norwick (6-0, 234) and Zeimetz (6-1, 207) at center. The tight ends — Jack Novak (6-4, 239) and Ron Egloff (6-4, 206) — were also in this close-knit fraternity.

The loss of three seniors from the 1973 offense-center Mike Webster and guards Dennis Manic and Bob Braun—meant the offensive line really hadn't yet jelled as a unit, or played its best football, according to Stieve.

"We had a poor game against Nebraska, probably the worst in two years," he said, suggesting the Badgers had upset the Cornhuskers in late September without much help from the O-line. "That's when we got together and decided to do something about it."

As an influential senior leader, the 219-pound Webster had raised the bar for the running game during the 1973 season, and Marek was the beneficiary.

Run, Billy, run.

"He was so fun to watch because of his ability to bob and weave," Webster said years later, after making All-Pro with the Pittsburgh Steelers. "And he was a great back to block for. If you got him just a crack, he would squirt past you. He made quick reads which allowed him to get into the hole quickly. And he had tremendous balance. He was moving all the time."

As a sophomore, Marek rushed 241 times for 1,207 yards and 13 touchdowns. He set the school record for single game rushing against Wyoming, rambling for 226 yards on 29 carries in a 37-28 win over the Cowboys. He had three touchdowns.

The game plan was vanilla. The Badgers ran on 70 of 78 plays and rolled up 548 yards, with Starch carrying 13 times for 184 yards. Wyoming head coach Fritz Shurmur (who would later serve as defensive coordinator for the Packers) cited the physical domination up front.

"We had trouble slugging it out with them — they controlled the line of scrimmage" Shurmur said. "That little Billy Marek was something, though. It looked like we had him boxed in a couple of times, and he just got away from us."

That same year, the Iowa defense had a similar problem tackling Marek. On the third play of the game, Marek raced 45 yards for a touchdown, setting the tone for a 35-7 pasting of the Hawks at Camp Randall. In the first quarter alone, Marek rushed for 131 yards and three scores. He didn't play in the second quarter and still finished with 203 yards.

"You've got to wrap-tackle runners like him," said Iowa head coach Frank Lauterbur. "You can't block-tackle him or he'll just keep falling forward."

Lauterbur took the fall at the end of the '73 season. He was fired. His replacement, Bob Commings, was a slow learner. He stated emphatically the Hawks would not key on Marek. "Everybody is aware of Billy Marek as one of the premier running backs in America," Commings said. "But you can't go into a football game watching one guy."

Famous last words.

After a cautious first half, Marek ran through the Iowa defense for 206 yards and four touchdowns during a 28-15 victory in Iowa City. Marek had 34 carries (22 in the fourth quarter), tying a Kinnick Stadium record. And he made a believer out of a skeptic.

"He did it when they needed him the most," Commings conceded. "We had some good hits on him, but he just seemed to bounce off."

He's not a one-shot artist. I would say that next to Archie Griffin at Ohio State, he's the best runner in the Big Ten."

Marek made an adjustment at halftime by lining up a foot deeper in the backfield. That made a world of difference, especially during a signature drive in the fourth quarter. Marek got the ball nine straight times as the Badgers marched 79 yards for the clinching score. "He wasn't getting smeared, so we kept giving it to him," reasoned UW coach John Jardine.

Marek welcomed the workload. So did his Grunts, his Marauders. Even though Reimer was nursing a sore back and tender ankle, he said, "You can't feel anything (but a high) when you see Billy 10 or 15 yards downfield. It's such an unbelievable feeling."

And momentum was building. The following Saturday, the Badgers were back on the road at Northwestern. The pre-game hype was on a Chicago Catholic League match-up between St. Rita's Marek and Loyola's Jim Pooler, the Wildcats leading rusher.

"Marek lulls a defense to sleep," Northwestern coach John Pont told the Chicago media. "The pursuit doesn't see a blur like it does when Archie Griffin runs. The outside men see Marek and think they have time to get to him.

"But he glides, he slides and he has the ability to hurdle without breaking stride. The outside people who are the ones who stop the big gains think they can get to him. But when they do, he has gained nine yards instead of four. He carried every time in that 79-yard drive against Iowa and didn't run a single sweep. Every rush was from tackle to tackle."

And the Wildcats didn't have anyone who could tackle Marek, who moved closer to that 1,000-yard season by rushing 29 times for 230 yards and four touchdowns during a 52-7 blowout that assured Wisconsin of its first winning season since 1963.

The Badgers rushed for 551 yards at Northwestern. Quarterback Gregg Bohlig attempted eight passes, one more than he had at Iowa. Another Chicago area product, Morgan, took part in the fun with 100 yards on 14 rushes. Pooler added 67 yards on 17 carries.

The Marauders were feeling good about themselves, Marek and the momentum they were generating together. "We're all out to get 1,000 for Billy," said Stieve, reiterating the rallying cry. "We're going to be immortal." On second thought, Stieve added, "Maybe nobody will remember us, but we still love blocking for him."

Next was Minnesota, the 1974 season finale in Madison. Marek was now just 89 yards away from 1,000. Stieve talked about how everyone on the line was conscious of Marek's penchant for breaking tackles and cutting back against the grain.

"We try to sustain our blocks longer because with Billy we have to be more aware of his cutback ability and what he can do once he gets into the open field," said Stieve. "It's been fun to be an offensive lineman this year. And it's great to humiliate your opponent."

Particularly the Gophers. Leading up to the game, Marek said of his Marauders, "They're pretty gung-ho on getting 1,000 yards for me." He chuckled and pointed to the irony, "They're more worried about me getting 1,000 yards than I am."

Marek's personal quest attracted a crowd of 55,869 on a cold, rainy, foggy, miserable day. As many fans were still settling in, Minnesota's Rick Upchurch was returning the opening kickoff 100 yards for a touchdown. The Gophers appeared to be in pretty good shape, except for one thing: they had to kick it back to the Badgers.

At halftime, Wisconsin led 28-14, and Marek was well on his way to another record-setting performance and one of the greatest moments in Camp Randall history. During the second half, he got a standing ovation whenever he left the field. And while on the sidelines, he was serenaded with chants of "We Want Marek."

The Badgers blew out the Gophers, 49-14.

And when Jardine pulled him from the game for the final time — late in the fourth quarter — Marek had 43 carries for 304 yards and five scores, despite having a 65-yard touchdown run called back because of a clipping penalty. "I don't think the offensive line can take credit today," Stieve said. "He looked like he was doing it all on his own."

Jardine made sure Marek got over 300. "Once they told me he needed three more yards, I said, 'Hell, yeah, let's get it for him,'" Jardine related afterward.

Marek was grateful — to his coach, his Marauders, and the fans. "Sure, I heard them," he said. "How can I not say it felt great to hear them cheering like that."

Some of those cheers were for Wisconsin cornerback Ken Simmons who had a "Marek-like" game on defense. Simmons recovered two fumbles, forced another, and intercepted one of Tony Dungy's passes. Simmons' play was overshadowed, though.

Not that he minded.

"You're kind of excited about what you're doing," Simmons said, "and, at the same time, whenever you get a turnover, Billy is turning it into points, so you're excited because it's giving him more touches. I know the one play I'll always remember is where he goes into a pile of bodies about 10 yards downfield and the next thing you know Number 26 is squirting out the back end and running for a long touchdown."

That was a 32-yard scoring run, which Marek described thusly: "It just seemed like they all let go. First, I felt a lot of big guys grabbing me, and then all of a sudden I didn't feel anything. All I know is that when I broke away I had a lot of room and I just took off."

Simmons had the experience of tackling Marek in practice so he knew how difficult he was to bring down. "He had a low center of gravity and really quick feet," he said. "Just when you'd think you might have him, he would make a quick cut, like all great backs.

"Billy was really tough-minded in addition to being really tough physically. The other thing that would come to mind is that he was extremely determined. I think he always had a little bit of a chip on his shoulder. I think he was out to prove something."

Did Marek ever worry about his size? "I just never thought about it," he said. "It never really entered the picture. You were playing, and you didn't worry about it. I wasn't real tall, but I had a decent weight. So I really didn't feel small."

Did he ever worry about his confidence? "I don't think it's something you think about," he said. "They've asked you to come [to Wisconsin] because they think you can play. You also think you can play, so you just go out and do it. You don't worry about it."

What did he see on film when he broke down his running style? "I really just tried to avoid taking the big hit," he said. "I worked at sliding, picking a hole, finding daylight."

His favorite play? "A rollout over the right tackle," he said. "It gave you a chance to square your shoulders to the line of scrimmage and see the whole field."

Did he use his lack of height to an advantage? "I'm sure the guys on the other side of the line wished I was bigger," he said. "It was like, 'Where the hell is he?'"

In 1974, he was all over the record books, that's where.

Marek's three straight games over 200 yards tied the NCAA record set the year before by Penn State's John Cappelletti. Over the final three games, Marek rushed for 740 yards, falling just shy of the NCAA mark set by Roosevelt Leakes' rushing for 744 yards.

"If there is a back with greater impact, pound for pound," Gus Schrader wrote in the *Cedar Rapids Gazette*, "well, we'd like to see what he registers on the Richter scale."

Marek wasn't interested in publicity or drawing attention to himself. He used to take incredibly long showers after games with the fervent hope that the sportswriters and sportscasters would grow weary of waiting for him outside his locker.

Courtesy of UW Sports Information

Ron Pollard rushes to the end zone to celebrate with Billy Marek after one of his five touchdown runs against Minnesota. Pollard, a sophomore from Columbus, Georgia, was used at both flanker and tailback during the '74 season. Replacing an injured Marek in the opener at Purdue, the shifty Pollard rushed for 72 yards and caught three passes

"A lot of people could have done the same job if they had my line blocking for me," Marek said humbly. "The records and touchdowns feel good, but those things really don't matter to me. I don't want to get involved with that All-American stuff, either."

Despite leading the nation in scoring with 114 points and ranking third in rushing, Marek wasn't a first team All-American in 1974. He was voted to the second team. No biggie. The individual accolades were never important. Marek was more focused on the team and his teammates, which is why the Grunts, the Marauders, thought so highly of him.

Stieve, for instance, tore cartilage in his right knee against Ohio State in mid-October and played through the pain, rarely missing a snap over the final seven games. He had surgery at the end of the season. Why did he do it? "I didn't want to sit out," Stieve said. "We were winning, and I wanted to be a part of it." It including Marek's run to greatness.

73

Wisconsin 14 Ohio State 14
November 6, 1993

A small but attentive crowd of more than 300 students attended the Thursday night pep rally at Camp Randall Stadium. They clapped along to the band, boogied with Bucky, listened to a select list of speakers, and rallied around the players, still in practice gear.

"Ohio State is talking about revenge," barked head coach Barry Alvarez, reminding the gathering of the Badgers' 20-16 upset victory over the Buckeyes the year before in Madison. "Let me say this to you — they're damn lucky that the game was that close."

Wisconsin nose guard Lamark Shackerford, a co-captain, encouraged the fans to be vocal during Saturday's rematch. "We want the same enthusiasm as the Michigan game," he implored. "Make Ohio State afraid to come out of that tunnel."

One by one the seniors were introduced. Shackerford, defensive tackle Carlos Fowler, fullback Mark Montgomery, and cornerback Henry Searcy were all members of Alvarez's first recruiting class. (Linebacker Yusef Burgess was not present because of a late class.)

Offensive tackle Tyler Adam, strong safety Reggie Holt, nose tackle Lee Krueger, free safety Scott Nelson, inside linebacker Todd Orlando, and outside linebacker Nick Rafko were the fifth-year seniors who would be making their final home appearance.

"These are the guys who have been here for the duration, and I'm proud of all of them," Alvarez said. "They were here when there were people who didn't quite understand what we wanted or the type of commitment we

Students come to the rescue of fellow students who had been trampled or pinned against a railing at the base of the stands during a crowd surge at the end of the Michigan-Wisconsin game. Others look on in stunned disbelief. Pam Zimmerman, a UW sophomore, told the Capital Times, "I was in about the fifth or sixth row and people just kept coming down and down and I ended up right up against [the railing]. You couldn't move anywhere. And then, all of a sudden, the fence collapsed. I just tried to keep my head above people so that I could breathe. And then someone just pulled me out."

wanted (52 players left the program).

"They stuck with us. They believed in the coaching staff. They opened their arms to new recruits and new additions to the team. Now, they're seeing the benefits of what we've been telling them all these years, the benefits for all of their hard work."

Offensive tackle Joe Panos, the other senior co-captain, shared the small stage with Shackerford and revved up the fans. It was the brash, outspoken Panos who in late September first alerted the college football world to the emerging Badgers.

After a 27-15 victory at Indiana in the Big Ten opener, Panos declared of the conference race, "It's wide open, and why not Wisconsin? We haven't shown a reason yet that we can't play with the big boys. Why not us?"

Others may have been asking, 'Why us?" Mary Mann, for one, arrived at the pep rally on crutches. She had been seated in the bottom row of the student section for the Michigan game and sprained a knee when the surging crowd engulfed her like a tidal wave washing down from the top rows of the stadium.

"I won't be in the same seat [for Ohio State]," Mann told the *State Journal*. "I'm going to move up to whatever the top seats are. I'm a little leery, but it's important that people cheer the team. What happened is no one's fault. That's why I'm here tonight, to get rid of those ghosts before I come back Saturday."

The pep rally was part of the healing process. While two students remained hospitalized in good condition, everyone else was still trying to pick up the pieces after more than 70 people were injured the previous Saturday at the end of the Wisconsin-Michigan game. In some circles, it was called a "stampede" — the Camp

Row after row of students pushed forward from the top, creating a human tidal wave that washed over helpless people at the bottom and crushed the field railing and chain link fence in front of Section P. "It was the scariest thing I've ever seen," recounted UW tackle Joe Panos. "I had to hop the fence to pull some people out of there who were unconscious. A couple of them were blue, literally blue. I thought they were goners."

Randall Stampede.

Hundreds were trapped or trampled from the force of the surge at the northeast end of the stadium, primarily Sections O, P and Q. The cascading force was so powerful that an iron railing at the base of the stands was lifted from its concrete moorings, leaving bodies piled one on top of another, four and five deep.

Miraculously, no one was killed. Many will remember the work of the stadium public address announcer, Jack Rane, who calmly urged fans to move to the south end zone so the paramedics could work on the injured. Few will forget Rane's chilling words, "We have a pulseless non-breather at the north end of the field. This is not a joke."

There was no laughter, no post-game celebration after a rare Wisconsin win over the Wolverines. The turf was turned into a triage center as emergency medical squads tended to the injured. Instead of the merriment of a Fifth Quarter, the sirens from rescue teams and ambulances sounded throughout the Monroe Street neighborhood hours after the game.

According to UW band director Michael Leckrone, two band members had taken part in the rescue, helping to pull an injured fan who had a broken leg from the collapsed fence. "There was a pall cast over the whole thing," Leckrone said. "I talked with a lot of students, both in and out of the band, and the feeling I got was it was a tough lesson to learn."

Questions outnumbered answers. What happened? Why did it happen? Could it happen again? Everybody had a theory, an opinion, from Keith Jackson to *Sports Illustrated*.

Jackson, the longtime "voice" of college football, was coming off an ABC assignment in Columbus, Ohio, where security guards had to spray mace on unruly students and fans who rushed the field after the Buckeyes' victory over Penn State.

On crowds, in general, Jackson said, "They're meaner. They've grown steadily meaner....Maybe I'm too old to understand this business of mob mentality....I don't know what you do. It ultimately will come back to the behavior of the individual."

Sports Illustrated proposed, "It's no excuse that unruly crowd behavior is well rooted in Wisconsin, going back to at least the Vietnam War years, when some anti-establishment demonstrations were led by none other than the current mayor, [Paul] Soglin."

From the sublime to the ridiculous. Such was the rhetoric. Wisconsin sports information director Steve Malchow was in the middle of the media frenzy. Obviously, this type of story — the Camp Randall Stampede — created intense national interest.

"I remember the sheer volume of calls from around the country," he said. "And it felt like I was on the radio most of the week talking about the incident. Early on, I thought I could keep recounting this story, or I could use it as a teaching tool. Even though I knew nothing about crowd control, I tried to share the message: unruly crowd behavior is unacceptable."

With potentially tragic consequences, he emphasized.

Four days before the Ohio State-Wisconsin game, Malchow was in his office entertaining some writers from Los Angeles, Chicago and New York, when his phone rang. The caller wanted some help in identifying a Badger football player, No. 3, a number shared by Ken Gales, a starting cornerback, and Michael Brin, a walk-on receiver.

When Malchow asked the female caller why she wanted the information, she replied matter-of-factly, "Well, he saved my life, and I need to reach him."

Knowing the reporters could overhear the conversation and were fishing for a human interest angle, Malchow asked the caller if she would mind if he put her on speaker phone so she could tell her story. Not at all, she informed Malchow. She was proud to do so, especially after getting a name to go along with a number, the No. 3, the life-saver, Michael Brin.

"I don't see myself as a hero," Brin insisted later to everyone who wanted to dwell on his heroic deeds. "I'm just an everyday kid. I'm not a hero. I'm just Mike Brin."

Brin helped pull Aimee Jansen from the crush of bodies, and he also came to the aid of Sari Weinstein, administering mouth-to-mouth resuscitation. He said he acted on instincts. As a result of his actions, Brin was selected as Peter Jennings' *ABC Person of the Week*.

On the 10-year anniversary of the Michigan-Wisconsin game, Brin thought about going from an "incredible high to an incredible low" when the post-game nearly turned into a post-mortem. "Every once in a while," he said, "I'll look back and think about the incident. That episode, whether I want to think about it or not, was a big part of that season."

(At the time of his reflection, Brin was serving his residency in emergency medicine as an ER doctor in Chicago, where he also attended medical school. Brin earned his undergrad degree in zoology at Wisconsin, and a master's in public health at Illinois-Chicago.)

Brin didn't act alone. Brent Moss, Mike Thompson, Brian Patterson, Joe Rudolph, and Tyler Adam also assisted fallen classmates who had been pinned under the avalanche of bodies. In turn, they singled out Panos for again leading by example. Helmet off, tears streaming down his face, Panos jumped into the fray and dragged people to safety.

"I remember going to the hospital afterward and visiting one of the girls [injured during the stampede]," Panos related. "I was wondering how she was doing. I was wondering if she was angry at Wisconsin. I was wondering if she was angry at the football team."

He needed those answers before he could move on. Reassured by her sincerity — she thanked him for being there for her in a time of peril and wished the team good luck against Ohio State — he could give his full attention to the Buckeyes. During the Thursday pep rally, Panos pleaded for everyone "to use their head and keep yourself under control."

Alvarez was extremely conscious of his players' heads — their mental frame of mind. Some were more fragile than others, particularly in the aftermath of the stampede. "We had a lot of different people talk with the kids," he said. "We told them we had counseling available. And we ran through the whole gamut just to clear their minds."

That was the backdrop to the Ohio State game. "When you take a look at what our kids went through that week, it's amazing," Alvarez said. "They were emotionally spent, and I had to back off [in practice]. We still had to get them ready to play. But it couldn't be a rah-rah thing, or we would have zapped them to the point where they would have had nothing left."

In the next breath, he confided, "We put a lot of emotion into that Michigan game."

As a head coach, Alvarez had faced the Wolverines just once previously, during his forgettable 1-10 first season, and the Badgers got spanked, 41-3, in Madison. The Badgers rushed for just 18 yards on 26 carries. The Wolverines had 534 yards of total offense, 360 on the ground. Freshman Ricky Powers was the leading rusher with 106 yards.

On Michigan's return engagement at Camp Randall — October 30, 1993 — the Wolverines were without injured tailback Tyrone Wheatley. That put additional pressure on Powers, who got a rude reception from the fired-up Wisconsin defense. Powers managed just 34 rushing yards and lost a fumble as the Badgers hung on for a hard-fought 13-10 victory, only the second win over Michigan since 1962. (The other was in 1981).

Rick Schnetzky, a walk-on placekicker, was an unlikely contributor. On his first career attempts, he booted field goals of 25 and 26 yards in relief of John Hall, who was in a 1-for-7 slump. (Schnetzky, a

Courtesy of University of Wisconsin Archives

The Buckeyes had trouble getting consistent pressure on quarterback Darrell Bevell with their front four. On this pass play, Joe Rudolph (63) has locked up Matt Finkes (92).

prep soccer player, came to the UW hoping to tryout for the hockey team. But after the junior varsity program was dropped, his dad talked him into specializing as a kicker. On his own, he kicked in the McClain Facility until he was "discovered.")

Brent Moss rushed for 128 yards, and Terrell Fletcher scored Wisconsin's only touchdown against the Wolverines on a beautifully executed draw play. "Fletch made a couple of guys miss, and the place went crazy," remembered Bevell, who was looking for his own personal redemption after throwing five interceptions at Minnesota the previous week.

Even though Bevell set a school record with 423 passing yards, it wasn't enough to overcome the mistakes or the Gophers, who handed Wisconsin its first loss, 28-21. So Michigan was a bounce back game. And a lot more. "It was the two big boys, and we were going to find out who the bully really was," said Panos. "And we ended up being the bully."

Not that the Wolverines didn't attempt to bully the Badgers by dancing and woofing on the W-logo in the center of the field during warm-ups. "That got my blood boiling," said UW defensive tackle Carlos Fowler. "That's like a slap in the face. Camp Randall is my home. You don't invade my home and take something from me. I took it as a personal insult."

It didn't stop there, either. "They were yelling, 'You haven't won anything, you don't have any tradition,'" Fowler went on. "Thing is, we stressed that we weren't playing Michigan tradition. We were playing the team that came out on the field."

That was the approach for the Ohio State game. "You've got an undefeated Ohio State coming in here talking about how they 'owe

Courtesy of University of Wisconsin Archives

J.C. Dawkins stretches out to make a finger-tip grab of a pass in front of Ohio State coach John Cooper. The 29-yard completion was Dawkins' only reception of the game.

you' for beating them last year," Alvarez lectured his players. "To me, this stuff about owing us something was like they were looking down their noses at us. Let's line up and play. We sure as hell are not going to take a backseat to Ohio State or anybody else. We respect them, but we're not in awe of them."

On Friday night, Alvarez had the team watch the movie *Rudy*, based on the true story of a Notre Dame walk-on who refused to let anyone take away his dream. Alvarez took it a step further by having Rudy — Dan Ruettiger — join his players. He talked about believing in themselves, believing that they can get the job done, no matter the odds.

Rudy had a sidelines pass the next day, along with 140 others. Normally about 90 such passes are issued. The press box was full, too, with 175 credentials having been approved by Malchow. "It was off the charts — by far the most inquiries we've ever received," he said. Just about every major newspaper in the country was represented at Camp Randall.

Big on big. No. 3 Ohio State vs. No. 15 Wisconsin. Big on big. The Buckeyes vs. the Badgers. Big-time. That was how Alvarez sold the game to his players. "There was a lot of emotion in the stadium that

day," remembered another "Rudy" — Joe Rudolph. "Everybody was still worked █ from the week before because of what had happened with the fans."

The primetime kickoff (2:30 p.m.) and the presence of ABC's No. 1 broadcasting team — Jackson, Bob Griese and Lynn Swann — validated the match-up as big on big. The Buckeyes, unbeaten in their last 14 regular season games, were a six-point favorite. They owned wins over three Top 25 opponents, including No. 12 Penn State, 24-6.

"I'm not going to fight the temptation — we smell roses out there," Ohio State offensive guard Jason Winrow was quoted as saying in a Columbus newspaper after beating the Nittany Lions. "That's what's pushing us right now."

Winrow was not the best player on the O-line. Not even close. Korey Stringer was the right tackle, and Alan Kline was on the left side. And they were largely responsible for protecting quarterbacks Bobby Hoying and Bret Powers and creating running seams for the rock-steady tailbacks Raymond Harris, and Butler By'not'e.

Wide receiver Joey Galloway was the game-breaker, the difference-maker on offense. His All-American counterpart on defense was Big Daddy Wilkinson. The Buckeyes were a cocky bunch. But then, so were the Badgers. "We wanted to put a stamp on our program," Gales boasted. "Teams weren't going to walk into Camp Randall and walk out with a win. This was our house, and we wanted to defend it."

Lightly falling snow framed the picture. "It was real soft snow with big flakes," Bevell recalled vividly. "It wasn't coming down hard enough to accumulate, but with the darkness and the bright lights, it made for a pretty cool atmosphere."

The Badgers gave up an early score but knotted the game in the second quarter on a Bevell touchdown pass to Lee DeRamus. Bevell completed just enough passes to keep drives alive and the Ohio State defense off balance. Relying on the slashing runs of Moss (25 carries, 129 yards), the quick feet of Fletcher (12 carries, 58 yards), and the muscle of fullback Mark Montgomery (8 carries, 53 yards) the Badgers dictated the tempo by controlling the football for more than 10 minutes in both the third and fourth quarters.

And they were in a position for a kill shot with 4 minutes and 34 seconds left when J.C. Dawkins downed a Sam Veit punt at the Ohio State 1-yard line. "The thing I remember was Coach [John] Cooper coming up to me and saying, 'You've got to make some plays,'" Galloway told the *Capital Times*. "And I said I was ready."

It took all of 46 seconds for the Buckeyes to cover 99 yards. It was Powers to Galloway for 15, Powers to Galloway for 47, Powers to Cedric Saunders for 11, Powers to Galloway for 26 and the touchdown. During this sequence, Galloway victimized UW defensive back Donny Brady, a backup, who was playing because of an injury to free safety Scott Nelson. (Jeff Messenger moved from corner to safety, and Brady took over as the boundary corner.)

The Badgers were in Cover 3, which meant Brady, who had an

interception earlier in the game, was responsible for a deep third. Nobody was supposed to get behind Brady. Galloway did. "If you're going to pick on anybody," Cooper cooed, "you pick on that substitute." (Years later, Cooper confessed to Alvarez that when he saw Brady wearing a knee brace, it was a no-brainer to challenge him with Galloway, the fastest Buckeye.)

The Badgers still had plenty of time for a counter punch, and one of the key plays in an 11-play, 54-yard march was a 13-yard off-tackle run by Moss on third-and-10 from the Ohio State 36. "A great call," Cooper told the *State Journal*. "If I did that [in Columbus] on third-and-10, and we didn't make it, Coop would probably be opening a bait shop somewhere."

When the possession began, Alvarez relayed a message to offensive coordinator Brad Childress in the press box. "Get us to the 20, and we'll kick to win."

The Badgers had all of their timeouts and a first down on the OSU 23 with 1 minute remaining. Alvarez was cognizant of two fumbled quarterback-center exchanges, one in each half, between Bevell and Cory Raymer. And he was cognizant of the clock.

Alvarez didn't want to give the ball back to the Buckeyes, not after watching the Powers-Galloway connection eat up so much ground in so little time. So he called for a couple of fullback dives. That put the ball on the OSU 15 (the left hash) with 7 seconds left.

Kick to win.

"I remember walking over and talking to Barry before mentally going through what I needed to get done," Schnetzky said. Both teams called timeouts. After going over his check list, twice, he was ready. Kick to win. Once he got over the ball and lined up the 32-yard field goal, Schnetzky entered his own world where "you don't hear anything."

Except a solid thump, the sound of foot on ball.

Only there were two thumps in this case.

"It was like a damn cannon going off in my ear," Panos said. "And I knew immediately what had happened because I didn't see the ball going through the uprights."

"After the second thump," said Bevell, the holder, "I jumped up and started backpedaling, looking for the ball. I didn't want them coming out of there and scoring."

"When I heard the thump of the ball being blocked," Schnetzky said, "that's when I first realized what had actually happened out there."

Kerner blocked the kick. Matt Nyquist, the wing on the right side of the formation, followed procedure. Ohio State's Craig Powell lined up on his left shoulder, and Nyquist was responsible for the inside gap. He blocked down.

"If [Nyquist] keeps his right foot in cement," Alvarez said, "and secures the inside gap, theoretically they can't get to the kicker. Matt may have slid his right foot three inches. But it's a case where a great athlete made a great play. He got a great jump."

Kerner, who also blocked a field goal in the Penn State game, told

the *State Journal*, "I was stretched out as far as I could. It was, 'Please, please, please, let me block.' Then I felt the ball hit my hand, and it was 'Thank you, thank you, thank you.'"

Cooper could live with a 14-14 verdict. "The second half they completely dominated," he told the Associated Press. "Any time they dominate a game that long against you, and you have to block a field goal to tie it, you've got to consider yourself fortunate."

To this day, Panos still gets upset thinking about the ending and the emptiness of a tie. "I was disappointed that we lost the game." Catching himself, he said, "Or, rather, we tied the game. It was more of a victory for them than it was for us. How's that sound?"

It sounded much better after the Buckeyes got skunked 28-0 at Michigan in the regular season finale, reopening the door for a Badger trip to Pasadena.

"It was a roller-coaster ride," Dr. Michael Brin concluded of the '93 season. "Some of the most exciting times in my life and probably the one year that has changed me personally the most. And it probably changed Wisconsin football as much as any other season."

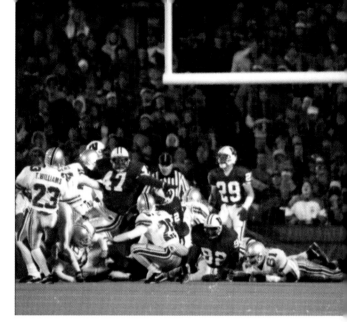

Courtesy of University of Wisconsin Archives

Tim Williams' extra point capped Ohio State's 99-yard touchdown march (in 46 seconds) that tied the game, 14-14.

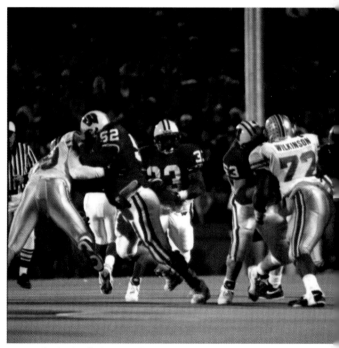

Courtesy of University of Wisconsin Archives

Tailback Brent Moss gets ready to accelerate through a crease in the Ohio State defense created by offensive center Cory Raymer (52), who has a good grip on Luke Fickell, and guard Joe Rudolph (63), who has tied up Big Daddy Wilkinson.

Wisconsin 7 Minnesota 6

On June 7, 1965, U.S. General William Westmoreland reported that North Vietnamese troops had infiltrated South Vietnam. Westmoreland called for another 41,000 combat troops right away and another 52,000 later. "Studies must continue and plans developed," he insisted, "to deploy even greater forces, if and when required."

On July 28, 1965, President Lyndon Johnson ordered the Airmobile Division and other forces to Vietnam, raising the fighting strength from 75,000 to 125,000 men.

"Additional forces will be sent as requested," Johnson pledged. "We do not want an expanding struggle with consequences that no one can foresee, nor will we bluster or bully or flaunt our power. But we will not surrender, and we will not retreat."

The world was changing. And so was the Madison campus: a tinderbox and growing source of political activism and dissent. One of the earliest reported anti-war protests had been staged in front of the Wisconsin student union in 1963.

With the 1967 Dow Chemical riot as a focal point, David Maraniss, a Madisonian, documented the rapidly changing landscape in his book *They Marched into Sunlight.*

Wrote Maraniss, "...for old schoolers like Arlie Mucks, the longtime director of the Wisconsin Alumni Association, a man who bled Badger red, there was grave concern that long-haired 'outside agitators' were sullying the image of his beloved alma mater."

The Wisconsin football program was undergoing changes, too. And there were pressing concerns about the image being projected. Coincidence? Or cause and effect?

"We had already started a cycle of campus revolution and unrest and that really hurt our recruiting," said LaVern Van Dyke, the venerable UW assistant coach who loyally served four head coaches: Ivy Williamson, Milt Bruhn, John Coatta and John Jardine.

"There were just so many rumors out there about what was going on in Madison," continued Van Dyke, who tutored the defensive line

Courtesy of UW Sports Information

Opposite page: Head coach Milt Bruhn (left) and athletic director Ivy Williamson strike a winning pose before the 1956 opener against Marquette. Upon the death of Guy Sundt midway through the '55 season, Williamson took over the dual role of coach and AD and named Bruhn, a trusty assistant, as his successor on the sidelines.

and freshmen for Bruhn. "The campus was changing, and it was tough on all of us. We'd go out and talk with parents, and they were afraid to send their kids here because of the trouble."

After captivating a sporting nation with a pulsating 23-point fourth quarter comeback against USC in the 1963 Rose Bowl—a rally that fell short of victory by a score of 42-37— the Badgers had fallen on hard times, struggling to 5-4 and 3-6 records in their post-Big Ten title seasons.

Bruhn was hoping to reverse the trend in 1965. But it turned out to be the worst team that he had fielded since going 1-5-3 during his rookie season in 1956.

The last four games were a nightmare for the overmatched Badgers, starting with a 50-14 loss to a below-average Michigan team in Ann Arbor. The Wolverines scored on their first offensive play, a 52-yard pass from Wally Gabler to Jack Clancy, and never let up.

Another road loss, 45-7, followed at Purdue before the Badgers returned home for a mid-November beating against Illinois. And what a beating it was. The Illini's 51-0 victory was Wisconsin's worst defeat in 49 years, dating to a 54-0 loss to Minnesota in 1916.

The Illini scored 37 points in the second half and controlled the ball, with 219-pound fullback Jim Grabowski rushing 38 times (tying a Big Ten record) for 196 yards and two scores. In lifting his season total to 1,071 yards, Grabowski became the first running back in conference history to rush for over 1,000-yards in two different seasons.

After another UW pratfall on offense (four lost fumbles, three interceptions), Bruhn was at a loss for words. "What can you say at a time like this?" he posed to the local press corps.

The *State Journal* observed "for one brief moment a big sign— 'Ostracize Milton. Losers Never Win'—unfurled along the top of the east stadium, but it was quickly torn to bits and shoved over the rim. There was some chanting directed at the Wisconsin bench. Camp Randall may have emptied in record time."

The following week, Bruhn had to deal with a far more serious crisis. After Tuesday's practice, one of his assistants, Clark Van Galder, died from a heart attack. He was 54.

Van Galder was in the company of fellow assistants at the Shrine

Courtesy of UW Sports Information

Milt Bruhn prepares to lead his charges onto the field.

All-City banquet at the Masonic Temple when he collapsed in the lobby. He had been hospitalized for several weeks in August after suffering an apparent mild heart attack.

"Clark was a very popular guy with the kids," Van Dyke said. "He had a lot of pep and desire, and he had a great rapport with everybody on the team."

Bruhn told the *State Journal*, "Clark Van Galder's sudden death is a great shock to me, my staff, and our squad....He imparted to many his enthusiasm for athletics...and he played a vital role in the success enjoyed by our teams in recent years."

That Saturday the Badgers took another beating, 42-7, at Minnesota. "There's no question about it," Bruhn confided to the Madison media, "this is the longest season I've ever had. It seems like an eternity, especially the last four games."

The Badgers were outscored 188-28 during that stretch and finished with a 2-7-1 record. A lot of people now had concerns about the direction of the program. Influential people. As such, the athletic board recommended that Bruhn be replaced by a vote of 4-3.

Professor V.W. Meloche, the board chairman, originally abstained but later voted to keep Bruhn, thus reversing the board decision and recommending that Bruhn be retained.

That sentiment was shared by UW President Fred Harvey Harrington and Madison Chancellor Robben Fleming. The Board of Regents voted 7-3 in support of Bruhn.

There were some stipulations, among them that Bruhn shake up his staff. To that end, Bruhn hired four new assistants: Mike McGee, Roger French, Les Ritcherson and Harland Carl. They joined the holdovers: Van Dyke, Deral Teteak and John Coatta.

What the Badgers really needed was a personnel transfusion: better players, and more of them. They were thin at most spots. A week before the 1966 opener, the depth question was raised again when Gary Bandor, a flanker-defensive back, was inducted into the Army.

Dwindling fan interest was another issue. Getting a bump from their Rose Bowl trip, the Badgers averaged 61,223 in 1963. However, attendance dropped to 56,428 in 1965.

Bruhn's timing couldn't have been worse. In 1966, he had more seats to fill because of the opening of the upper deck and communication center at Camp Randall Stadium. The $2.8 million project (paid by athletic gate receipts) increased capacity from 63,435 to 77,280.

Opening day drew a crowd of 51,051. Part of the attraction was 50 area high school bands and a halftime show conducted by Broadway composer Meredith Willson. The outcome was music to Bruhn's ears. The Badgers beat Iowa State, 20-10.

Outside of a couple ticket holders who discovered their seats had been eliminated to make room for an aisle, the upper deck passed inspection. "The view," Fred Harrington told the *State Journal*, "is much better than I expected, and I am very pleased."

But the majority viewpoint was that the Badgers were still not a very good football team. November was particularly unforgiving for the beleaguered Bruhn.

On November 5, Purdue quarterback Bob Griese guided the Boilermakers to a 23-0 win over Wisconsin before a disillusioned Homecoming gathering of 56,475 at Camp Randall. The hand-writing was already on the wall—spurring the hand-wringing in the papers.

"Wisconsin's football season is rapidly drawing towards a close," wrote *Capital Times* sports editor Harry Golden, "and perhaps, in a very few words, it is a good deal after the horrendous exhibition the Badgers put forth against Purdue....It was really a sad exhibition of Big Ten football and there are few who deserve any praise for the miserable play.

"With the exception of hard running sophomore Wayne Todd at fullback, battling Bob Richter at linebacker and pass-catching Tom McCauley, the Badgers had little to offer."

They offered up even less the following Saturday during a dismal 49-14 loss at Illinois. The Illini scored four touchdowns in the second quarter and led 49-0 in the fourth quarter before emptying the bench. The helpless Badgers had six turnovers, and no excuses.

"They were trying so damn hard to make it go, and then things started happening," Bruhn told the *State Journal*. Bruhn then instructed his players to stay away from the stadium on Sunday, canceling the regularly scheduled meetings and workout. "They've been getting too much football. We won't hit 'em at all this week. We'll just hit the dummies and play."

That was the week that was.

The Gemini 12 astronauts—James Lovell, who had attended the UW, and space walker Buzz Aldrin—completed a successful mission; President Johnson underwent surgery to remove a benign polyp from his throat; Los Angeles Dodgers ace Sandy Koufax retired, fearing permanent harm to his arthritic left arm; and Dr. Samuel Sheppard, who served nine years in prison before earning a new trial, was acquitted for the murder of his first wife.

Bruhn's program was also on trial. On Thursday, the *Capital Times* ran a front page story headlined "Foes Open 'Dump Bruhn' Drive Again."

Wrote Matt Pommer, "Alumni and sportswriter pressure again is building for the ouster of Milt Bruhn....The cast of characters and the arguments are almost the same as last year....Most rumors point to John Coatta as the number one prospect if this happens."

That same day, the 54-year-old Bruhn announced his resignation, effective after the season finale against Minnesota. Following practice, he met with reporters and confessed, "When you have a season like we had this year, if a change can be made that will help, I'm for it. I intend to do everything I can to create winning football at Wisconsin."

Williamson, the athletic director, announced that Bruhn will be "assigned to appropriate duties and responsibilities" within the department. He noted, "As a member of the faculty with the rank of professor, Milt has tenure and this will be honored."

With one game yet to be recorded, Bruhn's 11-year record was 51-45-6 with two undisputed Big Ten titles. The Badgers definitely got their money's worth. Bruhn's salary was $20,228, and he worked on a year-to-year basis with no contract.

The athletic board voted that Bruhn's replacement—and Coatta wound up getting the job—would get a three-year contract. But there would be no faculty tenure.

"The contract would tend to defray some of the outside pressure that comes with the year-to-year approach," athletic board member Professor Arthur Robinson told the *State Journal*. "The university is no place for taking care of somebody. If a person enters big-time coaching, he knows what he's getting into."

Harrington and Fleming released a joint statement and thanked Bruhn "for the quality of leadership he has provided....Wisconsin football has flourished under his coaching."

Capital Times sportswriter Bonnie Ryan contended that Harrington fired Bruhn. That drew strong denials from all the involved parties, including Bruhn, who insisted to the *State Journal*, "It was my own decision. Nobody fired me."

Fired? Or resigned? Decades later, Van Dyke agreed there might have been a compromise between Bruhn and Williamson, old allies. Bruhn moved from an assistant on Williamson's staff to head coach when Williamson took over as the AD. "Nobody on the inside really knew," Van Dyke said. "It was a sad time, I remember that very well. But Milt showed a great deal of professionalism. He could have ranted and

Courtesy of UW Sports Information

Pat Richter with Head Coach Milt Bruhn. "I think his players appreciated him as a man and a coach," Richter once said of his mentor, "but I'm not sure if the public fully appreciated his coaching."

Linebacker Bob Richter (66) and defensive tackle Tom Domres (79) gang up to make a big defensive stop behind the line of scrimmage.

Senior linebacker Bob Richter, a former walk-on from Milwaukee Lutheran, was one of the team leaders during the '66 season.

raved, but he didn't."

Tom Butler covered the Badgers for the *State Journal* and opined of Bruhn's trials and tribulations, "The pressures got to him this fall. All kinds of pressures. The snipers, the win-or-else alumni, the fair-weather fans took their toll. But Milt was under another pressure that had more effect on him, his wife Helen and their daughter Mary Ann than any indignity thrust upon them by a disconsolate football fan.

"Milt's only son, Pete, a center on Wisconsin's 1962 Big Ten championship and Rose Bowl team, has been in combat all fall as an Air Force pilot over Viet Nam. The big coach never said much, but it gnawed at him. The pressure seemed infinitely more important to him than football. Still, Bruhn could be found at his stadium office early in the morning, late at night, seven days a week...."

And that was the agenda for his final week as Wisconsin's head coach. He had to get his players ready to go out and beat Minnesota, his alma mater.

Bruhn, a native of St. Bonifacius, Minnesota (Mound High School), was a starting guard on a couple of national championship teams in the mid-30s. "I have no plans beyond this weekend," Bruhn reiterated. "All I want to do is win this game and get lost for a few days."

Minnesota coach Murray Warmath offered a testimonial. "I regret his resigning," he said to the Associated Press. "I think college football needs men like Milt Bruhn. It's unfortunate that the pressure builds up like it does because the man has built a fine record....There's not a finer or nicer man in the country."

That was echoed by the Badger players. "It's a shame people have to be so cruel," senior defensive end Eric Rice told the local beat writers. "Because the pressures are so great to win, a coach just doesn't have a chance unless he wins every game. I don't know of anybody I have more respect for than Coach Bruhn except my own father."

His dad, Fred Rice, the coach at Nicolet High School, had a firm grasp of the pressures that can come to bear on a college head coach, having also coached at Colgate.

Another team leader, Bob Richter, a senior linebacker, recalled that Bruhn's resignation was "very emotional and kind of upsetting to the guys who were really close to him. I think there was a faction that wasn't exactly disappointed. But, overall, there was confusion."

Richter, a former walk-on from Milwaukee Lutheran High School, remembered walking into Bruhn's office for the first time. "It was like I was talking to the Wizard of Oz," he said. "Milt had that stately, overwhelming demeanor yet he was just one of the real nice guys."

Van Dyke admitted that the uncertainty was hard on the assistants, not knowing whether they would be retained by the new coach, or where they might land next.

"As I remember before the ballgame," Van Dyke said, "it was a very, very quiet locker room. But you could sense that the team really had a goal it wanted to accomplish. Everybody was focused on doing something for Milt."

From an artistic standpoint, the Minnesota-Wisconsin match-up was more Mautz than Picasso. Or what you would expect from two second division Big Ten teams. The Gophers had a couple of early scoring chances but failed to capitalize. The Badgers did nothing.

"I felt our team was fairly nervous in the beginning," Bruhn said. "Whenever a football team is filled with emotion, the defense benefits by it."

In the first half, the Badgers had three turnovers and 77 yards of total offense. "Perhaps I didn't do my part in the first half," Bruhn said. "It was difficult for me to talk to them."

Minnesota finally got on the board with 39 seconds left in the half on quarterback Larry Carlson's six-yard touchdown pass to Ken Last. The first extra point attempt was missed, but the Badgers were offsides. On the second attempt, the snap was dropped.

Despite trailing 6-0, the Badgers felt good about their chances. "As I recall when we came in at halftime, it felt like, 'Boy, this is the way it used to feel in the past,'" Van Dyke related. "The team was excited and there was a strong feeling that we could win."

In praising his defense for keeping the Badgers within striking distance of the lead, Bruhn said, "In the second half, I felt like my old self and I was able to growl again."

After intermission, Minnesota never crossed midfield and rushed for only nine yards. Wisconsin rallied around its defense, namely Rice, Richter, Gary Swalve, Tom Domres, Sam Wheeler, John Tietz, Gary Reineck, Bill Grisley, and Wayne Kostka.

Late in the third quarter, Swalve put a crunching hit on Gopher halfback John Wintermute, and Domres recovered the fumble on the Minnesota 33. The Badgers drove to the 3, but that's where the possession stalled, bringing up a fourth down and goal.

Bruhn sent in a play from the sidelines—the "Ameche play"—named in honor of former UW fullback Alan Ameche, the 1954 Heisman winner. The Baltimore Colts had designed the play for Ameche to take advantage of his receiving skills, according to Bruhn.

"And we just put that play in this week for the Minnesota game,"

Courtesy of UW Sports Information

An emotionally drained Milt Bruhn — showing the wear and strain of coaching his final game — gets a victory ride, culminating a season and career.

Bruhn told the *Capital Times*. "Bill Fritz was to go outside and hook, and [Tom] McCauley was to hook inside. The fullback was to delay, go over the line and become the free man."

That was the plan. But when it broke down, quarterback John Ryan improvised, rolled left, eluded a tackler, and found McCauley in the end zone for the touchdown. Tom Schinke kicked the extra point and Wisconsin held a 7-6 lead with 13:02 left in the game.

And that was all the scoring the Badgers needed as Minnesota was forced to abandon its run game and safety-first game plan and throw the ball more than it wanted. "I could say that it was a miserable game for us, but Wisconsin simply beat us," Warmath told the *State Journal*. "Milt's team just played a lot better than we did."

In raising his career record to 7-3-1 against the Gophers, Bruhn scored one of his most heartfelt wins given the circumstances. Recognizing the significance of the moment, the players hoisted Bruhn on their shoulders and rode him to the center of the field.

"It was tremendously satisfying to step out knowing that the kids were really battling," Bruhn said afterward. "I wanted them to win it for themselves, but I suppose they tried as well to do it for me. Yes, it was a great satisfaction for me."

While the nation's focus was on East Lansing, Michigan, where Ara Parseghian would be harshly criticized for his conservative play-calling in a 10-10 tie with Michigan State, there was plenty to recommend being in Madison that day. Not that there were many witnesses in the Camp Randall seats (45,372) for Bruhn's last hurrah.

Didn't matter. Bruhn went out a winner. The Badgers didn't win again until October 11, 1969, a span of two-plus seasons, countless heartaches and 23 games (0-22-1).

"I think his players appreciated him as a man and as a coach," Pat Richter once said of his mentor, "but I'm not sure if the public fully appreciated his coaching."

Bruhn left the field, clutching the game ball. During his post-game, post-career press conference, he patiently answered all questions, knowing that when it was over it was really over. He then got up, shook hands with each sportswriter, and concluded wistfully, "Gentlemen, I'm going to miss working with you. It's been a pleasure."

Wisconsin 31 Purdue 24

October 10, 1998

Pack it up, pack it in
Let me begin
I came to win

Years removed from their classic quarterback-cornerback duals as collegians, Drew Brees and Jamar Fletcher were back at it again, challenging each other. Only this time, they were on the same team, the San Diego Chargers of the National Football League. And their competitive jousts were on the practice field during the 2004 season.

"When he's at quarterback and I'm on the corner, I'm going after him and I know he's going after me," said Fletcher, a consensus All-American at Wisconsin. "That's the same with any quarterback. But it's a little more so when I see Drew under center."

Brees, the Big Ten's all-time leading passer, silenced his pro critics by sparking a San Diego revival in '04. The Chargers went from 4-12 to 12-4 and won the AFC West title behind Brees, a second round pick out of Purdue in the 2001 draft. Brees threw for 3,159 yards, and completed 65 percent of his passes. His TD-to-interception ratio was 27-to-7.

"From Day One, I've always said that he's the best quarterback I've ever played against, period, at Wisconsin," noted Fletcher, a first round selection (26th pick overall) of the Miami Dolphins in the 2001 draft. "At that point in my career, he was the best in the pocket—Mr. Sharp, Mr. Precise—at Purdue. Now, we're teammates. It's crazy."

In mid-March, 2004, the Chargers acquired Fletcher as part of a trade that sent wide receiver David Boston to Miami. There was no question that Fletcher needed a change of scenery after an unproductive start to his pro career. As a sometimes nickel back with the Dolphins, he started six of 41 games and picked off only two passes.

"In college, the Wisconsin coaches let me play my game, they let me do my thing," said Fletcher, who set school records with 21 interceptions (five returned for touchdowns) and 57 passes defended. "But in

Photos Courtesy of Craig Schreiner/Wisconsin State Journal

Opposite page: Cornerback Jamar Fletcher anticipated the play -a quick out to wide receiver Randall Lane (84) - as soon as Purdue quarterback Drew Brees took the snap in the shotgun formation. That allowed Fletcher to step in front of Lane, pick off the throw and return the interception 52 yards for a touchdown, pushing the Badgers into a 24-17 lead late in the third quarter.

[the NFL], you can't give a quarterback or a coordinator the same looks. It's a chess match, and you've got to switch it up.

"I came into the league just not knowing, not really understanding what it was all about. I was just out there playing, trying to get by on my athletic ability, and I wasn't thinking enough about the game. I didn't study the game as much as I needed. But everything is beautiful now. I believe I've earned the respect of my teammates and the coaches."

During the 2004 season, Fletcher appeared in 16 Charger games, mostly on special teams, and collected one pick and 36 tackles. Occasionally, he will think about his playmaking past at Wisconsin. And when he does, he can't help but think of Brees, a dramatic interception return for a score, and a memorable 1998 night game in Madtown.

"We haven't really talked about that game, or gone into detail about it since I've been here [with Brees]," Fletcher said. "But that was the interception that put me on the map. People really started looking at me and understanding that this dude could play football."

When Brees was asked if he remembered Fletcher's pick, he said, "I do, I do." Laughing, he added that he didn't have good memories of the play or the outcome. "Fletch was a redshirt freshman, just a lowly freshman. And I threw a risky pass out there...."

One of 83 passes.

Hit rewind.

Brees will never forget that raucous Camp Randall crowd. Or the fact that it was a 7:30 p.m. kickoff, which "allows the Cheeseheads to drink all day long or until game time."

That was a genuine concern on the part of school officials, uncertain of what they were getting themselves into. Only two previous games had been staged at night, a 34-17 loss to Michigan in 1986 and a 43-7 loss to Colorado in 1995.

Moreover, the Purdue game was Homecoming. "We're always a little more worried about a night game because people have a lot longer to party before it starts," Al Fish told the *State Journal*. Fish was the athletic department's administrative officer and worry-wart. "When we have a full stadium," he said, "we become the fifth-largest city in

87

Photos Courtesy of Craig Schreiner/Wisconsin State Journal

Defensive tackle Eric Mahlik (98) whips a blocker on the line of scrimmage and pressures Purdue quarterback Drew Brees.

Wisconsin for those three hours. And we have to take care of all the things those 80,000 people need."

UW coach Barry Alvarez, of course, welcomed the opportunity to play the Boilermakers under the lights. "People around the Big Ten realize how difficult it is for teams to play here," he said.

"And when our crowd gets into it, it's even more difficult. It's very hard to execute when the crowd is at a fever pitch."

Tom Burke, the resident maniac at defensive end for the Badgers, cut to the chase. "The fans will be pretty lit up by that time of night and rowdier than they've been all year."

With a great sense of humor and timing, Purdue coach Joe Tiller commented on the extended tailgating and anticipated environment. "I don't know why it would be louder unless everyone partakes, you know, for strictly medicinal purposes."

The Badgers needed any edge they could get against Tiller's creative, fast-break offense (i.e., basketball on grass). The year before, Tiller's first season in the Big Ten, the unranked Boilermakers embarrassed No. 24 Wisconsin by jumping off to a startling 21-0 lead in the first 10 minutes and cruising to a 45-20 Homecoming win in West Lafayette.

"They found our weaknesses," lamented UW linebacker David Lysek, "and they capitalized on all of our mistakes. We had trouble doing anything right."

Purdue had seven plays of over 30 yards, averaged 11 yards per play (to the UW's 5.5) and finished with 559 yards of total offense. The Badgers had problems containing quarterback Billy Dicken, who completed 16 of 22 passes for 311 yards and three scores.

Dicken flourished in Tiller's system and led the Boilermakers to their best record (9-3) since 1980. The scary thing? Tiller viewed

Dicken, a senior, as a stopgap until the unheralded Brees came of age. And it didn't take long for that to happen during the 1998 season.

Through the first five games, Brees completed more than 66 percent of his passes for 1,504 yards and 14 touchdowns. Although the Boilermakers lost twice during that stretch—27-17 at No. 19 USC, and 31-30 at No. 22 Notre Dame—it was hard to find fault with Brees, who had 600 more passing yards than any other quarterback in the Big Ten.

The Badgers didn't catch any breaks, either, because Brees was coming off a record-setting performance the week before against Minnesota. The Boilermakers crushed the Gophers, 56-21, as Brees completed 31 of 36 passes for 522 yards and six scores. After breaking down the video, UW coach Barry Alvarez labeled it "a horror show."

Brees, who didn't even play in the fourth quarter, hooked up with 10 different receivers—four caught scoring passes and three had over 100 receiving yards. In the first half alone, Brees threw for 368 yards and four touchdowns. He was 21-of-25. As a team, the Boilermakers had a school-record 692 yards of total offense.

While this ambush was taking place in West Lafayette, the Badgers were struggling to keep their record unblemished in Bloomington, Indiana. The pesky Hoosiers dominated the play statistically in front of 32,328 indifferent spectators at Memorial Stadium and took a stunning 13-3 lead when Derin Graham returned the second half kickoff 100 yards.

But the UW rallied behind some clutch throws from quarterback Mike Samuel and finger-tip receptions from wide receiver Chris Chambers. Tailback Ron Dayne picked up 98 of his 130 yards in the second half and helped the Badgers overcome a 20-17 fourth quarter deficit by scoring the winning touchdown. (Fletcher also had a key pick that was converted into points, giving Wisconsin its first lead of the game in the third quarter.)

The Badgers didn't exhale until Indiana quarterback Antwaan Randle El came up empty on his team's last-ditch possession (17 plays and 0 points). The final score, 24-20. "I don't think I'd be sane enough to play football any more," an exhausted Burke said afterward, "if I had to go against a quarterback like Randle El every Saturday."

Not to worry. No one has accused Burke of being sane. Consider these words from Burke after chasing Randle El from sideline to sideline: "I never felt that kind of emotion in a football game before. I felt like I had Gibby's size, Echols' speed, and Faulkner's quickness. I felt like they all jumped inside of my body and nobody was going to stop me."

Faulkner is Eddie Faulkner, the backup to Dayne. Echols is Mike Echols, a starting corner, whose 4.3 40 is the fastest among the Badgers. And Gibby is Gibby. That would be the 378-pound Aaron

Gibson (47-inch waist, 33-inch thighs, 20-inch neck).

In 1996, Gibson made his first career start against the Boilermakers as a pseudo tight end. He wore No. 81, and according to Alvarez, "One of the officials told me one of the Purdue kids wanted to know if there was a weight limit for players in the 80 numbers."

Back to Burke, and more insanity.

"When I was sitting on the sidelines (at Indiana) I was going nuts," he said. "I could feel the tears coming down my face, not because I was sad or hurting but just because of the feeling I had. It felt like my hair was standing on end. And it felt like someone poured scalding hot water on my rear. I'd like to play a whole game with that feeling."

You get the picture. And so did Burke—that Brees was going to pose a far different challenge to the Wisconsin defense than Randle El. "He's going to complete some passes, and he's going to do a lot of good things," Burke said of Brees. "When he does, we just have to keep our confidence. We know that he's going to make some plays out there."

Rick Trefzger was in charge of the offense the last time the Boilermakers traveled to Madison, and the crafty lefty put a scare into the Badgers, who nearly squandered a 24-0 lead. Trefzger passed for 328 yards in three quarters and fell just short, 33-25, of the upset.

Dayne was the difference, rushing for 244 yards. Nonetheless, Purdue still ran an astounding 104 plays and produced 540 yards of total offense. "It was not a typical bend-but-don't-break defense," Alvarez said. "I thought we broke a few times."

Bend-but-don't break—bleed slow—was also the strategy for Brees.

"We knew that he was going to throw for a bunch of yards," said UW defensive line coach John Palermo. "We were going to play a soft zone against him and let him throw the ball underneath (the coverage). But we wouldn't let him run the ball. And when they got into the red zone, we wanted to make them kick field goals or force Brees into errors.

"If we weren't giving up big plays, we were hoping we could frustrate him. You know what I'm saying? We wanted to keep the ball in his hands, but we wanted to make sure he was running sideways and not up the field because he's very dangerous when he pulls it down."

Because of Purdue's quick game, Palermo realized that it would be nearly impossible to get much pressure on Brees, which put more pressure on the secondary. To prevent big plays, home runs, the

Photos Courtesy of Craig Schreiner/Wisconsin State Journal

Top right: Tailback Ron Dayne breaks free for his longest run of the night, 11 yards, against a stingy Purdue defense that revolves around defensive ends Roosevelt Colvin and Chike Okeafor. Dayne finished with 33 rushes for 127 yards.

Bottom right:
By his own admission, UW defensive end Tom Burke played the game "like my hair was on fire." During the 1998 season, Burke was virtually unblockable, recording 31 tackles behind the line of scrimmage, including 22 quarterback sacks.

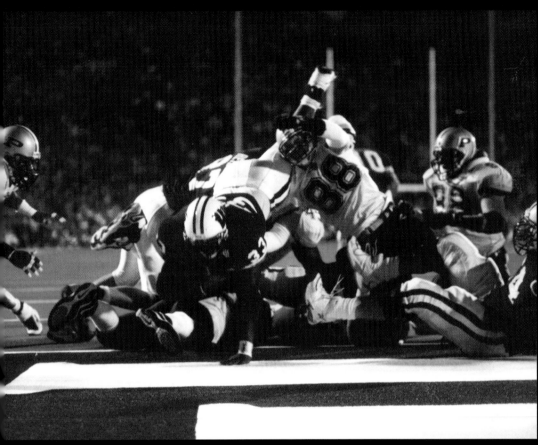

Purdue defensive tackle Matt Mitrione (98) upends UW tailback Ron Dayne but not before Dayne dives into the end zone for a touchdown with 7:38 left in the fourth quarter. Dayne's only rushing touchdown of the night gave the Badgers a 31-17 lead and capped a 12-play, 67-yard drive.

Badgers wanted to get mileage out of a four-deep zone.

In this coverage, Fletcher, Echols, Jason Doering and Leonard Taylor or Bobby Myers are each responsible for a quarter of the field. Taking away Purdue's deep game came at the expense of giving up the short game, the quick outs. Such was the give and take.

"They can move the ball up and down, and you can't get impatient," Alvarez said. "I know people always want you to crowd the receivers and not give them the out cut. But as soon as you start crowding them, the ball is going down the field.

"We just had to be patient...knowing that when they got closer to the goal line, they would run out of room, and our guys could squeeze on them a little more."

Let the chess game begin.

Purdue defensive coordinator Brock Spack replaced defensive back Henry Bell with an additional run-stopper, Chuckie Nwokorie, on running downs.

Wisconsin defensive coordinator Kevin Cosgrove replaced inside linebacker Donnel Thompson with an additional pass defender (Myers) on passing downs.

Cosgrove, at times, also replaced outside linebacker Bob Adamov with pass defender Joey Boese to give the Badgers six defensive backs in passing situations.

Who knew that Purdue would be in passing situations all night?

In what amounted to the greatest aerial show this side of the Pete "Maverick" Mitchell (Tom Cruise) and Tom "Iceman" Kazanski (Val Kilmer) dogfight scenes, Hurricane Drew was the Top Gun in Camp Randall's airspace. Brees set an NCAA record with 83 pass attempts, tied another mark with 55 completions, and threw for 494 yards.

Brees was in such a zone, he probably didn't want it to end. And it nearly didn't. This was a marathon, not a sprint, a 3-hour and 37-minute mini-drama that came down to mistakes. Brees was picked off four times, the Boilermakers lost a fumble and twice failed in short yardage (fourth-and-1), whereas the Badgers stayed patient and survived, 31-24.

"It was one of the craziest games I ever played in—ever, ever in my life," Brees said from the Chargers' training base. "It felt like we threw the ball on every play. We were in the two-minute drill basically the entire game. At the end of the game, I was thinking, 'Gosh, I could have thrown the ball 100 times, if it had gone into overtime.' It was just crazy."

Brees took what the Badgers gave him defensively, and kept taking. "I felt like Drew Brees' press agent all week, and I think you can see why," Alvarez said. "He's as fine a quarterback as I've faced. He's fantastic. I don't think I'll have to answer any more questions on whether our secondary has been tested. They had a lifetime of tests."

Call it Late Night with Bucky and Brees. Looking up at the clock during his post-game press conference, Alvarez mused, "That's the trouble with those guys who throw too much-the game takes too long. I thought our fans were starting to fall asleep it was so darn long."

The Badgers definitely answered an early wake-up call, taking a 14-3 lead in the first quarter. Field position was the storyline. Purdue's Da'Shann Austin fumbled a punt, and Donte King recovered on the 9-yard-line, setting up the first score (Samuel's option run). A Nick Davis punt return, and a subsequent personal foul on the Boilermakers, set up the second touchdown (another Samuel run). The length of the drives: three plays, 29 yards.

It looked like it was going to be a breeze. It wasn't. Purdue scored 11 points over the final four minutes of the first half to pull into a 17-17 tie. And the Boilermakers had a golden opportunity to forge into the lead on the first possession of the third quarter, driving to the UW 10. But on third-and-4, Echols intercepted a Brees pass in the end zone.

Offensively, the Badgers couldn't stay on the field. They didn't pick up a first down in the entire third quarter, elevating the stress level of the defense, notably the secondary.

"The coaches told us all week that they would complete some passes," Fletcher said, "and when you throw the ball 83 times, you can't help but complete some. It's very tempting when you see all those little short passes being completed in front of you the whole game, and you can get a little frustrated out there. But you have to sit back and be patient."

That's what Fletcher did with Purdue receiver Randall Lane, who caught short pass after short pass in Fletcher's zone. (Lane finished with 18 catches for 178 yards.) "There comes a time during a game when you have to do something," Fletcher said. "So I decided that I was going to sit on one of those quick outs that they had been throwing all night."

On a second-and-8 from the Purdue 47, Brees lined up in the shotgun. Fletcher, a former prep quarterback, kept his eyes on Brees' eyes and pointed out, "He was looking at Lane from the beginning of the play to the end."

Brees released the pass, and Fletcher stepped in front of Lane, intercepted, and returned the gift 52 yards, breaking the 17-17 tie. "It put me on the map," Fletcher repeated. (With the five turnovers, the Badgers improved to a plus-13 in takeaways-giveaways.) "We knew Drew was going to dissect and work the offense. We just waited for him to make a mistake."

So, despite running 103 offensive plays, which added up to 33 first downs and 570 yards of total offense, Brees guided Purdue to only two touchdowns, the second coming with just 22 seconds left in the game. And despite all those completions, just one was completed for longer than 20 yards, and that was for 21. "They can pass for 1,000 yards," Echols told the *State Journal*. "But as long as they don't get in the end zone, then we're doing our job."

The fans also did their job.

"It was an electric atmosphere," Palermo said. "I remember telling Barry when we were both at Notre Dame that I swear to God when we'd come out of the tunnel I'd see sparks coming off our helmets. Well, it was that kind of night. There were sparks everywhere."

Brees had a curious recollection of the crowd when contacted in San Diego.

Believe what you want.

"I remember walking out before the game, and they were dumping beer on our heads," he claimed. "Fans would come out of the stands and walk over to our sidelines, and they'd be like a foot away, screaming obscenities. There were security guards posted every 20 yards along this area. So when one fan would come and yell at you, the guard would get him.

"That fan would walk back to the stands and another guy would

UW defensive line coach John Palermo (left), head coach Barry Alvarez, and defensive coordinator Kevin Cosgrove implemented the bend-but-don't break game plan for Purdue and leave the field victorious after surviving Hurricane Drew and 83 pass attempts.

come and replace him and start yelling at us again. This went on all game long. I never wanted to go over there and sit on the bench because all I was going to do is get some fan in my ear."

Brees probably left Madison with one song ringing in his ears, "Jump Around" by House of Pain. That made its debut during the third and fourth quarter exchange. Previously, the band had struck up, "If you Want to be a Badger Just Come Along with Me."

Although UW band director Mike Leckrone was not necessarily a big fan of the choice of music ("I don't have too many CDs of House of Pain"), he went along with the marketing concept. And it has turned out to be a smash hit, a new Camp Randall tradition.

"I've had people from around the country," Fletcher said, "tell me that they've heard how crazy our stadium gets when everybody is jumping around to House of Pain."

Put 'em on the map, you might say.

Pack it up, pack it in
Let me begin
I came to win

(chorus)

I came to get down
So get out your seats and jump around
Jump around
Jump up, jump up and get down
Jump

Illinois 29 Wisconsin 28
October 23, 1982

Always on the lookout for a new wrinkle to add to his offensive playbook, Monona Grove High School coach Dick Rundle was intrigued by a "double-pass" that he saw executed successfully in a televised college football game.

The trick play—originating with a bounce pass or lateral from the quarterback to the flanker—allowed a huge underdog to pull the upset over a traditional rival; it was love at first sight for the innovative Rundle, a Hall of Fame prep coach.

"They threw the ball on a bounce to the flanker and the cornerback came right up and grabbed a hold of him," Rundle related. "Then the flanker turned his back on the line of scrimmage and threw the ball down on the ground. The corner let go, the ball bounced back up into the flanker's hand, and he threw it again for a touchdown."

Rundle felt that was one too many bounces. "So I took the second bounce out of the play and left the first bounce in," he said, adopting the "bounce pass" into his system. "I believe 1965 was the first time we used the play at Monona Grove—and we used it a long time after that—and scored the first seven times, three by running and four by throwing."

Rundle, who won two WIAA state titles with the Silver Eagles (1977 and 1984), ran the play out of different formations. In the huddle, the call was simply "Bounce Left" or "Bounce Right." Rundle had so much success with the bounce pass that he wasn't afraid to use it in any situation, even with the Badger Conference championship on the line.

"Sun Prairie had the ball and the lead with a fourth down and inches to go in their own territory," remembered Rundle. "Their quarterback got

Courtesy of UW Sports Information

Linebacker Jim Melka (33) bolts across the line of scrimmage and makes a crunching hit on Illinois running back Mitch Brookins while defensive tackle Scott Bergold (92) bowls over Jim Juriga (71) and safety John Josten (13) fills quickly.

knocked backwards (on a sneak), and they turned over the ball to us with something like 11 seconds left in the game."

Rundle signaled for the bounce pass. "We threw the ball on the bounce and as soon as it hit the ground, the Sun Prairie defense ran together," Rundle said, picking up the play-by-play. "On the film, you can see their players jumping up and down together while we're throwing the ball for a touchdown. We kicked the extra point, and won the championship."

That was one of 15 Badger Conference titles that Rundle won. From 1962 through '84, the Silver Eagles never finished lower than second. He coached 34 years and his overall record was 164-50-3 (with most of the losses coming late in his career after the school's enrollment began to decline). Rundle guessed that he called for the bounce pass maybe 18 to 20 times.

"We didn't need to use it that much," he said, "because whenever we split or spread the formation, the threat was always there and people thought it was coming."

Rundle fielded a lot of inquiries about the bounce pass. In fact, Wisconsin head coach John Jardine came out and watched a Monona Grove practice. Jardine even had some of his assistants visit with Rundle over the feasibility of running such a play with the Badgers.

"We would run the play for them on our practice field," Rundle said, "and they just couldn't get over the fact that the possibility of fumble just didn't exist when the ball hit on its point. It's almost impossible to not make that ball bounce directly."

Rundle claimed that he could get a true bounce on a gravel road. Others still had reservations. And Jardine passed—on the double pass. "John thought it was a great play and I think he really wanted to run it," Rundle said. "But if it went wrong in front of [78,000 at Camp Randall] it would

Courtesy of UW Sports Information

Opposite page: The Badger defense attempted to get pressure on Illinois quarterback "Champaign"Tony Eason all day with little success. Here Tim Krumrie #50 gets double-teamed by two Illini offensive linemen. Eason finished the day 37 for 51 with 479 yards.

Courtesy of UW Sports Information

Above: Al Toon scores on a 46-yard pass from Randy Wright - easily gaining separation on Illinois linebacker Clint Haynes and cornerback Mike Heaven (No. 9).

Courtesy of UW Sports Information

Left: Wisconsin offensive coordinator Bill Dudley.

Courtesy of UW Sports Information

Quarterback Randy Wright hands off to fullback Gerald Green on a draw play. A big hole opens up between left guard Mark Subach (53) and center Ron Versnik.

make you look like an amateur."

Jardine's successor, Dave McClain, also attended a Silver Eagles practice, according to Rundle, and expressed some interest in the bounce pass. But Rundle didn't hear back from him or anybody else connected with the Badger program.

"When my kids were in trouble out there I wanted to be able to come up with something that would maybe get them over the hump," Rundle said of his philosophy behind implementing such trickery into a game plan. "A lot of people didn't like it that we were doing this kind of thing because it's an opportunity to be embarrassed.

"But I threw all these plays under one heading: momentum changers. When your kids are out there pulling on their chin straps, with their hands on their hips, and you know they're confused and need help, you better have one of those plays to come up with."

There's always an element of surprise and luck involved with the execution of trick plays. Not that the 1982 Badgers needed a lucky horse shoe or a rabbit's foot. Not when they could count on divine intervention. McClain contended "God had a plan" for his players after Wisconsin's improbable rally and victory at Purdue in early October.

In one of the wildest comebacks in school history, the Badgers scored two touchdowns in the final 89 seconds to shock the Boilermakers, 35-31. "To tell you the truth," said UW quarterback Randy Wright, "my first thought was that all the praying that I did during the year that I spent at Notre Dame must have paid off."

Purdue coach Leon Burtnett called it, "the worst loss I've ever been associated with in coaching." He was left dumbfounded by the closing sequence of events which played out to the remnants of a big crowd (69,131) in Ross-Ade Stadium. Many began to leave after the Boilermakers took a 31-23 lead with 2:24 remaining in the game.

"We preach all the time to our football team that you can never give up," McClain said. "I'm probably getting a little into Christianity, but we do tell our young men that God has a plan for them and if you keep believing...it will be carried out."

It took 55 seconds for Wright to carry out his assignment as he drove the Badgers 70 yards for a touchdown. That made it 31-29. The two point conversion failed when Purdue linebacker Brock Spack batted down a pass in the end zone. (Spack later became the defensive coordinator under Joe Tiller in West Lafayette.)

The Boilermakers recovered the ensuing on-side kick at their own 47-yard line, the cue for Purdue's Golden Girl to begin limbering up for the postgame show.

(Insert Lee Corso here and a "Not so fast, my friend.")

That was also the cue for Purdue to begin unraveling like a team that had lost seven games in a row. On second down, the Boilermakers were guilty of a delay of game penalty. Quarterback Scott Campbell was then tackled for no gain, and the Badgers called their final timeout.

On a third down rollout, designed to eat up precious seconds, Campbell had a brain lapse and kept rolling and rolling and rolling until he rolled out of bounds—with a shove from UW linebacker Kyle Borland—and stopped

Courtesy of UW Sports Information

Right: Tight end Jeff Nault (88) had to first decoy the Illinois defense by holding a count or two on the line of scrimmage before releasing into this pattern.

the clock.

That forced a Purdue punt. Standing on his own 26, Matt Kinzer called for the ball, but it was snapped over his head. Kinzer chased it down, picked it up, and got off a lame kick that was deflected by Clint Sims into the hands of UW linebacker Jim Melka, a former 1,000-yard rusher as a prep running back. Melka needed no directions to the end zone.

Melka was credited with a 30-yard punt return for a touchdown. "I looked up," Sims said, "and thanked the Lord. It was a miracle come true."

The following Saturday, the Badgers again accomplished the improbable: they won a football game at Ohio State. Will miracles never cease? The last time Wisconsin won in Columbus was 1918. Over the last 64 years, the Badgers were 0-19-3. And they had never before won in the devil's playground, Ohio Stadium.

But on a gloomy, rainy day, they scored on their first possession and made it stand up for a satisfying 6-0 victory. In the end, they beat the Buckeyes at their own game, power football, Woody Hayes football. Wright had injured his thumb in the first half and couldn't throw the ball, so the Badgers slammed it at 'em—17 straight running plays, which consumed the final 8 minutes and 33 seconds on the clock.

It was an especially satisfying triumph for McClain, who once coached for Hayes. "It's a great victory," McClain said, explaining "because a lot of these guys stood in this locker room three years ago when we got beat here, 59-0."

The Badgers were on a roll, riding the momentum of back-to-back road victories. And they were returning home to face a beatable and winless Michigan State team, coached by sad sack Muddy Waters. The Spartans were 0-3 in the Big Ten and 0-5 overall.

Prior to the Thursday practice, UW offensive coordinator Bill Dudley had the quarterbacks scuffing up the game balls, standard operating procedure. One of the best ways to take the shine off a new ball was to bounce it off the turf.

While the quarterbacks were playing catch, Wisconsin's first-year offensive line coach, Dick Scesniak (who had worked as an offensive coordinator under the wily Don James at Washington) approached Dudley and asked, "Ever thrown a bounce pass?"

"No," Dudley replied. "Have you?"

"No," Scesniak answered. "But, geez, your guys are pretty good."

Pretty good at skipping the ball off the turf and making it catchable. "We hadn't done it," Dudley rationalized of a bounce pass, "and nobody had much experience with it."

So the discussion was tabled. For a while.

The focus returned to Michigan State. Not that the Badgers were focused, in any respect. They had a quarterback who couldn't talk (Wright had laryngitis) and a tailback who couldn't breathe (Chucky Davis had asthma). And they lacked the jump that they had shown in beating Purdue and Ohio State. A letdown was predictable.

True to form, though, the Badgers found a way to win and escaped with a 24-23 decision over the Spartans. The outcome was in doubt until the final 13 seconds when UW safety David Greenwood foiled

Courtesy of UW Sports Information

After fielding quarterback Randy Wright's skip pass, Al Toon cooly ignores the pressure from Illinois defensive end Terry Cole and outside linebacker Pete Brugard and delivers a perfect strike to tight end Jeff Nault. Offensive tackle Kevin Belcher watches as the trick play unfolds. Said UW offensive lineman Bob Landsee, "Never thought it would work. But Toon had the best arm on the team. He could throw it 75 yards with a flick of his wrist."

Courtesy of UW Sports Information

MSU's two-point conversion attempt by intercepting John Leister's pass in the end zone, a play that was warmly received in Camp Randall.

Still, the loudest cheers of the day were reserved for the Brewers, not the Badgers. Thanks to the stadium message board, the fans were kept updated on the progress of the World Series match-up between the St. Louis Cardinals and the Brewers in Milwaukee.

Much to the bewilderment of the Michigan State and Wisconsin football players, the crowd erupted when the Brewers scored six runs with two outs in the seventh and rallied for a 7-5 win at County Stadium, tying the series at two games each.

Before Cecil Cooper stepped to the plate in that fateful seventh, Badger football fans, many of whom were listening to transistor radios, serenaded the Milwaukee first sacker with "Cooooooop," not unlike the "Tooooooon" that they would one day bellow out for Al Toon, then a promising but still unproven sophomore.

Such was the state-wide appeal of the Brewers back in the day. The Badgers were winning over new converts, too, with their late comebacks and growing confidence, the byproduct of four consecutive victories. That set the stage for a Big Ten showdown between the teams chasing first-place Michigan (4-0): Illinois (4-1) and Wisconsin (3-1).

The following Monday, the bounce pass plot thickened. The Badgers actually started practicing the play, with Wright throwing the lateral to Toon, who would then throw a pass to tight end Jeff Nault. Nobody else was needed because the three-step drop protection was not going to change for the interior line or the running backs.

"We did it maybe once in team period," Dudley said, "because with such a trick play you hated to spend too many reps on it during the week."

UW safety Matt Vanden Boom got a hint of what was going on. "We'd walk out of meetings on to the field before stretching," he said, "and we'd see this goofy stuff going on with Randy and Al and Jeff. And they'd all have a wry little smile on their faces."

In the huddle, the play was "62 Skip Pass Left." (Consider: any past reference to the "Bounce Pass Game" was a misnomer. It was a skip pass, not a bounce pass.)

The play was run to the left because it was easier for Wright, a righthander, to skip the ball in that direction and easier for Toon to catch the lateral and make the throw to Nault.

"When I was in high school," said Nault, a sophomore from Escanaba, Michigan, "Menominee used to run that same play against us year after year after year. And it worked every time, and they were doing it on grass. We knew that they had the play, but we still didn't stop it. You wouldn't believe how many teams were stung by it."

Bret Pearson was Nault's backup at tight end with the Badgers. And Pearson just happened to be Menominee's triggerman (Toon's role) on the bounce pass.

Meanwhile, the Badger defense was concentrating on Illinois quarterback Charles Carroll Eason IV—Champaign Tony—who had one of the itchiest trigger-fingers in college football. In 18 career starts, he had thrown for less than 200 yards just once. Eason had thrown for over 300 yards nine times,

including 357 yards against Wisconsin in '81.

"He has a pro's arm and the kind of mobility they drool over," Illinois head coach Mike White said of Eason, a JUCO transfer from California, who "watched Joe Namath on television and from a mechanical standpoint" modeled himself after Broadway Joe.

Eason lived up to expectations and once again made believers out of the Badgers by completing 37 of 51 passes for a career-high 479 yards. But few will likely ever forget the one pass that Toon completed to Nault. The skip pass. (Truth is, few will likely remember the Badgers had a 20-9 lead with 4 minutes left in the third quarter, and blew it.)

Before the opening kickoff, McClain had huddled with the game officials and gave them a heads-up on the possibility of a trick play. "We had to brief the refs," Dudley said, "because an inadvertent whistle could kill you."

Timing was everything. So was field position. With less than two minutes left, and Illinois leading 26-20, White ordered his punter, Chris Sigourney, to run out of the south end zone. White wanted the safety and free kick rather than risking a punt from inside the 10.

That made it 26-22.

"Ideally, we wanted to use the skip pass from the 30-yard and in," Dudley said. "And, honest to God, I had not thought of the play when Dave comes by me on the sidelines and says, 'Run that pass.' He couldn't remember what the play was called. I go, 'okay.'"

On second-and-10 from the Illinois 40, the Badgers lined up in a formation that Rundle recognized immediately from his perch in Camp Randall. "As soon as they split out, I said to my wife, 'They're going to throw the damn thing,'" he recalled.

Sure enough, Wright tossed a one-hop lateral to Toon, who was positioned three yards behind the line of scrimmage. When Toon fielded the ball on the skip, he carried out his fake, freezing the Illini secondary and drawing a groan from the sell-out crowd of 78,406. "They went Awwwwwwww (bleep),'" Dudley remembered.

As soon as the ball was snapped, Nault was decoying the secondary. "When the ball was thrown to Al, I pulled up, took a couple of walking steps, and blasted off again," he said. "I really didn't have to give their safety much of a fake, though, because he stopped dead.

"He was flat-footed. And as soon as I saw that I knew if someone up front didn't read the play, it was a touchdown. It was a real shot in the dark. But it worked."

Toon, who had one of the better arms on the team, threw a perfect pass to Nault, who had gotten behind the unsuspecting Illinois defense and romped into the end zone, triggering a crazy, albeit premature, celebration on the field and in the stands.

"I didn't know what happened, it just came out of the blue sky," Illini safety Craig Swoope told the *State Journal*. "The last time I saw that was back when I was playing in the Pop Warner League," said Illini receiver Oliver Williams. "You just have to watch those plays," added Illini placekicker Mike Bass, "and then clap."

That was the ecstasy. What followed was the agony. Wendell Gladem doinked the left upright with his extra point attempt, a continuation of a season-long problem with special teams. Gladem also had an extra point kick blocked earlier in the game.

Wisconsin led, 28-26. But the Illini had the ball, 52 seconds, and, most importantly, total faith in the unflappable Eason. "That's the spot you want to be in," he said. "Shooting free throws in the closing seconds. Game on the line. I'm the last guy who can get emotional at a point like that. That's what I get paid for." (Insert your own punch line here.)

It took five plays for Eason to move the Illini 51 yards to the UW 29. Two of the biggest plays were a 22-yard completion to Williams and a 23-yard completion to tight end Tim Brewster. Eason did make one mistake, misfiring on a pass over the middle that skipped through the hands of Wisconsin linebacker Jody O'Donnell.

That could have ended the game. Instead, the bare-footed Bass got the honors. The portly 5-foot-10, 210-pound Bass, the son of NFL assistant Tom Bass, had had a 56-yard field goal attempt deflect off the upright the week before against Ohio State. "The guy really looked fat, and I thought he might choke a little bit," observed UW receiver Tim Stracka.

Fat chance. With three seconds left, Bass calmly nailed a 46-yard field goal (his fifth of the game). That kick would have been good from 56. And it was like a kick in the groin to the Badgers, and their fans, numb as they were to the reality of a 29-28 defeat.

"I was as high as I've ever been when we scored that [skip pass] touchdown," said UW safety John Josten. "And 52 seconds later, I was on the bottom floor." Interjected Kyle Borland, "This is the way we've been beating people. I guess our bubble burst."

Upon further review, Nault said, "Maybe I should have looped around a little bit before I got to the goal line [after catching Toon's pass]. Maybe I should have gone to the 5-yard-line and just died on the ball. That would have gotten the clock down some. But in the heat of the game, you're going for the touchdown and the win right away and nothing else."

Dudley is retired from coaching. But, along with McClain, he always believed that Illinois had tape of the skip pass. He said two unauthorized people were spotted in the north end zone during one of the practices leading up to the game. A UW graduate assistant, Guy Boliaux, tried to chase them down, but the trespassers got away.

Hence, the grassy knoll theory, which was partly reinforced after the game by something Swoope told the *State Journal.* "I've seen [the skip pass] before, and when I saw [Toon] take a few steps back, I said to myself, 'Oh, oh, that's the play.'"

In particular, Dudley always had his suspicions about two young, aggressive assistants on White's coaching staff: Bill Callahan and Kevin Cosgrove. All of which has introduced a little bit more intrigue and mystery to the Bounce Pass Game.

Check that.

The Skip Pass Game.

Courtesy of UW Sports Information

The UW coaches watch as Mike Bass attempts the game-winning field goal. UW offensive coordinator Bill Dudley (third from left) is flanked by team physician William Clancy (second from left). To the right of Dudley is graduate assistant Dave Mohapp, and Andy North, the two-time U.S. Open champion, holding the clipboard. North, who volunteered his time, was very good friends with head coach Dave McClain.

Courtesy of UW Sports Information

Illinois placekicker Mike Bass focuses on the ball and his follow-through on the game-winning field goal. The Badgers positioned safety David Greenwood under the goal posts with the hope that the kick might be low enough to knock away. Greenwood had mad hops. He was a 7-foot high jumper and the Big Ten outdoor champion.

Wisconsin 27 Minnesota 0
November 20, 1954

Movie goers had plenty of viewing options the second week of November, 1953, including the sci-fi thriller The *War of the Worlds*, starring Gene Barry, Ann Robinson and Les Tremayne. Byron Haski█ directed the film adaptation of the H.G. Wells novel.

While The *War of the Worlds* was playing at the Parkway Theater in Madison, the Capitol had the premier showing of *Crazylegs*, starring none other than Wisconsin's folk hero, Elroy Hirsch, as himself. The film got banned. But Hirsch drew raves.

"Hirsch does show a great ease with the camera," wrote one review-er and his 'Aw, shucks' acting style is endearing. He seems to have been a sweet and kind individual. His craggy face and build would put him in the hunk category."

That same weekend, a record-breaking crowd of 52,887 watched another smash hit, "The Horse," starring Alan Ameche as himself. The reviews were terrific for Ameche, who buried the needle on the hunk meter, too. His unsung supporting cast with the Badgers also got high marks after a 34-7 stomping of previously unbeaten Illinois at Camp Randall.

"Wisconsin was a great football team on this golden afternoon," wrote *State Journal* sports editor Henry J. McCormick, "one that will stand comparison with the greatest teams that ever wore the Cardinal. It had to be that good to win handily from a team that had won four previous Big Ten starts by margins never thinner than 16 points."

The Badgers' productive one-two punch of Ameche (17 carries for 145 yards) and Harland Carl (seven for 103 yards) bested the highly-touted Illinois tandem of J.C. Caroline (25 carries for 83 yards) and Mickey Bates (14 carries for 67 yards). Jim Miller, Norbert Esser, and Bobby Gingrass also had key contributing roles in the UW pro-duction.

Ameche really was a horse, a work horse. Some say UW assistant coach George Lanphear tagged him with the moniker because Ameche worked like a horse in practice. Some say Ameche ran with high-knee action and pranced like a horse. Some say Ameche threw off tacklers like an ill-tempered rodeo bronc. Some say "Horse" was short for "Iron Horse" which was a testimonial to Ameche's durability as a two-way player.

By any name, the reviewers loved The Horse.

Dick Hackenberg, *Chicago Sun-Times*: "A 'horse'-drawn vehicle got in the way of Illinois' touchdown express and the wreckage was awful to behold."

Oliver Kuechle, *Milwaukee Journal*: "Ameche was nothing less than spectacular as he bulled and stormed and time after time carried two or three or even four men on his back before sheer weight forced him to the ground."

Red Smith, a Cheesehead from Green Bay and the *New York Herald Tribune*: "Illinois stopped at the sign of the Flying Red Horse."

Smith was referencing a popular slogan du jour, linking Ameche to Pegasus, the mythological winged horse and the corporate logo of the Magnolia Petroleum Company (Mobil Oil) in Dallas. A large oil der-rick, erected on the city's first skyscraper, supported two red neon signs (35 by 50 feet) that formed the image of the Flying Red Horse.

Ameche's teammates had their own images of The Horse.

"Playing with Alan was exciting because the kid had no fear," said Jim Temp, a defensive end from LaCrosse. "He was as hard as a rock from the top of his head to his toes. His thighs were not quite as big as Jimmy Taylor's, who I played with later (in Green Bay from 1957-1960). Nevertheless, when you hit him—with your head or your shoulders or whatever part of your anatomy—you got hit BY him, and you felt it."

"Ameche was a great athlete," added Gary Messner, a center from Madison East. "He was a real good basketball player, good at any-thing he did. He sure was a competitor. And he appreciated every-body else doing their job. But he was good enough if somebody missed a block, he ran over the guy in most cases.

"He made everyone feel part of the team, he made everyone feel part

Courtesy of University of Wisconsin Archives

Opposite page: Once the Horse - Alan Ameche - picked up a head of steam he was almost impossible to haul down as a colle-gian. And he was no easier to bring down as a pro with the Baltimore Colts. Ameche is still best remembered for scoring the sudden death touchdown in the 1958 NFL championship game ("The Greatest Game Ever Played") between the Colts and the New York Giants at Yankee Stadium. The game featured 15 future NFL Hall of Famers and was watched nationally in black and white on NBC by over 50 million people.

Jim Temp, No. 82, a 6-4, 228-pound senior end from LaCrosse. "Alan Ameche was an everyday guy, he really was," Temp said. "Fact is, for that whole four years, we had great team chemistry. Plus, we had great examples to follow with the Hard Rocks."

of his success. No one was better than Ameche. He was one of those guys where success came easily to him. Not that he didn't work hard, he just expected to be successful, and he was."

At the end of the 1953 season, Notre Dame quarterback Johnny Lattner won the Heisman Trophy. Lattner edged out Minnesota halfback Paul Giel by 56 points (1,850 to 1,794). Rounding out the top five were UCLA halfback Paul Cameron, Maryland quarterback Bernie Faloney, and Stanford quarterback Bob Garrett.

Ameche finished sixth with 211 points. Because he was the only junior in this group, he was the Heisman frontrunner going into the 1954 season. And he would live up to those high expectations, bringing home the trophy to Wisconsin for the first time.

There was an ironic twist to all of this horseplay. In his final home appearance, his final game as a Badger, Ameche had little impact on the outcome of the game. But this special "Senior Day" still ranks as one of the great moments in Camp Randall history.

After the energized Badgers buried Minnesota 27-0, McCormick wrote of the 10 seniors, "They were determined to close out their college careers with a victory, and they made it obvious from the start of the game until the finish, when the other nine hoisted Ameche on their shoulders and carried him off the field."

Man bites dog.

Horse rides man.

"You never forget those moments," Temp recalled nostalgically. "And we all did carry him off the field, you're darn right we did, and we were proud to do it."

Carrying Ameche off the field was not solely a symbolic gesture of respect. "He could hardly walk, much less go out on the field," Messner remembered.

The Madison writers were promoting the Minnesota game as "the last roundup for the Horse." But physically, Ameche was hurting. He played just three minutes the week before against Illinois. McCormick wrote, "It remains a question as to how close Ameche will be to top physical condition [for the Gophers]. The belief is that the brilliant Wisconsin senior will go all out to close his intercollegiate career with a top effort."

Not that Ameche needed any more incentive to play, but the Minnesota papers were touting Bob McNamara as "the greatest fullback in the country." McCormick implied that type of boast didn't sit well with Ameche's teammates. Nor did some biting commentary from Paul Giel, the former Gopher All-American.

"Whether the players saw it or not, I do not know," McCormick wrote, "but the remark that Giel is said to have made wouldn't be calculated to make the Badgers feel anything but savage. It doesn't sound like the Giel I know, but Sid Hartman of the Minneapolis *Tribune* quoted Giel as saying, 'I think Ivy Williamson and the Badgers are afraid of us.'"

Sounds like the Hartman everyone in the Midwest had grown to know.

A shorthanded Minnesota team—playing without injured quarterback Geno Cappelletti—was no match for the fired-up Badgers, who delivered an early knockout punch by scoring three first-half touchdowns in the span of four minutes and five seconds.

Because Ameche's mobility was limited because of a sprained ankle, he finished with just 13 rushes for 26 yards. But he did manage to get into the end zone a couple of times before re-injuring the ankle in the third quarter. He also played a strong game at linebacker.

"[Ameche] couldn't turn or cut, although he did pretty well when he could go straight ahead," Williamson told the *Capital Times*. "Those ankle injuries don't heal fast; one little twist and it's as painful as ever. The defensive job he did was quite a tribute to him. I was surprised he did so well in the condition he was in, but, of course, he's a team player."

Team defense erased McNamara, who rushed 19 times for 68 yards. "Playing cleanly but with a savage vengeance," McCormick wrote, "[the Badgers] gave McNamara one of the most rugged afternoons any player ever has had at Camp Randall."

Hartman described McNamara as "looking like a street fighter who had just gone 15 rounds with Rocky Marciano"—the heavyweight champ. "They had the toughest defense I've faced in my four years at Minnesota," McNamara said. "I was hit by three Badgers on every play. They seemed to spread their defense across the entire field."

It was duly recorded that the 1954 Badgers bowed out with a defensive performance the famed 1951 Hard Rocks might well have envied. Nobody personified that compliment better than Clarence (Clary) Bratt, who set a Big Ten record with four interceptions.

Courtesy of UW Sports Information

Gary Messner, No. 54, a 5-11, 198-pound offensive center from Madison East, was the captain of the 1954 Badgers. During his UW playing days, Messner was a mentor for a young athlete in the neighborhood, Pat Richter, who grew up a few houses down the street.

Above: Ameche accepts the 1954 Chicago Tribune Trophy given to the Big Ten MVP.
Legend has it that Ameche, born in Italy, changed his name from Lino - Lino Dante Ameche - to Alan Ameche at age 16
because Lino didn't sound tough enough. As a youth, he was a Golden Gloves boxing champion in Kenosha. He won the light
heavyweight division by default when all of the other boxers dropped out when they learned that they might have to fight
Ameche.

Right: Wisconsin's nine other seniors hoisted Alan Ameche on their shoulders and carried the Horse off the field after his final
appearance at Camp Randall Stadium. "It was a nice way for the seniors to bow out," said UW coach Ivy Williamson. "They
were a fine group, and there will be others, besides Ameche, who will be hard to replace. But Ameche is a truly great football
player, a team player."

Three others have since matched that feat, but nobody within the conference has topped it.

Bratt was one of the busiest players on the field against Minnesota. He also rushed 10 times for 67 yards and a touchdown, and returned two punts and one kickoff. As a team, the Badgers established another Big Ten record with seven interceptions (six off Don Swanson, one off Shorty Cockran). Messner, Gingrass and Jim Miller had one pick each.

Miller, the junior quarterback, received praise for how he managed the Wisconsin offense. "He's another Giel," said Minnesota guard Mike Falls. "Playing against him is like scrimmaging against Giel. He's not fast, but he is shifty and hard to get a clean shot at."

All of the underclassmen, including Miller, recognized that this spotlight dance was reserved for the seniors: Ameche, Temp, Messner, Bratt, Gingrass, Norm Amundsen, Ronnie Locklin, Clarence Stensby, Don Ursin and Glen Wilson. It was their day to remember.

"Those four years were the most wonderful time of my life," Temp said. "We had great examples to follow with the Hard Rocks (in '51). And we had team chemistry. Messner was our offensive captain and a helluva kid. And Alan was an everyday guy, he really was."

Temp still thinks of Ameche—whenever he smells garlic. "When they put him on defense at weakside linebacker (in '53 and '54) and he came into the huddle," Temp said, "he was garlic king. All he did was burp. To this day, I can't eat anything with garlic."

Married with two children, Ameche recounted to a UPI writer that his one-year-old son Brian had startled nutritionists at the university by eating spaghetti at the age of only two months. Ameche said it proved that the boy "is a real Italian, just like his father."

Temp had another memory. "Alan used to stand in front of the mirror in the training room," he said. "He'd always grease back his hair and stand and pose. He'd pull his chest out and squeeze his biceps and turn sideways to the mirror until everyone told him, 'Get the hell out of here.' But he was no prima donna by any stretch of the imagination."

"He was a body builder," Messner pointed out. "Everybody else [in that era] thought it would make you muscle bound. But he was lifting weights in the eighth grade."

That accounted for his leg drive. Said UCLA coach Red Sanders, "Ameche is the strongest runner in football history, not even excepting Bronko Nagurski."

A vocal, sign-carrying Kenosha contingent was on hand to celebrate their Favorite Son's final game as a Badger. "We want the Horse," they chanted during the fourth quarter. "Ameche sat on the bench, smiling," John Dutton wrote in the *State Journal*.

"It was a sad sort of smile. The fans who have watched him become one of America's great fullbacks will never forget the four years when the Horse helped Wisconsin plow its way into becoming one of the nation's great teams."

The 10 seniors were freshmen in 1951 and eligible then for competition under Big Ten rules. As a class, they were 26-8-3 overall: 18-5-3 in the Big Ten and 16-2-2 at Camp Randall. They were on board for Wisconsin's first share of a conference title in 40 years, a Rose Bowl trip, and a No. 1 national ranking, which has happened just once in school history.

(In 1952, the Badgers jumped from No. 8 to No. 1 in the Associated Press football poll after a 20-6 victory over defending Rose Bowl champion Illinois at Camp Randall. They were ranked No. 3 in the UPI poll behind Michigan State and California.

Wisconsin didn't hold on to the No. 1 ranking for very long—losing 23-14 at Ohio State the following Saturday. "My boys won't forget that ball game for 50 years," yipped Buckeye coach Woody Hayes, who was carried off the field on the shoulders of fans and players. The next week, the Badgers dropped to No. 12 in the AP poll.)

At the end of his UW career, Alan Dante (The Horse) Ameche was No. 1—on the 1954 Heisman Trophy ballot. Ameche received 1,068 points to beat out Oklahoma's All-American center Kurt Burris, who had 838 points. Ohio State's Howard (Hopalong) Cassady was third, and he came back the following year and won the 1955 Heisman.

When he left Wisconsin, Ameche was the NCAA's all-time leading rusher with 673 carries for 3,212 yards (4.8). His No. 35 is one of four retired numbers at the school, joining No. 40 (Elroy Hirsch), No. 83 (Allen Shafer), and No. 80 (Dave Schreiner).

Most people felt Ameche was deserving of the Heisman. "I think Ameche was the one that should have won—I had selected him myself," said Edith Heisman, wife of John Heisman, the trophy's namesake. Heisman was a successful coach and innovator as well as the former director of the New York Downtown Athletic Club.

"I think I'm going to send [Ameche] a telegram," she told the Associated Press. "I've never done that before in all the years the trophy has been given, but since he's a Wisconsin boy I believe I'm going to do it." (Edith Heisman, a Wisconsin native, had a sister who lived in Rhinelander, and on Edith's request, John Heisman was buried there in 1936.)

Alan Ameche is part of Heisman lore for another reason. After Ameche's death from a heart attack in 1988, his wife Yvonne remarried in 1996, exchanging vows with Glenn Davis (Mr. Outside), the 1946 Heisman Trophy winner from Army.

The *Washington Post* wrote of Yvonne Ameche, "She was a young wife, the mother of two, when Wisconsin's stampeding fullback won the Heisman in 1954. Fans knew the two-way star as 'The Horse.' To Yvonne, smitten since she sat behind him in social studies in junior high, Ameche was the cutest thing she ever saw." A real hunk.

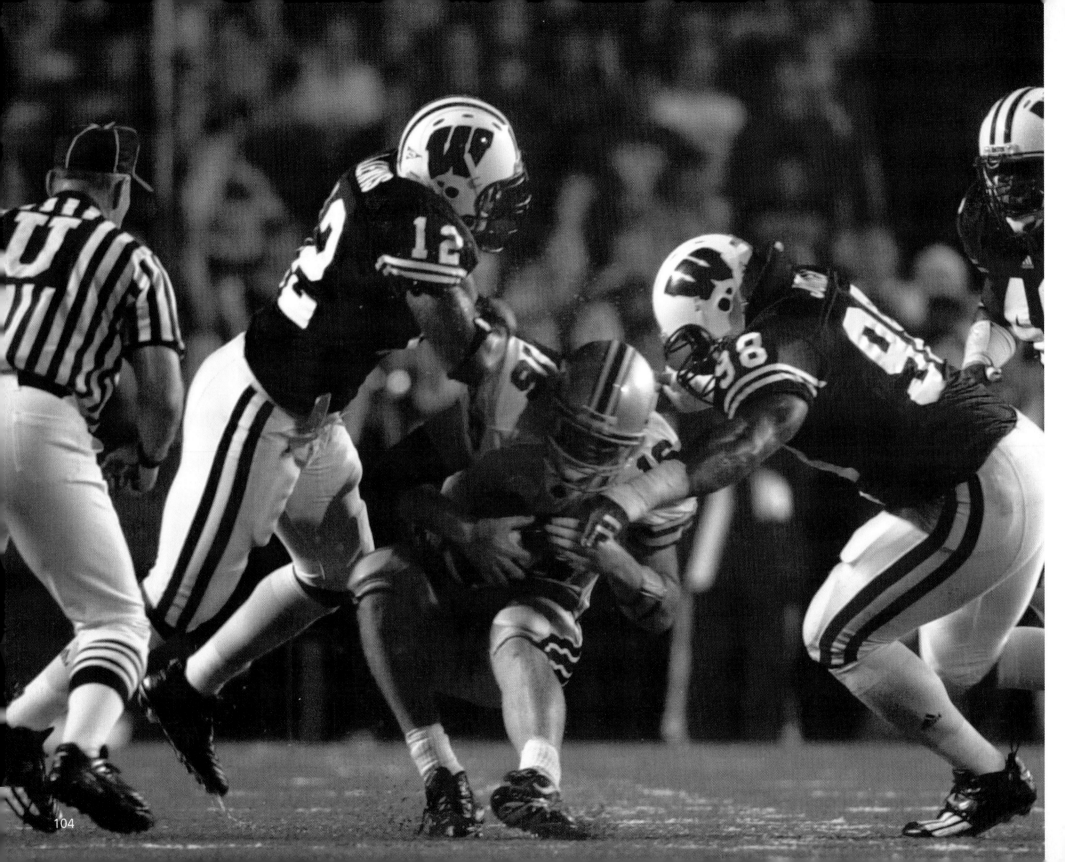

"It was one of the most special moments in my athletic career. Going through everything I went through, just to come back and mak■ a play like that to help our team win against the defending natio■al champions....I'm overwhelmed with joy."

—Lee Evans

Wisconsin assistant coach Henry Mason decided the timing was right to have a little chat with senior wide receiver Lee Evans. The Badgers were gearing up for a Saturday night date with Ohio State, and Mason wanted to mak■ sure that his marquee player knew what was ■■ the line, besides the Buckeyes' highly publicized 19-game winning streak. From Mason's perspective, this was not a pep talk. It was an infomercial.

"I can remember saying to him, 'Hey, this is goi■■ be the tape that the scouts are going to put on to see what you can do because you're going up against a quality, quality defensive back in [Chris] Gamble,'" Mason said. Did he understand the ramifications?

"No question, because Lee is such a competitor, I really wasn't challenging him, but throughout his whole career he's a guy who has always taken advantage of opportunities. And I just wanted to make sure that he understood that this was an opportunity for him to get what he really wanted—and that was to be a first round draft pick."

Mason ended their friendly conversation this

Courtesy of John Maniaci/Wisconsin State Journal

UW guard Jonathan Clinkscale (50) helps create a gapping hole in the Ohio State defense for tailback Booker Stanley. Subbing for the injured Anthony Davis, the hard-running Stanley scored the Badgers first touchdown on a 2-yard run in the second quarter.

Courtesy of John Maniaci/Wisconsin State Journal

Opposite page: Blitzing linebacker Alex Lewis (12) and defensive tackle Darius Jones (98) sack Ohio State quarterback Craig Krenzel.

way. "The tape of the Ohio State game will go a long way in determining whether people think that you're 100 percent healthy and whether you can do all the things you did before [the injury]."

Funny thing about tape—Mason wasn't sure what kind of college player Evans was going to be after watching his high school tape.

"You could see that he could run, and there wasn't any question that he was a good player and a competitive kid," said Mason. "But they ran a Wing-T offense where they didn't throw it a bunch, and he played as much defensive back as he did receiver. Off the film, you just had no idea that he was going to be the player that he turned out to be, no idea."

Mason had scored a recruiting coup from this same Bedford, Ohio, high school when he sold Chris Chambers on becoming a Badger. In this case, Mason got a big assist from former Wisconsin basketball assistant coach Shawn Hood, who had Cleveland roots and had first identified Chambers as a blue chip prospect—in both sports.

"Chris came up here for a basketball camp, not a football camp," Mason recalled. "Shawn alerted me to the fact that he was a good football player, too. We visited with Chris, and he came back in August, looked over the place, and jumped in the boat."

Michigan and Ohio State were also aggressively recruiting Chambers for football. But the deal-maker for the Badgers was basketball. Neither the Wolverines nor the Buckeyes were willing to allow Chambers to go out for hoops. Wisconsin supplied that option.

(As a true freshman, Chambers saw limited action in seven games for the Badgers as a defensive stopper for UW basketball coach Dick

Attempting to make an over-the-shoulder catch, Ohio State punt returner Chris Gamble (7) mishandles an R.J. Morse kick in the third quarter. Byron Brown (1) is the first player downfield while long snapper Matt Katula (86) recovers the loose ball (page 107) and the Badgers convert the turnover into a 10-3 lead on Mike Allen's 38-yard field goal.

Bennett. But the negatives outweighed the positives, and Chambers gave up his dual-sport dream to focus on football.)

Chambers' success at Wisconsin opened doors in Bedford. "Could we have gotten Lee without Chris?" Mason posed. "I think we could have. But it would have been harder."

Again, the hardest thing for Mason was evaluating Evans off his high school tape. Mason can still remember walking into Jim Hodakievic's office and hearing the Bedford head coach say, "I've got one better than Chris."

Mason did a double-take.

"I kind of looked at him like he had 10 heads," he said. "How can you have another receiver here that's better? But I trusted [Hodakievic]. I wasn't sure he was going to be better than Chambers, but I believed the coach that Lee was going to be a Division I player."

Mason proceeded to do his homework on Evans. He checked out his grades and

talked to people in the high school to learn more about Evans and the kind of person he was. Everything checked out. Good grades, great kid. But what would be the deal-closer?

On Hodakievic's advice, Mason stuck around for the conference track meet that spring. Evans, then a junior, was running the 300 intermediate hurdles for Bedford.

The overwhelming favorite in the event was a powerful running back from Euclid High School named Tony Fisher. Euclid High had previously sent Robert Smith and Pepe Pearson to Ohio State, and Fisher was destined to wind up at Notre Dame on a football ride.

"It was a big meet and there were a lot of people, a lot of publicity," said Evans, backtracking in his own mind. "I was all juiced up and I'm sure [Fisher] was, too. He hadn't lost all year, and he had this aura about him. His whole school did. It was like they were the best, and they tried to intimidate us that way."

Evans didn't flinch. Instead, he won the race.

"They were running side-by-side," Mason said of Evans and Fisher, "and Lee kind of looked over at the guy, and he had this look that he wasn't going to get beat. After I watched him attack that race, I looked at his high school coach and said, 'Lee needs to know that he's got a scholarship right now, period, end of story.'"

That was just a beginning for Evans. As a UW freshman, he gave everyone a glimpse of his potential when he caught a 64-yard touchdown pass against Ball State. The following week, he caught what would have been the game-winning pass against Cincinnati in the closing seconds. But it was washed out because of a motion penalty on the tight end.

In the Big Ten opener, Evans suffered a high ankle sprain against Michigan. And the timing of the injury couldn't have been worse—Evans missed the subsequent Ohio State game in Columbus. That was going to be the triumphant homecoming for the Bedford kid. The rest of his first season was also a washout because of the injury.

"But from the first day he got here," Mason said, "you knew he could run, and you could see that he could catch the ball and then his instincts just took over."

As a sophomore, Evans caught a game-winning 45-yard touchdown pass from Jim Sorgi (subbing for the injured Brooks Bollinger) with 29 seconds left in the fourth quarter at Michigan State. "You always dream about that type of thing when you're little," Evans said afterward. "You dream about coming down with the ball and winning a game."

As a junior, Evans caught 75 passes for 1,545 yards, a Big Ten record. He finally got to play against Ohio State, too, and helped rally the Badgers to a 20-17 win in Columbus. Evans had three catches for 92 yards, including an ESPN *SportsCenter* highlight. In the fourth quarter, Evans reached over OSU cornerback Derek Ross for a 30-yard gain that set up the game-tying field goal. He later had a 35-yard reception on the game-winning possession.

"It's one of those backyard things," Evans said of his personal dual with Ross. "It's just you and him going out there playing." And the better man is going to win.

Evans' winning streak ended the following spring when he blew out his knee during a meaningless intra-squad game at Camp Randall. Although he embarked on an aggressive rehab program with the hope of returning for the Big Ten season, he never made it back. He required a second surgery and was forced to redshirt.

"I really didn't know if he could make it back," Mason admitted. "Lee was my first ACL, the first player I had with that kind of surgery, so I really didn't know. I felt pretty comfortable the summer before his senior year that he was going to be healthy enough physically to make it back. But he had to get over the mental part of the injury."

In the 2003 opener at West Virginia, Evans answered some questions by scoring on a 20-yard touchdown pass from Sorgi, tying the game in the opening minutes of the fourth quarter. Evans finished with seven catches, and the Badgers went on to a 24-17 win.

Akron was next, and once again, Evans had plenty of answers, catching nine passes for 214 yards. Most of the yardage came from one play: 56 Jerk. UW offensive coordinator Brian White relayed the play call to quarterbacks coach Jeff Horton who kidded afterward that he wanted to look up at the press box and give White a feigned look of disbelief.

Rightly so. The Badgers had a slim fourth quarter lead (34-31) over the underdog Zips and the ball on their own 1-yard-line. "Every once in awhile," White said of his first down call, "you have to change up tendencies and take a shot."

Courtesy of John Maniaci/Wisconsin State Journal

See caption on page 106.

56 Jerk was that shot. The number refers to the blocking protection: maximum protection, with two tight ends and a fullback. Jerk is code for the flanker, Evans, to execute a double move—out and up. Akron corner Rickey McKenzie bit on the out cut, Evans flew past him, and Sorgi dropped the ball into his hands. Evans didn't have to break stride and ran away from McKenzie for a 99-yard score, the longest in UW history.

"That play," Mason said of 56 Jerk, "has been here since I walked in the door [in 1995] and it has stood the test of time. It's a route that we've hit over and over with different receivers. In the time I've been here, it has probably resulted in five or six touchdowns."

Mason remembered Tony Simmons executing the 56 Jerk and scoring on a 53-yard touchdown pass from Mike Samuel in a 1997 victory at Minnesota. "Tony was not a good 'out' runner," Mason said. "But he could sure transition." Touchdown Tony.

The out and up was designed for the flanker, whether it was Simmons or Evans. Donald Hayes and Chambers were split ends, and their specialty was the slant and go.

Like most teams, the Badgers were playing to the strength of their receivers. And despite the gaudy numbers in the Akron game, Evans was still working on returning to full strength.

"I thought he was a little sluggish early in the year, a little rusty and that's to be expected," said Mason, knowing that Ohio State and Chris Gamble would be the ultimate test for Evans. "If you look at the game within the game, you've got maybe the best receiver in the league and maybe the best D-back in the league. It's like a heavyweight fight.

"Gamble vs. Evans. This would be the game within the game (a primetime night game) between Ohio State and Wisconsin. The Buckeyes were playing on the road for the first time since winning the national title in double-overtime over Miami. They were also coming off a bye, so they had two weeks to prepare. That was offset by the Badgers' record under the lights. They were 15-5, and winners of 14 of their last 15 under UW coach Barry Alvarez.

"We wanted to make this game, the Ohio State game, one of the biggest games in the country on this day," Evans said. "And the stage was set. It's big, really big."

After Wednesday's practice, Evans talked about his respect for Gamble, a former receiver, and said, "I don't know if [Gamble] will follow me around the entire game. But I definitely think, in certain situations, he'll follow me."

After Thursday's practice in

Courtesy of John Maniaci/Wisconsin State Journal

Top: Ohio State linebacker Robert Reynolds (top) applies a choke hold to quarterback Jim Sorgi, who's also being pinned to the turf by linebacker A.J. Hawk (47).
Bottom: Offensive center Donovan Raiola (53) and guard Jonathan Clinkscale (50) come to the aid of their fallen teammate, Sorgi, who's surrounded by Buckeyes. Pictured are Nate Salley (21), Will Allen (4), Quinn Pitcock (90) and Tim Anderson.

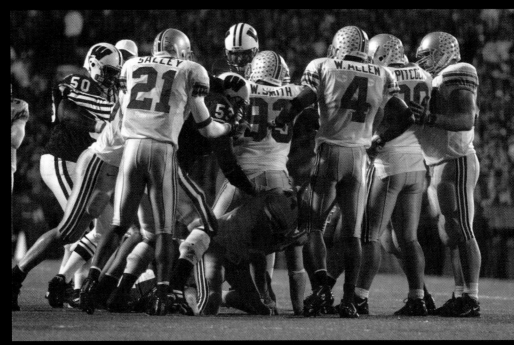

Courtesy of John Maniaci/Wisconsin State Journal

Columbus, Gamble talked about his respect for Evans and said, "I think they'll come after me. But I'll just let them know that Chris Gamble can go out there and play the game. I like playing against the top receivers in the country, and I like showing everybody that Chris Gamble can play with the best."

Gamble vs. Evans. Speaking to the match-up, Ohio State secondary coach Mel Tucker said, "When you have two great players, there are a lot of different things that go into it."

Tucker, a former UW defensive back recruited by Alvarez, listed the variables.

"What type of pressure we're able to put on the quarterback," he said. "What type of throws he's able to make. How much man coverage we're going to play as opposed to zone coverage. How much help is he going to get as opposed to not getting any help at all. All those things can be determining factors in how that match-up plays out.

"But obviously, there's going to be a couple of times in the game where there's going to be a one-on-one, *mano-a-mano* type of play, and it will be a situation where one guy is going to come out on top. Those moments are bound to happen."

In sum, Evans said, "This is what you play college football for—to play in big games. So when you get the opportunity you have to embrace it and take advantage of it."

Regarding the challenge that Gamble presented, he added confidently, "It's going to come down to who outworks who for

Courtesy of John Maniaci/Wisconsin State Journal

Backup quarterback Matt Schabert rolls away from the pressure of linebacker Robert Reynolds and spots Lee Evans running behind Ohio State cornerback Chris Gamble on an out-and-up pattern ("56 Jerk"). Looking for the interception, Gamble bites on the fake and jumps the route. Schabert lofts the ball into Evans' soft hands and Evans does the rest, sprinting 79 yards, untouched, to the North end zone (page 111), where he's finally tackled - by a teammate, Jonathan Orr. Let the celebration begin.

the ball. Whoever can make the play."

Alvarez played to his team's emotions the previous Saturday at Penn State. After the Badgers struggled to a sloppy 30-23 win, Alvarez demanded that his players forget about the Nittany Lions and anything not related to Ohio State. He used his entire post-game forum to fan the flames of their passion for the Buckeyes. Nothing else mattered.

"I'm sure you heard us yelling in [the locker room]," said UW tight end Tony Paciotti. "You could feel the electricity rolling through everyone."

This is where Brian Curtis, a free lance writer from Los Angeles, picked up the Wisconsin storyline for his book *Every Week A Season: A Journey Inside Big-time College Football*. This was the insider's slant and go. Curtis wrote about what happened behind the scenes in nine programs: Colorado State, Georgia, Boston College, Tennessee, Maryland, LSU, Florida State, Arizona State and Wisconsin. Armed with an all-access pass, Curtis spent one week on each campus and chronicled the build-up to game day.

The Wisconsin chapter was entitled "I'm in, I'm on." For certain big games, Alvarez has had the players wear rubber bands on their wrists as a reminder of resiliency and maximum concentration. The

rationale for the rubber bands has varied over the years, but the message behind the motivational tactic was generally the same: focus, 24/7.

Follow the Alvarez theme through these Curtis snippets:

On Monday, Alvarez tells the players, "If we play our best, we are a better team than them and will win." On Tuesday, he tells them, "When you are in and on, committed to playing your best, get your [rubber] bands from your coaches. Listen, you gotta believe you can win. You HAVE to believe you can win." On Wednesday, he reminds them, "You can have no hesitation when you step on the field Saturday—none at all."

On Thursday, Alvarez says of the Buckeyes and their 19-game winning streak, "They believe they are going to win. And on their opponents, one or two guys get doubts, thinking, 'We're not supposed to win,' so they don't break up a pass or make the catch. If you guys go out there and give it your best shot, we'll win."

During Saturday morning's 40-minute walk-through at Camp Randall, he stresses to his players, "You can't be in awe of them. Yes, they are a good football team and you have to respect them, but you can't be in awe of them."

Minutes before the kickoff, Alvarez pulls all his themes together in

Courtesy of John Maniaci/Wisconsin State Journal

See caption on page 109.

Reported Curtis of the emotion in the UW locker room, "Before the team walks out [for the second half], Anthony Davis, he of the high-ankle sprain, becomes enraged. The offense huddles around him as he releases his energy in a 10-second pep talk that concludes with him slamming his helmet into the floor so hard that pieces fly off."

The only scoring in the third quarter was a Mike Allen field goal, making it 10-3. The score was set up by a Gamble fumble on a punt return. Late in the quarter, the Badgers lost their quarterback, Sorgi, when he was tackled and mugged by Ohio State linebacker Robert (Hacksaw) Reynolds. In one of the all-time punk moves—a WWE trademark—Reynolds applied a choke hold to Sorgi's wind pipe.

No flag, no Sorgi. Couldn't breathe. ("It was kind of scary," Sorgi would say after regaining his ability to communicate. "I think the team rallied around me. It gave us a willingness to fight for the win, more-so than a willingness to retaliate.")

As Sorgi was helped off the field, UW offensive center Donovan Raiola was breathing fire and challenging the Ohio State bench to a no-holds barred cage match, Hawaiian style. No takers. "I lost all respect for them," Raiola said.

Enter Matt Schabert. (Memo to ESPN: it's Shay-bert, not Shah-bert.)

the locker room. "You are ready for this," he says. "You had a great week of practice and you are ready. No hesitation now." As he speaks, according to Curtis, his voice grows louder, and the players begin to shout and hop around. Curtis wrote, "They are raging by the time Alvarez shouts, 'Let's go kick their (bleeps).'"

Camp Randall Stadium was rain-swept and up-for-grabs. And with starting tailback Anthony Davis still nursing an ankle injury, Booker Stanley gave the Badgers a huge lift in the first half, rushing 10 times for 38 yards and the first score of the game. Stanley was in a groove, having rushed for 119 yards against both North Carolina and Penn State. Smash-mouth was the order of the night. At halftime, Wisconsin led, 7-3.

On his first series (third-and-4), he ran for 12 yards and a first down on a quarterback draw. "It gave me a chance to get in there and get some confidence," said Schabert, who deked out OSU linebacker A.J. Hawk. "It was pretty much run for your life (with Hawk pursuing)...but once I got that first down, I settled in, and I was ready to lead the guys."

On his second series (third-and-15), he read Ohio State's cover 2 defense and lofted a perfect pass into the hands of Brandon Williams, who picked up 25 yards.

On his third series (second-and-9), Schabert got the call from the sidelines: 56 Jerk. The game was tied, 10-10—Michael Jenkins had caught a 6-yard touchdown pass from Craig Krenzel with 6:09 left in the fourth quarter. Perfect timing, Mason thought.

"We had hit a couple of outs against their man-to-man, but it wasn't Lee, it was Brandon Williams running the out," Mason said. "They were breaking on it pretty hard."

Evans was still without a reception. "But if you look at the game tape," Mason said, "Lee handled [Gamble] pretty much all night long, beat him a majority of the time, but we just weren't able to hook up with him."

To his thinking, Evans was setting up Gamble. "Somewhere along the line, Lee is going to run that route on a running play, and he's going to get a feel for how hard the guy is playing it," Mason said. "Lee was a veteran, he could bait you into that route by running a real bad or lazy out route. So you know what? I'm thinking, 'We need a play.' It's time."

Evans was on the same page. "They were rolling up tight, playing me hard underneath and rolling the safety over the top," he said. "[Gamble] bit hard on the out fake."

Gamble likes to gamble. That's his calling card. He has great ball skills. In 2002, he intercepted a Sorgi pass targeted for Jonathan Orr in the end zone. The following week, he returned an interception 40 yards for a touchdown against Penn State.

"We didn't go into the game saying we could beat Gamble," Mason said. "We just trusted Lee and the fact that he could beat anybody on that route. If we throw the out there, Gamble is going to pick it and walk into the end zone the other way, and they win."

Much to Gamble's chagrin, it was not an out route. But he had already bit. "The pre-snap read wasn't good. It kind of looked tough to run [56 Jerk]," Schabert said. "But halfway through, I kind of looked at the backside route and as soon as I did, I saw Lee taking off behind [Gamble]. I threw to a spot and let Lee run under it."

Evans caught the ball in stride and ran away from Gamble, who had no place to hide after the Badgers took a 17-10 lead on the 79-yard touchdown play. "It's kind of pure excitement, pure joy, running down that sideline," Schabert said, sprinting towards the north end zone. "I was thinking maybe I should do a cartwheel."

He wisely backed off. There was still 5:20 remaining. And the Badgers needed one more play from Schabert to seal the victory. On third-and-2, he ran a naked bootleg and picked up the first down. For good measure, he stayed inbounds to keep the clock running. "You dream about playing in a game like this," Schabert said.

A coach can dream, too. "This is one of my most gratifying wins,"

Courtesy of John Maniaci/Wisconsin State Journal

Jonathan Orr and Lee celebrate after Evan scores on a 79-yard touchdown pass.

Alvarez said. "I've never seen an atmosphere where it was prolonged like it was. I thought the fans were at a fever pitch for every snap. There was never a play that they took off."

Beating Ohio State was particularly gratifying for Evans, the Ohio native. In mid-November, he would add to his legacy by catching 10 passes for 258 yards and five touchdowns in a 56-21 blowout of Michigan State at Camp Randall. (Sorgi completed 16 of 24 for 380 yards). That was a great moment. But this may have been his greatest.

"When he catches the ball, he's still got about 40 yards to run. And there are so many things going on in your mind as you're watching him run, watching him stride out," Mason said. "It was one of those great moments captured in time." And on tape.

Wisconsin 21 Nebraska 20
September 21, 1974

When you walk into the Eau Claire insurance agency, you will not be overwhelmed by the Badger memorabilia celebrating the college football career of native son Gregg Bohlig. That's by design. Old news is just that to the soft-spoken Bohlig, who didn't bring a lot of attention to himself as an industrious, overachieving player. So why start now?

Regardless if the Badgers were good or bad, regardless if he played well or poorly, Bohlig always could see the big picture. Still can. And if you walk into Bohlig's office, you can see it, too—an aerial shot of Camp Randall Stadium taken from the Goodyear blimp. The large blow-up picture was a cherished gift from his dad.

The inscription reads: Wisconsin 21 Nebraska 20.

"I walk by that picture every day, and I do enjoy having it in my office; I was very proud of my involvement [in that win]," said Bohlig in an almost reverent voice. "I'll have clients in here and almost daily someone mentions something about [that outcome]. It's kind of amazing how far- reaching that game was to a lot of people."

You get the picture. So did Bohlig and his teammates. In order to beat a powerhouse like a Nebraska in 1974, they first had to believe that they could measure up and stay on the field with the Cornhuskers, which they proved to themselves conclusively in 1973. "We felt like we could have won that game in Lincoln," Bohlig said.

They were the only ones that felt that way BEFORE the game. The early betting line was unflattering to the Little Red, a 28 to 35-point underdog to the Big Red.

The perceived slight was a slap in the face to senior offensive center

QB Gregg Bohlig

Mike Webster, who didn't take kindly to the not so subtle implication that the Badgers were a bunch of patsies. "That made us all kind of mad," growled Iron Mike. "After all, I don' think anyone deserves to be a four touchdown underdog."

By Friday, the Badgers had earned a modicum of respect from the odds-makers. Nebraska was now a three-touchdown favorite. "It should still make our team mad and ready to play," said UW assistant coach Dick Teteak. "We have something to show people."

By contrast, the Big Red, the truly Big Red, had nothing to prove, at least not against a lightweight like Wisconsin. Nebraska had not lost to a Big Ten opponent since 1960, so the 21-point spread was justified for the 1973 intersectional game. Especially since the Cornhuskers were coming off back-to-back national championships.

The locals welcomed the Cheeseheads to Lincoln, and not only because the Badgers represented, in their mind, little more than a speed bump. They were most grateful for the exports from the Dairy State: quarterback Jerry Tagge and defensive back Jim Anderson, the co-captains of the 1972 title squad. Tagge and Anderson prepped at Green Bay West (which also turned out Dave Mason, the starting monster back for the Cornhuskers).

The Badgers did catch Nebraska in transition. Johnny Rodgers had moved on after winning the 1972 Heisman. Tagge had moved on after being drafted in the first round by the Packers. Husker icon Bob Devaney was still calling shots as the athletic director, but he had reduced his work load by turning over the head coaching chores to Tom Osborne.

Not much else had changed in Lincoln (where Northeast High School had an up and coming assistant, a former Husker linebacker by the name of Barry Alvarez). Going into the Wisconsin game, the Cornhuskers were ranked No. 2 in the country behind USC. The dream of a three-peat was still alive among the frenzied Big Red

Opposite page: Although Gregg Bohlig was not the biggest, strongest or fastest quarterback in college football, he was smart (a two-time academic All-Big Ten selection) and never hesitated to take advantage of an opportunity, whether by throwing or running. Overcoming a knee injury as a freshman, Bohlig was motivated to prove his mettle. In retrospect, he said, being selected as the Most Valuable Player of the 1974 team was the ultimate reward and keepsake.

faithful.

"The people come from all over the state and they really support the team" marveled UW assistant coach George Chryst (the father of Paul Chryst, a former UW player, who rejoined Alvarez's staff in 2005 as the co-offensive coordinator). "They're good fans, too. They even throw the footballs back on the field after extra points."

As such, with the Badgers in town, there was a rotator cuff warning for those hearty Husker fans seated behind the goal posts. They expected to be arm weary.

Imagine the shock, though, when Wisconsin and Nebraska played to a 7-7 first half tie. Imagine the shock when the Badgers took a 10-7 lead midway through the fourth quarter. After the Cornhuskers countered with a long scoring drive to go back on top, 14-10, imagine the shock when UW's Selvie Washington returned the ensuing kickoff 96 yards.

Never have so many—76, 279 in Memorial Stadium—sounded so meek. Or looked so red-faced. Wisconsin 16, Nebraska 14. Shocking.

"There were about four minutes left in the game when I got in the huddle," said Nebraska quarterback David Humm, a poised lefty from Las Vegas. (His dad was a cashier at Caesar's Palace). "We all knew we could score again. The momentum was still with us. We were all a little tired, but there was a tremendous amount at stake."

Humm took charge and averted the upset by marching the Huskers 83 yards in seven plays for the winning touchdown. He converted on 4 of 5 passes on the penultimate drive and wound up breaking two school records by completing 25 of 36 for 297 passing yards.

The Badgers had held their ground, getting 143 rushing yards from Billy Marek. And they proved that they were no patsies. For now, a moral victory was something that they could build on, particularly with the Cornhuskers coming to Madison in 1974.

So when the returning Wisconsin players got together and watched the film of their 20-16 loss, they could see how close

Courtesy of UW Sports Information

Jeff Mack, senior flanker from Chicago Farragut.

Courtesy of UW Sports Information

Jeff Mack had a simple philosophy whenever he ran a pass route. "A big play can happen anytime," he said. "And as far as I'm concerned, a pass is a big play every time." As a sophomore, he caught a 77-yard touchdown pass from Rudy Steiner at LSU; a preview of his game-winning catch covering the same distance against Nebraska. As a senior, Mack had modest numbers: 16 receptions for 353 yards and two touchdowns; and 19 rushes for 124 yards and one score. But he usually came up big when the Badgers needed a big play.

they had come to winning the game, and how vulnerable and beatable Nebraska had been on its hallowed home turf.

Preparing for the rematch, Bohlig said, "The mindset was pretty positive really. We were feeling good about ourselves. We felt like we belonged on the field with them in Lincoln. We felt like we had a year more experience under our belt, and we felt like we were a better team [in 1974]. And we were confident coming off the Purdue game."

Playing without the injured Marek, the Badgers still pounded the Boilermakers, 28-14, in the 1974 opener at West Lafayette. It was an historic win, Wisconsin's first road win since 1970, a 14 game span (0-13-1), and first win at Ross-Ade Stadium since 1957 (dating back to when UW head coach John Jardine was PLAYING for Purdue).

The co-captains, Bohlig and linebacker-defensive end Mark Zakula, presented the game ball to Jardine, who probably wanted to share it with Marek's replacement, Ron Pollard. Despite a couple of fumbles, Pollard filled the void by rushing for 72 yards and two scores.

Pollard could have been speaking for everyone in the UW locker room when he boasted, "We're confident and cocky. And we'll play that way the rest of the year."

Senior offensive tackle Bob Johnson seconded the notion of a possible turnaround. "Look around here, the atmosphere has changed," he said. "Everyone believes we can win. It's a close team and a happy team. It's a lot different from past years."

Bring on the Huskers, ranked No. 4 nationally behind Notre Dame, Ohio State and Oklahoma. The Badgers started the week as a 17-point underdog. The spread dropped to 15 by kickoff, which was moved to 12:50 p.m. to accommodate ABC's regional telecast.

Jardine figured the TV exposure—to about 70 percent of the nation—would be a natural stimulant to the high-profile Huskers. "Plus, they're only fourth in the polls this week, so they'll probably be mad," Jardine cracked. "We won't catch them by surprise this time. Unlike last year, they might have even practiced for us this year."

Nebraska did respect Bohlig. "He could play quarterback for almost any football team in the country," volunteered Husker assistant coach Jim Ross.

Except, of course, for the Cornhuskers,

who were touting their returning starter, Humm, for the Heisman Trophy. In the season opener, Humm guided Nebraska to scores in six of their first seven possessions during a 61-7 rout of Oregon.

With 31 career touchdown passes, he was one shy of Tagge's school record. "He's a better quarterback now," Jardine said. "And he has as quick a release as I've ever seen."

The Badgers inadvertently stumbled upon the perfect way to defend Humm: knock him out of the game. Humm suffered a hip pointer in the first half and was sidelined the rest of the day. He completed just 2 of 6 passes for 20 yards before leaving.

"In a way, I kinda pulled myself out of the game," Humm told the *State Journal*. "We talked about it, and Coach Osborne said, 'If you can't go full speed, we'll keep you out.' After I got hurt, I couldn't throw. I couldn't set up. I couldn't step into my throws."

Bohlig confirmed that the loss of Humm "was just huge, and not just psychologically because it obviously impacted what they could do offensively."

Humm's backup was sophomore Earl Everett, a runner, not a thrower. "I was afraid to have him throw the ball," Osborne confided to the *State Journal*.

That turned the Cornhuskers into a one-dimensional team: run, run, run. Everett attempted just seven passes and completed three for 27 yards. Everett's inexperience in managing the offense was also a factor because of the crowd noise in Camp Randall.

"It was kinda loud," Everett said. "In the second half, we couldn't audible too much. The split ends and wide men were going on the movement of the ball instead of the count. It's an advantage to the defense when they know you're going to do that."

Still, without Humm and with Everett's predictability, the Cornhuskers took a 17-7 lead into the fourth quarter. Turnovers hurt Wisconsin in the first half. Due to a lack of practice reps, Marek was rusty and lost two fumbles. Bohlig threw two picks.

Defensively, the Badgers were having trouble slowing down Nebraska's ground game. The Huskers finished with 258 rushing yards compared to Wisconsin's 77.

That all changed in the fourth quarter as the Badgers grabbed the momentum from the Cornhuskers, thanks to a memorable goal line stand. "Our defense rose up and stopped them," Jardine said proudly, "and that was the key to the game."

Leading 17-14, Nebraska didn't get fancy. Staying in character, the Huskers started to grind out yardage, controlling the ball and the clock. Ten straight running plays left them with a first-and-goal on the UW 2-yard line. A touchdown would likely close out the Badgers.

"We just looked at each other in the huddle," said Wisconsin defensive end Mike Vesperman, a senior from Platteville, "and the feeling went through us. We just knew we could do it. We knew that we could stop them there despite the odds."

On first down, Vesperman, Ken Simmons and Rick Jakious (who

Courtesy of UW Sports Information

Feeling like he had just been run over by a Mack truck, Nebraska coach Tom Osborne tried to jog his memory. "We haven't had a long touchdown scored on us since I don't know when," he said after Jeff Mack crossed the goal line, punctuating a 77-yard pass completion from Gregg Bohlig. "Our safety went for the interception instead of playing behind the man," Osborne lamented. "And it was all over once Mack caught the ball."

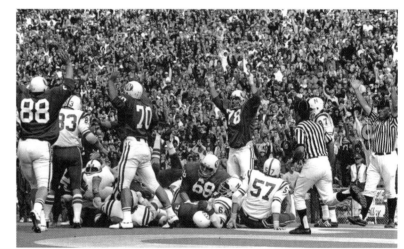

Courtesy of UW Sports Information

Tight end Jack Novak (88) and tackles Dennis Lick (70) and John Reimer (78) signal touchdown after Billy Marek scores on a 1-yard run in the fourth quarter.

Courtesy of UW Sports Information

The Wisconsin-Nebraska start time was moved to 12:50 pm to accommodate ABC's telecast.

ended up with 19 tackles) threw Nebraska I-back Jeff Moran for a three-yard loss. Two more Moran rushes came up short, and Osborne settled for the field goal, making it 20-14 with 4:21 remaining.

Plenty of time, Dennis Lick thought. "We were kind of down," said the UW right offensive tackle. "But after they kicked the field goal, I looked up at the scoreboard and I realized that we could still win this game. The defensive stand really got us going."

After Nebraska nose guard John Lee sacked Bohlig for a six-yard loss on first down, the Badgers were in desperate need of a play, and a play-maker. And they found both in No. 39, Jeff Mack, a senior flanker from Chicago Farragut.

"Jeff was a tremendous natural athlete and a very gifted receiver, and he could really run once he got the ball," Bohlig said. "Looking back, when you've got a weapon like that it would have been nice to get him involved a little more. But we were built around the run first. We had a great offensive line and great running backs and that was our bread and butter."

Bohlig had no problem with the plan or the planners: offensive coordinator Ellis Rainsberger and quarterback coach Bob Spoo. "They were both really savvy," he said.

On second down, Bohlig rolled right with his two running backs in front of him for protection. Split receiver Art Sanger was running a 10-yard out pattern to the sideline. Mack was splitting the defensive seam some five yards farther downfield.

Bohlig looked first at Sanger and then lofted a pass to Mack, who was nudged by Nebraska safety George Kyros in his anxiety to go for the interception. An official threw down his flag on contact, signaling pass interference. Never mind. Mack was already on his way to the end zone, completing a beautifully executed 77-yard pitch and catch.

Kyros stood at midfield, his hands at his side—the loneliest figure

Courtesy of UW Sports Information

Gregg Bohlig rolls left behind offensive guard Bob Braun (63) during the 1973 season, Bohlig's first season as a starter. As a junior, he finished No. 2 in the Big Ten in passing, completing 63 of 138 attempts for 953 yards. He was also No. 2 in total offense, averaging 131.5 yards.

in a delirious stadium, rocking to the cheers of 73,381 fanatics. Kyros had intercepted Bohlig earlier on a similar roll-out, but this time his gamble was costly to Nebraska. Vince Lamia kicked the extra point, ABC had a ratings winner, and, more importantly, Wisconsin had a 21-20 lead.

Although there was still 3:29 on the clock, Humm remained on the sidelines so Everett was forced to do something he couldn't do: throw the ball. Steve Wagner intercepted Everett's desperation pass and the fans stormed the field to celebrate the upset.

Years later, Mack told the *Capital Times*, "That's a highlight I'll never forget." It ranked up there, he said, with watching his son, Jeff, play linebacker for the Badgers.

"It was kind of Jeff's job to read the defense and run the route that they gave him," elaborated Bohlig. "When [Kyros] overcommitted, I saw what was happening. I had the right trajectory on the pass, and Jeff made the play. It was kind of out of the blue, really. It wasn't like we went into the huddle thinking, 'Okay, let's score a touchdown on this play.'"

Decades later, Bohlig conceded of the scoring play, "It's still pretty vivid. Once in a while, I'll pull out the TV tape of the game. I've never tried to break down what happened. I've just savored the excitement of it all. And you just kind of get chills because it was so unexpected, so out of the blue, like I said earlier."

Mack was a reliable target, a game-breaker. But Bohlig didn't play favorites. Against Nebraska, for instance, Mack had four catches. Sanger, Marek, fullback Ken Starch and tight end Jack Novak had two each. Tight end Ron Egloff had one catch, but it went for a score.

"We had a lot of guys who made plays for us," Bohlig said. "And I felt like I had a good rapport with all of them. We did a lot of extra stuff to try and develop that chemistry."

Marek, Sanger, and Bohlig didn't necessarily have the measurables that college recruiters seek out. They were too short, too small or too slow. "That happens anytime you don't fit the exact mold or have what people think are the perfect dimensions," Bohlig said. "We had a bunch of guys like that, and we all banded together and supported each other."

In 1975, the Big Ten opened up the bowl process to more teams than just the league champion. (Ohio State played in the Rose Bowl, Michigan played in the Orange Bowl.) But the ruling came too late for the '74 Badgers. "We would have been a very attractive bowl team," Bohlig said. "We scored a lot of points, and we were pretty exciting."

The Nebraska win was Exhibit A. Afterward, Jardine said of Bohlig, "Clutch-wise, he never had a better game. When the chips were down, he came through."

Jardine saw the irony in his own words because he was always looking for a reason to play someone else at quarterback, someone with more skill and speed than Bohlig.

"We had our differences at certain points because we didn't always agree whether I should be playing or not," Bohlig said. "But I also felt he was respectful. He told me what he thought, and I always felt like I was getting the straight story from him."

That was Jardine, a straight-shooter, for better or worse. UW athletic director Elroy Hirsch was largely responsible for the "Operation Turnaround" phrase. Hirsch hired Jardine and, together, they turned around the attitude, the way people looked at the program.

Alumni donations were up, attendance was up—even though Jardine never won more than four games in each of his first four seasons at Wisconsin.

After beating Nebraska, the Badgers surfaced in the national ratings for the first time in over 10 years. UPI had them No. 10 and the AP had them No. 11. Asked if this signaled a change of fortune, Jardine said, "Yes, this is the Turnaround."

Wisconsin went 7-4 in '74. That was Jardine's first and only winning season. In 1977, the Badgers won their first five games but didn't win again. Jardine personally reached a crossroads following an ugly 22-0 home loss to Purdue.

The booing was wide-spread and student sections had broken out into "Good-bye Johnny" serenades. Jardine had to restrain two of his players, Kevin Boodry and Thomas Houston, from going into the stands and taking on a wild, sick group of people. "The fans were throwing apples and pouring drinks on us," Houston said. "That's not right."

Jardine resigned the following Monday. "I just said, 'That's it,'" Jardine related of the Boodry-Houston incident. "I don't ever want to see that again."

He was not bitter. He just wanted to alleviate the pressure on his players and family. He had thought about the decision for a while, he had thought about making this his final season even before the

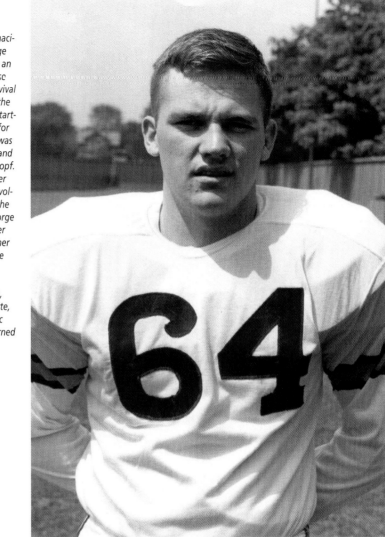

Courtesy of UW Sports Information

Much of John Jardine's tenacity stemmed from his college playing days at Purdue. As an undersized, 186 pound nose guard, Jardine learned survival instincts while captaining the 1954 freshman team and starting as a junior and senior for the Boilermakers. Jardine was recruited by Stu Holcomb and mentored by Jack Mollenkopf. In 1956, Jardine came under the influence of a Purdue volunteer assistant coach by the name of Steinbrenner, George Steinbrenner, who left after one season to help his father run the family business, the American Shipbuilding Company in Cleveland. Jardine's first coaching job, meanwhile, was in Lafayette, Indiana, at Central Catholic High School. He later returned as a Mollenkopf assistant.

season got under way, especially after eating became a challenge.

"I've never been sick in my life," he said the day after resigning, "but for the past two years, my stomach has tied up in knots so I don't digest my food.

"It's like a big lump, like someone's got a knife in there. I've had to go to the hospital six or seven times, usually at four or five o'clock in the morning. I've still got the pain right now. Maybe when it's all over, it will be gone. I hope so."

The memories have not gone away, the lasting memories of the good days under Jardine, like the day Bohlig and Mack worked their magic against Nebraska.

The big picture.

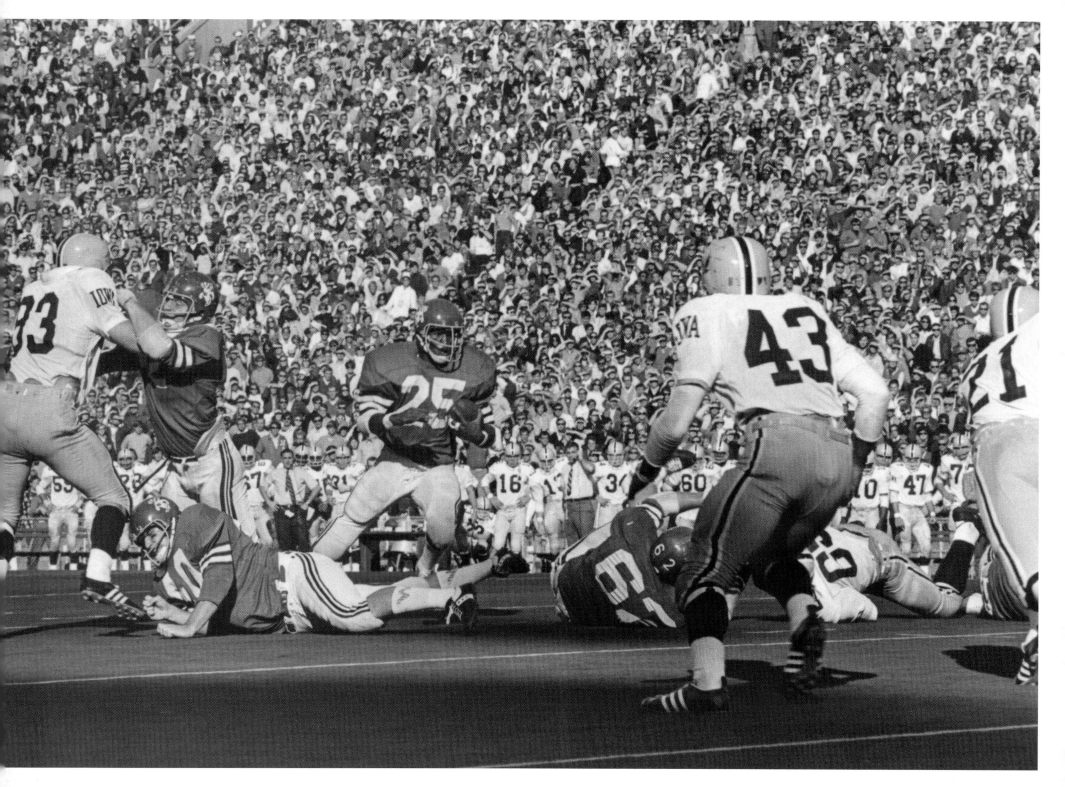

Wisconsin 23 Iowa 17
October 11, 1969

On the same week that Hubert H. Humphrey won the 1968 Democratic presidential nomination in a first ballot landslide and violence erupted on the streets of Chicago, with thousands of anti-war protesters and "hippies" clashing with police and national guardsmen, the Wisconsin football team reported for Picture Day and the opening of fall drills.

Camp Randall and the surrounding area was under construction. On the south end, a new roof was going on the Field House. On the north end, a new engineering building was going up. Inside the stadium, workmen were putting the finishing touches on a new artificial playing surface (Tartan Turf). Meanwhile, John Coatta was bracing for the second year of his rebuilding project after going 0-9-1 during his inaugural season as head coach.

This was the brave, new world that Neil Graff encountered.

The 18-year-old Graff, an All-State quarterback from Sioux Falls, South Dakota, was a member of Coatta's freshman class in '68. Growing up a Gopher fan, Graff envisioned playing in the Big Ten. But when Minnesota didn't recruit him as aggressively as Wisconsin, he packed his bags for Madison. He had already fallen in love with the natural beauty of the UW campus, and the business school had the type of quality reputation he was looking for.

Plus, there was another influential factor in his decision.

"I wanted to play as a sophomore," Graff admitted. "I never sat on the bench in any sport in my life, and I wanted to go to a place where I had a good chance of playing. As I looked at Wisconsin's personnel and record the last couple of years, I knew I would have

Courtesy of UW Sports Information

Quarterback Neil Graff gives a quick glance towards Stu Voigt #40 as he barks out the signals.

that chance. There was no guarantee, but I would have a chance anyway."

The Badgers' last winning season was 1963.

But there were other considerations—beyond the football team's lousy record—for anyone attending Wisconsin in the late '60s. In the aftermath of the Chicago disturbance, the Associated Press reported that there had been 221 student protests at 101 colleges and universities thus far in 1968. Not since the Civil War had there been such a high degree of social unrest in this nation, the AP researcher editorialized.

Wisconsin was among the national leaders in campus turmoil, jockeying for position at the top of the polls with Cal-Berkeley and Columbia University.

"I didn't have any reservations about coming here. That aspect of the Madison campus didn't enter into my decision whatsoever," said Graff, who realized that he was clearly the exception, not the rule. "In looking back, I always felt bad for Coatta and his staff. Part of the reason for the lack of success—and why Coatta's regime was never able to get over the top—was attributable to all the turmoil on campus."

By the end of 1968, there were 495,000 troops in Vietnam, and the death toll had reached 30,000. About 1,000 a month were dying. The turmoil was not going away.

At the end of spring drills in 1969, the UW sports information office turned out this bio on Graff, the co-captain of the freshman team: "A tall, cool-headed, strong-armed young man who could be the answer to the quarterback problem that dogged the Badgers over the past few years.... Rated as the number one man going into fall drills."

Wisconsin was still mired in a winless streak (0-19-1) when Graff made his starting debut in the 1969 season opener against Oklahoma. Even though the No. 6-ranked Sooners had a Heisman

Courtesy of UW Sports Information

Opposite page: Danny Crooks, a shifty junior tailback from Peoria, Illinois, finds a running crease between center Mike Musha (62) and Stu Voigt (40) and gets ready to take on Iowa defensive back Craig Clemons (43).

Sophomore quarterback Neil Graff threw for 1,086 yards and seven touchdowns during the 1969 season. His favorite target was Stu Voigt. "When the chips are down, you tend to move towards people that you know can come through when you need them the most," Graff said. "Stu was one of those guys. So when you needed a big play, or some crucial yardage, it was just natural to look in his direction."

Trophy-worthy running back in Steve Owens, their appearance at Camp Randall Stadium drew little more than a yawn and 43,000. On Bascom Hill, the campus hub, there was still more chatter about the National Guard than pulling guards.

"It was distracting, there's no doubt about it," Graff said. "You couldn't go to class without encountering the National Guard or some commotion to do with Vietnam and all of the related issues. I don't know how to put it any better than to say it WAS a distraction. To be successful at that level, the Big Ten level, in any sport, you have to be focused on what you're doing and putting your all in practicing and playing games. And during that period, particularly 1969, it was hard to do that with everything that was gong on."

There was one benefit: football players didn't have to worry about losing their privacy. "There was no adulation of athletes, the big men on campus type of thing that you see today," Graff said. "We weren't winning and the whole program just wasn't important in the eyes of the students and the Madison public. And the other reason was the stuff on campus. People had more important things going on with their lives than football."

Nobody understood the Madison climate and its politics better than Stu Voigt, the senior wingback from West High School. Certainly nobody had more athletic credentials than the talented Voigt, who excelled in football, track and baseball. And, perhaps, in retrospect, nobody gave up more by staying at home. Voigt could have gone to just about any school in the country and enjoyed team success. Instead, he stayed loyal to his Badgers.

"In the late '50s and early '60s, football was king here," Voigt reminisced. "I remember watching the Badgers when they had those white helmets with the big 'W' on them. I used to stand by the tunnel and get chin straps from the players when they came off the field. For a local kid, it was a dream come true to play for Wisconsin."

And a nightmare in waiting. "Football took on a low priority here, well down in the pecking order," Voigt said of the Coatta era and the anti-war protest years, which coincided. "If we could have won some more games maybe the fans would have come back. But in those days it was just the faithful attending Badger games.

"There were just so many things going on with the reaction to the war on campus. You tried to stay above the fray, but really you couldn't. Being from Madison, I went to high school with some of the people who were protesting. Some were friends of mine.

"It wasn't like this faction was all weirdos, way out in left field. These were people who really had some hardcore beliefs. So even if you didn't agree with what they were saying or doing, you certainly agreed that they had the right to say things. Madison was a hotbed of activism in the '60s, and it was impossible not to be influenced by what was going on."

Voigt remembered going out for track practice in the spring. "I was a shot putter," he recalled, "and I'd throw the shot and a national guardsman would throw it back to me."

Such was the landscape. Coatta remained upbeat, though. "It isn't optimism, it's confidence," he explained to visiting sportswriters making a tour of Big Ten campuses. "We will win some football games. We will have a chance to win in every game we play.

"We have sophomores who can play Big Ten football. Of our 22 starting players, 18 of them are sophomores or juniors. Good solid football timber. Basically, we're a young team. We have more speed. And we show promise at quarterback with Neil Graff."

Graff, for one, didn't feel the burden of the winless streak or any kind of expectations. "Maybe if I was a senior it would have been different," he said. "But I didn't feel any pressure because I hadn't been a part of [that streak]. I was out trying to create a new legacy, so to speak, for Wisconsin football, trying to start something new."

Starting out with non-conference games against Oklahoma, UCLA, and Syracuse was not a prescription for success, not for a doormat program. Predictably, the Badgers were overmatched and lost all three home games by scores of 48-21, 34-23 and 43-7.

"We didn't have any illusions that we were going to beat those guys," Graff said. "But we wanted to play them tough, and we played respectable enough in those first three games that it kind of set a positive tone for the start of the Big Ten season."

Left: Randy Marks hauls in a 17-yard Neil Graff touchdown pass on fourth down giving the Badgers a 21-17 lead with 2:08 left in the game. On the ensuing kickoff, Iowa's Dennis Green (the same Dennis Green who would later go on to coach the Minnesota Vikings) misplayed the ball, downing the football in the end zone for an automatic safety pushing the Wisconsin lead to 23-17.

Wisconsin drew Iowa for the conference opener at Camp Randall. The year before, the Hawkeyes mauled the Badgers, 41-0 in Iowa City, getting two touchdowns each from quarterbacks Larry Lawrence and Ed Podolak. A few UW players had shaved their heads the day of the game with the hope of reversing their luck. But if there was a change in the karma, it didn't show up in their blocking or tackling. Neither did they—show up.

"I think you go into every game where you think you have a chance to win, the hope springs eternal thing," Voigt said, assessing the damage of the winless streak. "We'd work hard as a team, and we had been knocking at the door a bunch of different times."

In '68, Voigt could have cited the ultimate frustration from a 21-20 loss to Indiana during which the Badgers missed six field goals, two in the last 85 seconds. That Sunday morning, the *State Journal* ran a most telling picture of Coatta on the front page of its sports section. He's shown kneeling on the turf, his head buried in his hands. And the caption reads, "Coatta sags under mounting pressure of Badger misfortunes."

And the beat goes on: 1,057 days since the last win. Coming to Madison, the Hawkeyes were a 10-point favorite to extend the losing streak to 19 and winless streak to 24. Lawrence was the catalyst as the Hawks were scoring in bunches: 61 on Washington State and 31 on Arizona. They ranked No. 1 nationally in total offense, averaging 538 yards per game.

Still, the Badgers felt good about the match-up. The only highlight

during the drought had been a 21-21 tie with Iowa. Moreover, Wisconsin had won five straight games in the series before that 1967 draw. And the Hawks hadn't won at Camp Randall since 1958.

"Iowa was not a powerhouse," Voigt remembered. "And we had some good players who from that point on would prove they were good players."

But the bad still outweighed the good. With 4:11 remaining in the third quarter, Iowa seemingly took a commanding 17-0 lead over the mistake-prone Badgers. One long, promising drive ended when Graff was intercepted in the end zone.

"I don't remember any specific play that turned it around, but I do remember the attitude," Graff said, adding that the younger players, the sophs, weren't about to throw in the towel. "We hadn't bought into the losing. And those first three games hardened us. It showed us what we had to do to be successful, the level of play we had to bring to the table.

"We were confident at some point in time that we were going to win. I recall we got a couple of breaks from the officials. Maybe it was a little of luck, but you could just feel things turning in our favor. Maybe we could finally see some light at the end of the tunnel."

On Wisconsin's first scoring drive, Graff attacked through the air with passes to Voigt and split end Mel Reddick. On the ground, A-Train Thompson, Joe Dawkins, and Danny Crooks ran hard behind the blocking of tackle Mike McClish and guard Brad Monroe. Thompson scored on a short run, making it 17-7 with 12:26 left in

The post-game celebration was historic. Tom Turman (50), a sophomore from Two Rivers, gets a ride from long-suffering fans who had waited a long time to party.

the fourth quarter.

Iowa lost a fumble on the next series, and the Badgers were now picking up momentum and punching holes in the defense with Thompson, Dawkins, and Crooks. Suddenly, the Hawks were vulnerable. Wisconsin scored again, making it 17-14 with 4:50 remaining, and 53,714 diehards starting to make a lot of noise in Camp Randall.

On the subsequent kickoff, Lee Wilder made a huge play on special

teams, dropping Dennis Green on the Iowa 13-yard line. (This is the same Dennis Green who became a part of the celebrated rivalry between the Vikings and Packers when he coached in Minnesota.)

An inspired Wisconsin defense, led by tackles Bill Gregory and Jim DeLisle, end Gary Buss, linebacker Chuck Winfrey, defensive backs Neovia Greyer and Dick Hyland, forced another Iowa punt, and the Badgers took over on the Hawkeyes' 36.

For what it's worth: Badgermania.

(with apologies to Buffalo Springfield and Stephen Stills):

There's something happening here
What it is ain't exactly clear

The next drive stalled, though, as the Hawkeyes stiffened defensively, and the Badgers were left with a fourth-and-11 from the 17. A field goal would tie it. But the harsh memory of the '69 Indiana game was still haunting Coatta, who wasn't about to turn back now.

"When it was fourth down," Coatta told the *State Journal*, "I thought it was another one of those dying efforts that wasn't going to connect." But he went for it.

"During the timeout, we talked it over," Coatta said. "We told Graff to have Reddick go at least 11 yards, if he threw to him, but to look for Randy Marks first. We got the message from the spotter [in the press box] that Marks was wide open on the play earlier in the game."

Graff still remembers the particulars.

"It was a bootleg to the right," he said. "I faked a handoff to Thompson, and I rolled out. Randy was on the left side of the field, and he was cutting across the back of the end zone, from left to right. I remember faking, getting outside of the rush and looking for Randy."

And that's when everything really slowed down.

"It was almost like he was running in slow motion when I threw the ball out in front of him," Graff said. "In reality, I think that's how things played out for me. To the fans in the stands, it was normal speed. But to me it was slow motion."

Marks, a converted tailback, made the catch just before stepping out. The Hawkeyes blew a coverage and the lead and were now trailing, 21-17, with 2:08 left in the game.

Green misplayed the ensuing kickoff and downed the football in the end zone for an automatic safety. That made it 23-17. The Badgers had a chance to ice the win but missed a 29-yard field goal, giving Iowa one last chance. The Hawks drove to the UW 46, but Greyer ended the scoring threat, and the ignominious winless streak, with an interception.

All of a sudden, 53,000-plus were on the field. Or so it seemed. Such was the bedlam, the relatively controlled chaos, if you will. Voigt was among those players who got a ride on the shoulders of long-suffering fans, one of whom was a fellow West High alum.

"Because the crowds were down, you were sharing this victory with friends," Voigt said. "The monkey was finally off our back. The players were not the only ones breathing a sigh of relief, a lot of fans were, too. I know my folks said, 'It's about time.'"

While witnessing the fans spill out of the stands and on to the playing surface, *Capital Times* columnist Miles McMillin had a most unique take on the experience.

"It was like the day the dam broke," he wrote. "The only thing you could compare it to was the rush of a body of water once it breaks its confinement...the players themselves were mainly responsible for restoring order. What a pity, I thought, that we can't find some heroes for our demonstrators so that the rip-tides of their efforts can be commanded.

"And we are left to ponder the problem of whether it is more meritorious to take over State Street in the name of football or in the name of peace."

Such was the battle ground.

Coatta was left to ponder other thoughts. He fielded this question to open his post-game press conference, "Do you know HOW to open a press conference after a victory?"

Coatta sighed and said, "That was a lovely sight, watching those seconds tick off and knowing you had the victory....I savored those moments watching the clock run out. The electricity through the whole crowd was fantastic. Those were really happy folks."

They stayed happy, if not sober. Shouting "We're Number One, We're Number One" and "Rose Bowl, Rose Bowl," they exited Camp Randall for a long-overdue victory march.

"We have a parade permit that was issued for the first game we won," said Wisconsin band director Michael Leckrone. "But I didn't think we'd be using it [after the Iowa game]. It's madness, just madness. Isn't it delightful?"

The campus was overrun by revelers, most of who headed downtown. The *State Journal* reported, "Fans passed bottles of liquor through the crowd and picked up pitchers of beer as they passed the Langdon Street fraternity houses...open convertibles, some loaded with as many as 20 students, drove down the center of the street; honking, screaming, drinking."

Some compared the party scene to New Year's Eve. "I can still remember Elroy [Hirsch] dancing on the top of a car on State Street," Voigt said, teasing, "Of course, Elroy would have been doing that even if we didn't get a win."

There was some property damage. Parking meters were carried from State Street to other parts of the city. At least three storefront windows were broken. Several police cars were stoned (not to mention the number of students who also fit that description).

The *Capital Times* reported that one youth was arrested because he "decked" three persons who told him they didn't "really care that Wisconsin had won."

The State Street crowd didn't begin to disperse until 3 a.m. Sunday. Police reports said most of the youths merely stood in the middle of the street hollering, "We're Number One."

Graff recalled the craziness of the victory celebration and said, "Socially, it kind of helped perk everybody up and gave people some-

thing else to focus on."

A few days later, there was another demonstration, and people took to the streets again. But it was for a far different cause—and for far different reasons.

"A massive, flickering sea of candles moving through Wednesday night's rainy darkness symbolized Madison's remembrance of its war dead and plea for peace," Rosemary Kendrick wrote in the *Capital Times*. "An estimated 15,000 persons attended a Vietnam Moratorium rally at the University of Wisconsin Field House and then marched to the State Capitol, chanting slogans such as "Peace Now.""

Wisconsin's one-game winning streak came to a crashing halt the following Saturday in a 27-7 loss at Northwestern. Mike Adamle rushed 40 times for a record 316 yards. The banner headline in the *State Journal* summed it up: "Badgers Back to Normal."

Wisconsin did win twice more during the 1969 season, but it wasn't enough to save Coatta's hide. He was fired and replaced by John Jardine.

I think it's time we stop, hey, what's that sound

Everybody look what's going down

On August 24, 1970, a van loaded with explosives blew up outside Sterling Hall, killing Robert Fassnacht, 33. The east wing of the building housed the Army Math Research Center. The blast could be heard from 20 miles away and damaged 26 buildings. Three days later, the Wisconsin football team reported for Picture Day and the opening of fall drills.

Courtesy of UW Sports Information

Top: Stu Voigt was one of the UW's last three-sport letterwinners (football, track and baseball). What was his best sport? Major league baseball scouts loved his power - he was a .350 career hitter for the Badgers - but Voigt opted for the NFL and went on to start in three Super Bowls for the Minnesota Vikings.

Bottom: John Coatta was one of four W-winners to come back and coach at his alma mater. The others were Art Curtis, Bill Juneau and John Richards.

Courtesy of UW Sports Information

123

Wisconsin 21 Michigan 14
September 12, 1981

Getting beat is one thing. Getting beat up is another. The scars belonging to Dave Levenick and his teammates were from a 1977 beating in Ann Arbor.

Final score: Michigan 56, Wisconsin 0.

The Wolverines, who were the No. 1 ranked team in college football, ran 88 plays from scrimmage and had 25 first downs and 546 yards of total offense.

The Badgers, who had been unbeaten, ran 56 plays and had eight first downs and 126 total yards. They didn't cross midfield until the closing minutes of the fourth quarter.

"We went into the game against Michigan hoping that we could win," said Levenick, a true freshman from Grafton, who appeared in seven games as a backup linebacker and went on to earn five letters. "If we got lucky, we thought we might be able to beat them."

Levenick had three tackles against the Wolverines and a keepsake—a gray sweatshirt with "Beat Michigan" in large blue letters across the front. Each of the UW players were issued one the week of the game for added inspiration when they went out to play with the big boys.

"We had high hopes of going to a bowl game that year," said Levenick, who was beat down by the end of the season, along with his teammates and the coaching staff.

The Badgers lost their final six games.

Coach John Jardine resigned under pressure.

"You reach a point where everything starts to bother you and get under your skin," said Jardine, who was not necessarily referring to the Wolverines.

Courtesy of The Capital Times

Opposite page: A swarming Badger defense - led by linebackers Larry Spurlin (49) and Dave Levenick (47) and safety Matt Vanden Boom (39) - reacts to the ball in the air and surrounds Wolverines wide receiver Vince Bean.

Courtesy of The Capital Times

UW tailback Chucky Davis catches a short pass and turns upfield with Michigan cornerback Brian Carpenter bearing down on him.

But could have been.

Getting beat is one thing. Getting beat up is another. The scars belonging to Guy Boliaux and his teammates were from a 1978 beating in Madison.

Final score: Michigan 42, Wisconsin 0.

The Wolverines led 14-0 in the first 11 minutes and "settled' for a 21-0 halftime lead behind the steady game management, running, and throwing of quarterback Rick Leach.

The Badgers couldn't get anything going offensively—they crossed midfield twice in 12 possessions—much to the displeasure of a record crowd of 80,024 at Camp Randall.

"When we were getting ready to play Michigan the feeling was, 'Let's try to make it close...maybe,'"said Boliaux, a true freshman from Des Plaines, Illinois, who started three games at linebacker. "I was in awe of Michigan. Here I was fresh out of high school, tackling [Leach] who was on the cover of *Sports Illustrated*. I thought they were all gods.

"I remember tackling Leach once and I was amazed to be so close to that maize and blue helmet. They could just throw their hats on the field and beat a lot of people, like us."

Boliaux had a couple of tackles against the Wolverines and a keepsake: an injury. Boliaux didn't play again during the 1978 season.

"When I lined up across from those guys," he said, "I thought they were above me-the high and mighty. We didn't have confidence in ourselves."

Getting beat is one thing. Getting beat up is another. The scars belonging to Tim Krumrie and his teammates were from a 1979 beating in Ann Arbor.

Final score: Michigan 54, Wisconsin 0.

Tailback Chucky Davis scores on a 1-yard touchdown run just before the end of the first half. Following a block by guard Carleton Walker (74), Davis drags Michigan linebacker Mike Boren (40) into the end zone, while Dave Mohapp (28) gets ready to celebrate.

The Wolverines scored 37 points in the second half, and tailback Butch Woolfolk rushed for 198 yards, including a school-record 92-yard dash from scrimmage.

The Badgers fumbled six times, losing three. They were also guilty of an interception while completing just eight passes. They gave up a safety, too.

"I don't remember the score, but I remember getting whupped pretty good," said Krumrie, a true freshman from Mondovi, who started every game as an undersized, 220-pound nose guard and finished second on the team in tackles. "It was a constant challenge to get your level of play up to Michigan's level of play. It was a struggle, a matter of will power.

"I was kind of a strong-headed guy anyway, and I just wanted to prove to everybody that I deserved to be in there. At times I was out-manned and overpowered. I just needed some time to grow up. That was the frustrating part. Knowing that I was good enough to play the position—or they wouldn't have put me in there—but also knowing I wasn't quite ready."

That same year, Ohio State gave the Badgers a 59-0 beating in Columbus.

"You just wanted to go and hide," Krumrie said. "But any time you're frustrated as a team, or as a player, it motivates you. When I first started playing as a freshman, there were a lot more negatives than positives. The positive was I was playing. The negative was losing."

Getting beat is one thing. Getting beat up is another. The scars belonging to Bob Winckler were the same as Krumrie's—from that inglorious 1979 beating in Ann Arbor.

"We thought we could compete at Michigan, but all of a sudden we got out there and we got killed," said Winckler, a true freshman from West Bend, who started four games at offensive guard. "It was disheartening. A lot of us were playing as freshmen. Maybe because we were freshmen it didn't affect us as much as it probably should have. We had three more years.

"Coming out of high school, there were a lot of us who weren't physically ready to play or nowhere near strong enough. But we had to play because there wasn't anyone better than us. It's embarrassing the way we lost to Michigan—54-0 is a shellacking."

Krumrie and Winckler were friends. They had the same likes and dislikes. They really disliked losing and the lack of respect that the Badgers were shown by Michigan.

"You could see that they didn't take us seriously," Winckler said of the Wolverines. "They had no respect at all for Wisconsin at that point. Looking back, we were the opponent for Michigan where everybody got a chance to play and earn their letters."

A function of Bo Schembechler emptying his bench.

"I don't know if they rubbed it in," Krumrie said. "But you kind of sensed when you were playing them that they just thought it was another easy win. We didn't have the credibility or the respect that we needed. You have to earn that every Saturday."

Levenick, Boliaux, Krumrie and Winckler suffered from similar growing pains as freshmen. In 1980, the losing didn't stop, but the beatings did. Physically, the Badgers stood toe to toe with the Wolverines in Madison. Final score: Michigan 24, Wisconsin 0.

That was the first step, albeit a small one, to personal redemption. Defensively, the Badgers held Michigan without a first down for the first 22 minutes of the game.

"We knew for the first time that we could compete and play with Michigan," Krumrie said. "We knew then the wins would come. First, you have to be able to compete and be respectable, and we weren't earlier in my career. But now they knew they were in a game."

Reiterated Winckler, "That's when we realized as a team, 'Wait a second, we can play with these guys.' It ended up 24-0, but it was a lot closer before they broke it open."

A fumbled punt set up Michigan's first score: an Ali Haji-Shjeikh 23-yard field goal with 2:33 left in the second quarter. Moments later, the Badgers went three-and-out and the subsequent 16-yard punt left the Wolverines with great field position at the UW 42.

With 13 seconds remaining in the first half, Michigan flanker Anthony Carter scored on a four-yard touchdown pass from quarterback John Wangler. It was Carter's only reception of the game, but it gave the Wolverines a 10-0 lead.

There was no more scoring until late in the third quarter. The Wolverines drove to the UW 4-yard-line where they faced a fourth-and-1. Wangler stepped up under his center to call signals, but he backed off and complained to referee Glen Fortin that his teammates couldn't hear because of the deafening noise from the students in the north end zone.

Seven times, Wangler stepped to the line. Seven times, the students roared. Seven times, Wangler threw his hands in the air and walked away from center. The Badgers were warned twice and then stripped of all their timeouts, one by one.

That was followed by two delay of game penalties, the first of which gave the Wolverines a first-and-goal. Wangler eventually took the snap—some 10 minutes after his initial refusal to call signals because of the noise—and Woolfolk scored, making it 17-0.

"I don't remember it ever being louder," said Wisconsin senior linebacker Dave Ahrens, an Oregon native. "I was standing right next to Wangler, and I couldn't hear a thing. I was kind of upset, but I wasn't mad [at the fans]. They pay money for those seats."

Orchestrating the Wangler scenario from the Michigan sideline was Schembechler and assistant coach Gary Moeller. Under the strict orders of a scowling Schembechler, who loved the gamesmanship, Wangler was instructed not to take a snap unless it quieted down.

(Earlier in the '80 season, the UW students created a similar disturbance at that end of the field—reacting wildly to the appearance of the Portage Plumber—but the referee handled it much differently, ordering BYU quarterback Jim McMahon to ignore the noise and go about his business. He did and the Badgers lost, 28-3. McMahon was 22 of 34 for 337 yards.)

Schembechler came out of the 1980 game complaining about the lack of sophistication of Wisconsin's fans. He strongly implied that they just weren't like Michigan fans. "I never heard a crowd that didn't realize what they were doing to their team," Schembechler said. "I can't believe they don't understand the game and the rules."

The Badgers took much more out of the game: confidence.

"If you want to be known as a good football team, you have to beat the guys who are ranked at the top," said Krumrie, who beat the maize and blue stuffing out of Michigan's All-American center George Lilja, a rag doll. Krumrie had 17 tackles, 12 solos. "We all knew we were playing Michigan in the [1981] opener and that motivated us the whole off-season."

The intensity was turned up even more after the Wolverines were ranked No. 1. And the Badgers practiced like a group of players who had learned the hard way from all of those beatings. They had not forgotten that they had been outscored 176-0 over the last four games against Michigan. And they weren't in a very forgiving mood, either.

"When you get knocked around—not just beaten on the scoreboard but beaten physically—that becomes something in the back of your mind and your heart that you want to change," said Wisconsin free safety Matt Vanden Boom. "In that '80 game, we knew something had changed. And that gave seed to our ambition for '81."

The draw and dish. Running the option to perfection, quarterback Jess Cole draws the Michigan defense — linebackers Rob Thompson (99) and Mike Boren (40) — before pitching the ball to the tailback.

On game week, Nick Savage, a senior backup, donned a No. 1 jersey and impersonated Anthony Carter for the No. 1 defense in practice. Carter, er, Savage took a beating.

"When I look at our people's faces now, and when you say 'Michigan,' they don't shy away," Boliaux said. "In last year's game, I stuck their running back and he went right down to the ground like anyone else would. If they can throw their hats on the field, so can we.

"We'll still be the underdogs. But we've got a chance to knock them off. In the past, we were the underdogs, and we were just trying to survive against them."

In Ann Arbor, the Wolverines prepared with their normal urgency, according to Schembechler, who made a point of saying Michigan wasn't overlooking Wisconsin.

"Without a doubt, they were the toughest team for us to move the football against last fall," he told the Associated Press. "Defense is the name of the game. I honestly believe Wisconsin is the most improved team in the league, no matter what happens against us."

Michigan fullback Stanley Edwards obviously didn't get that memo: Be humble and complimentary about your opponent. Not his style. (Like father, like son. Braylon Edwards exuded the same type of confidence and brashness. And also backed it up with results.)

Edwards personified Michigan's smugness about being Michigan.

"It's a business and we're somewhat professional entertainers," Edwards told the *Capital Times*. "People expect a certain performance out of us. We're accustomed to winning and I think we beat some teams on name and character alone. When we take the field and they see those maize and blue helmets, it strikes fear in some people's hearts."

In the early '60s, Wisconsin head coach Dave McClain had been an assistant on Schembechler's staff at Miami (Ohio) University. He was tired of the beatings, too.

On Thursday, McClain had the UW marching band show up for

Tim Krumrie (50) wraps up Michigan quarterback Steve Smith after overpowering offensive tackle Ed Muransky (72).

practice. He also sent a message to his players with a message on the scoreboard: Wisconsin 17, Michigan 14.

"I remember Coach McClain putting a lot of pressure on us to believe that we could win against the elite teams in the Big Ten," said Marvin Neal, a junior flanker from Peoria, Illinois. "I remember him saying, 'You're Big Ten players, but you haven't played well against Michigan yet.' He challenged us to win these big games. He asked, 'If not now, when?'"

On game day, McClain tacked another message to the bulletin board in the locker room. Mike Jolly, a safety on the 1977 Michigan team, had some inflammatory things to say about sensing fear in an opponent like Wisconsin, heretofore a punching bag.

Jolly was quoted as saying some players used to stand on the sidelines and bet on how many points the Wolverines would score against the Badgers. "Those comments made us really mad, that was an insult," said UW offensive guard Leo Joyce.

Saturday's pre-game warm-up featured more insulting behavior from Michigan. While the Badgers were loosening up in front of the North goal post, the Wolverines came out of the tunnel and jogged around the Wisconsin players, like they were circling their prey, before going down to the south end zone for calisthenics.

"They were trying to intimidate us," Levenick said. "It was tacky."

"They were shouting, 'We're No. 1,'" said Joyce. "It was poor sportsmanship."

"It annoyed me a lot," Krumrie said. "They were real cocky."

Why would anyone want to annoy Krumrie? "You can block him," McClain said, "but you better hang on until the whistle blows because he's never going to quit. He's not particularly fast, but he always seems to get there in an ugly mood."

Krumrie, a preseason All-American, had started 22 straight games. He was the hood ornament on a Wisconsin defense that also featured tackles Darryl Sims and Mark Shumate; linebackers Boliaux, Levenick, Larry Spurlin and Kyle Borland; safeties Vanden Boom and David Greenwood; and cornerbacks Von Mansfield and Clint Sims.

"We're forever holding Krumrie up as an example, and we have some people in our defense trying to emulate him," UW defensive coordinator Jim Hilles told the *State Journal.* "I see nothing wrong with that because he's everything I always respected in a player."

In 1979, the Badgers ranked 109th nationally in rushing defense. In 1980, they were No. 11. Such was the dramatic improvement once the young players, like Krumrie, grew up.

"The whole defense was just a bunch of tough guys," said Winckler, remembering how Krumrie had an odd-shaped head that made finding a properly-fitting helmet difficult. On contact, the helmet would slide down and open a cut on the bridge of his nose. "Tim didn't really start playing until his nose was bleeding and he was all bloody."

Few nose guards have ever played with the same resolve or range. "He made tackles from sideline to sideline," Winckler agreed. "You'd see his numbers from linebackers."

Pity the Michigan offensive center, Tom Dixon, a converted guard, replacing Lilja. On the first play of the game, Michigan gave the ball to Woolfolk. No gain.

"We put him flat on his back and that established the tempo," Levenick said.

"They figured that they would run right at me to see what I could do," Krumrie said.

That was one of many mistakes the Wolverines would make.

"I got ready for every game, as a collegian or a pro, the same way," said Krumrie, who had a productive career with the Cincinnati Bengals before moving into the NFL coaching ranks as a defensive line assistant with the Bengals and the Buffalo Bills.

"I was nervous because there was just a lot of anticipation for [the Michigan] game. In your mind, you're asking yourself, 'Are you prepared? Are you ready? Are you strong enough? Do you know what the hell you're doing?' I think I played pretty well."

Krumrie broke out in loud laughter. "I don't really remember who I played against," he said. "I can't remember the stats. But I think I had a pretty darn good football game."

Krumrie did, abusing Dixon and chalking up a team-high 13 tackles.

His teammates played pretty darn well, too.

Statistically, it was a mismatch. The Badgers had a big edge in most categories: plays (78-53), first downs (23-8), and total yards (439-229). In addition, 89 of Michigan's yards came on one play, a Woolfolk touchdown gallop.

"We caught them maybe on a sideways day and beat them in every phase," Vanden Boom said. "Every now and then, I'll pull out the tape of the game. It's interesting because you see something different each time you look at it. Reflecting back, we brought our 'A' game at every level, and the score was closer than it really should have been."

After a scoreless first quarter, Michigan got on the board first, taking advantage of David Keeling's fumbled punt. McClain later second-guessed himself for using a freshman in this capacity, especially since Keeling was fragile after the recent death of his father.

Michigan quarterback Steve Smith, making his first start, capped the scoring drive with a four-yard touchdown run. Smith was far more comfortable running than throwing. Later in the quarter, Neal caught a 17-yard touchdown pass from Jess Cole to tie the game, marking the first points Wisconsin had scored against the Wolverines since 1976.

Just before the end of the half, Cole flawlessly managed the clock and guided the Badgers to the go-ahead score: a Chucky Davis touchdown with two seconds left.

"Jess wasn't the most gifted quarterback in any aspect," Winckler said. "But he brought a toughness to the huddle. He wasn't going to let anything bother him."

Cole, a Mondovi sophomore, had made his first career start against Michigan. "He was a different breed of cat," said Krumrie, a close friend and prep teammate. "He had a lot of confidence in himself. Not cocky confidence. But somehow he was going to make a play."

Woolfolk's long touchdown run in the third quarter knotted the score again. But the Badgers countered on their next offensive possession. The key play was a screen play that McClain had added to the playbook specifically for the Wolverine defense.

"When you run screens in practice, they're never successful," said Winckler, the split tackle. Joyce was the split guard, Ron Versnik the center, Carlton Walker the tight guard, and Jerry Doerger the tight tackle. Jeff Nault and Craig Fredrick were the tight ends.

"Screens just don't work against your own teammates because they know what's coming so everybody cheats. We knew what to do even if it didn't work to perfection in practice. In a game, it's different because you've got people running up field and rushing."

McClain added another twist: running the screen out of the shot-

Badger fans celebrate their first victory over Michigan since 1962.

gun formation. The Wolverines didn't know what hit them. Winckler, Versnik, Walker, and Neal got blocks down field, springing tailback John Williams who went 71 yards for the score.

"I was just hoping to get a first down," Williams admitted. "But after I got past that first wave of people, I was thinking about only one thing: the touchdown."

That made it 21-14. The Wolverines still had all of the fourth quarter to work with. But they couldn't get anything going offensively. Smith kept finding the open man with his passes—not Carter, who managed just one reception all day—but the ball-hawking Vanden Boom, who had three interceptions in Michigan's final six possessions.

"Smith looked nervous," Levenick said.

You think? He was 3-of-18 for 39 yards.

"I'm not being a smart aleck," Schembechler told the *State Journal*, "but it's obvious we're not as good as people thought we were, and it's obvious Wisconsin is a lot better than people thought. I told you before and I'll tell you again, Wisconsin is a good football team."

The Badgers had great balance on offense: 182 passing yards, 257 rushing yards. (Fullback Dave Mohapp had 19 rushes for 87 yards; Davis had 15 carries for 69.)

"Our problem was simple," said Schembechler, growing a bit crankier with each post-game question. "Our offense wasn't any good, our defense wasn't any good, our kicking game wasn't any good, and our coaching was poor. When you have those four things going against you, and you only get beat by seven points, it's a miracle."

Only 68,733 paid to see this "miracle." But seeing was believing. And after all those beatings, the Badgers finally proved that they could beat the big boys.

Sunday afternoon, Levenick reported for team meetings at the stadium with a much different perspective on life—life in the Big Ten. "We're no longer peons at Wisconsin," he said, puffing out his chest under a ratty "Beat Michigan" sweatshirt.

On passing downs, the split receiver would read the defense before the snap and use hand signals to communicate with the quarterback, relaying the route that he was going to run against the coverage. Right hand across the chest might be a post pattern. Tapping the top of the helmet might be a curl. Touching the shoulder pad might be a hitch or corner route.

The split receiver was Pat Richter.

The quarterback was Ron VanderKelen.

"As a receiver, you loved it," Richter said of the freedom to read and react. "Basically, Vandy would call the formation in the huddle, 'Split Right' or whatever. Everybody knew when he checked off at the line that calling a number meant a pass."

"That allowed me to maybe go straight up the field if the defensive back was up tight. Or if he was playing off, maybe you'd go towards the post. It was up to Vandy to read it, and if they changed the defense, he could go to a different receiver."

UW coach Milt Bruhn was friends with Green Bay Packers coach Vince Lombardi, and they would annually exchange ideas on offensive trends, like the implementation of the power game with the pulling guards, pre-snap reads or check-off systems.

"As a result, we had about the most contemporary offense that you could have at the time," Richter said. "Milt felt if you were going to the primary receiver, you needed to identify the defense and come with up some variations. Just let Ron know."

Wisconsin offensive guard Steve Underwood always felt like he was left in the dark. "They'd change the play and we'd never know," he said of VanderKelen and Richter. "They were doing it all the time with their own signals. That's the way they played their game."

Courtesy of UW Sports Information

Quarterback Ron VanderKelen

Courtesy of UW Sports Information

Opposite page: Quarterback Ron VanderKelen rolls to his left and delivers a pass against Northwestern.

Richter noted that he tried to "make the signals as innocuous as possible" because he didn't want to draw attention to himself, and he didn't want to tip off the defense.

To his knowledge, nobody ever caught on to the hand signals. "Back in those days, you had film," Richter said, "but you didn't break it down like they do today."

When all else failed—fist, paper, scissors—VanderKelen had a distress call.

"Now and then, when I got myself in trouble, I'd yell, 'Help' and Pat would always find a way to get open," he said. "We made all kinds of adjustments. We just had a feeling for each other. It was just one of those situations where you'd know what somebody was going to run [for a pattern]. Pat was great at coming back and saying, 'I can do this or that.'

"And he was a guy I listened to. There were a lot of other people who would tell you they could do something, and you just said, 'Okay, I'll keep it in the back of my mind.' Not with Pat. And all I had to do was get the ball near him, and he'd catch it."

That was not a revelation—Richter catching the football. But who knew that VanderKelen would be the pitcher? Now that was a story with an ending nobody saw coming. And that's why it was so easy for VanderKelen to stay grounded during the 1962 season.

Prior to his senior year, he had 90 seconds of playing experience—that was all—and it came as a defensive back in the 1959 Marquette game, a 44-6 rout.

"I really hadn't even played here," said VanderKelen, who lettered in four sports at Green Bay Preble High School. "I mean, I was on the team as a sophomore, but I never really had a chance. I went to the Rose Bowl as a non-participant, so to speak. I sat on the bench."

VanderKelen injured his knee the following spring, had surgery that summer, and sat out the 1960 season. He had eligibility issues in 1961, dropping out of school to work in construction. But he stayed in touch with the program and was committed to returning. When he did return,

Left: Pat Richter was able to use his imposing size and reach to get leverage on smaller defensive backs, winning most of the jump balls. That was fitting since Richter saw himself as a basketball player, not a football player, coming out of Madison East High School. "I wasn't going to play football and I was thinking of going away from home for the first time and then I changed my mind," he said. Richter finished his career with 121 catches for 1,873 yards (15.5) and 15 touchdowns.

Right: Head Coach Milt Bruhn gets carried off of the field following a 37-6 victory over #1-ranked Northwestern.

he received another year of eligibility because of the injury.

Bruhn was hoping that extra year would go to another quarterback, Ron Miller, whose petition for additional eligibility was rejected. During his two seasons as Wisconsin's starter, Miller broke numerous school records while throwing for 2,838 yards and 19 touchdowns.

In his final game, Miller guided the underdog Badgers to a 23-21 upset win at Minnesota, handing the Gophers their only loss of the 1961 Big Ten season. Miller completed 19 of 37 passes for 297 yards. Playing on a bad knee, Richter caught two touchdown passes against the Gophs and set a conference record for receiving yards (36 catches for 656 yards).

"Pat's one of the greatest ends I've ever seen," Bruhn told the *State Journal.* "And that includes Mike Ditka of Pittsburgh and El Kimbrough of Northwestern."

Bruhn felt the Minnesota victory would be a springboard into the '62 season. All he needed to do was find a starting quarterback to replace Miller. And there was no shortage of candidates for that position when the team opened training camp.

That was illustrated by a staged photo in the *State Journal.*

UW offensive center Ken Bowman was poised over the ball, ready to make the snap. John Fabry was the first in line, hands under center. Seven other quarterback prospects fanned out behind Fabry in single file—forming a question mark.

In order, then, it was Fabry, Harold Brandt, Jim Hennig, Arnie Quaerna, Bob Allison, Greg Howey, Lew Fawbush, and VanderKelen—last in line.

Bruhn liked VanderKelen's mobility. But he was less enamored with his independent thinking. Bruhn wanted to toughen him up, to make sure he could handle the mental demands, so he made life miserable for

VanderKelen throughout the camp.

"He never backed off me," VanderKelen told the *Capital Times.* "He was very rough on me. Maybe that was the way he thought he had to develop me."

VanderKelen slowly put distance between himself and Brandt, Fabry, and Howey. One of his most memorable early starts came against Notre Dame at Camp Randall. VanderKelen completed his first eight passes in leading Wisconsin to a 17-8 victory. The Badgers had gone win-less in seven previous meetings with the Irish, dating to 1928.

"Even though they didn't have a great team that year, they were still Notre Dame," said VanderKelen. "For a kid from Green Bay, this was a big thrill."

Although VanderKelen was also picked off three times, Bruhn told the *State Journal*, "Vandy's the boy I'm going with from now on. He and Richter are going to be my offense."

The following Saturday, Wisconsin played host to Iowa at Camp Randall, and, for the first time, VanderKelen was starting to feel comfortable as the No. 1 quarterback.

"I had confidence, but everybody has confidence and you have to be able to perform," VanderKelen said. "For me, the turning point in the season came against Iowa. I had one of those breakout performances, where everything I did just happened to be the right thing.

"Even though you may have confidence in yourself, all of a sudden you really start believing in yourself. It's like, 'Hey, I'm not that bad. I can do this.'"

VanderKelen passed for 202 yards and three scores in Wisconsin's 42-14 win over the Hawkeyes. "It was really against Iowa that I felt confident," he said, "and it kept building each game. Things kept improving, and then you started feeling good about how you were calling plays because we called our own plays in those days and made the adjustments."

It really didn't matter what VanderKelen called the following Saturday in Wisconsin's first road game of the season. Not much worked in a 14-7 loss at Ohio State. The Badgers' only score came on a 47-yard pass from VanderKelen to Ron Smith late in the second quarter.

VanderKelen hit on just 7 of 22 throws. The Ohio State secondary, led by the all-around skills of Paul Warfield, put a blanket over the UW receivers, especially Richter who had caught TD passes in eight straight games before seeing the streak end in Columbus.

One week later, the Badgers were back in rhythm offensively and over-powered Michigan, 34-12, in Ann Arbor. VanderKelen and Richter hooked up repeatedly during a 20-point fourth quarter explosion. VanderKelen completed 17 of 25 passes for 202 yards. He also led Wisconsin in rushing with 13 carries for 59. Richter had eight catches for 104 yards.

Bruhn didn't dwell on the successful trip to Michigan Stadium (where only 53,789 fans bothered to show up). "Right now, we're thinking only about Northwestern," Bruhn told the *State Journal*. "We have a chance to stop them and that would give us a shot at the title."

Northwestern was one of five unbeaten teams—along with Alabama, USC, Mississippi and Dartmouth—and ranked No. 1 in both national polls. (The Badgers were ranked eighth in the AP poll and seventh in the UPI poll).

The Wildcats nearly got caught looking ahead to Wisconsin, too. Despite being a three touchdown favorite over Indiana, which had lost 17 previous Big Ten games, Northwestern needed a fourth quarter rally to edge the Hoosiers, 26-21, in Bloomington, Indiana.

Sophomore quarterback Tom Myers completed 16 of 26 passes for 243 yards and two touchdowns. But he was also intercepted three times. His favorite receiver, Paul Flatley, had trouble getting open against the Indiana secondary, which doubled him when possible.

The Northwestern-Wisconsin match-up was being marketed by (what else?) its quarterback-receiver match-ups: Myers vs. VanderKelen. Flatley vs. Richter.

"Maybe I was immune to all of that, I never really paid any attention," VanderKelen said. "I just knew there was an awful lot of publicity about, 'Who's going to win the battle, Richter or Flatley? Who's going to win the battle, VanderKelen or Myers?'"

In passing offense, Myers was No. 1 in the Big Ten. VanderKelen was No. 2. In total offense, VanderKelen was No. 1. Myers was No. 2.

Top: Ron VanderKelen was particularly shifty in space as Minnesota defensive back Jim Cairns (29) found out the hard way. "Every single game at Camp Randall Stadium was a thrill for me," VanderKelen said. "It was just a thrill to run out the tunnel and have that kind of support from the Wisconsin crowds."

Bottom: Wisconsin fullback Jim Purnell (38) and guard Dion Kempthorne are the lead blockers for quarterback Ron VanderKelen on this end around. "We played every game like it was the first game of the year," VanderKelen said of the 1962 season, "and we just went out and tried to win. We knew who we were, and we went out and played our game."

Lou Holland (27) was a dangerous open field runner whose quickness was a huge advantage. He was a smart runner, too. And an even smarter businessman. Quarterbacking his own Chicago-based capital management team, he became one of the most prominent and successful investment experts in the country. Holland told the Capital Times, ``When you're involved in sports, it creates a competitiveness that is very difficult to achieve in other things until you get older. It builds an inner toughness that is certainly important in the investment business.''

In receiving, Flatley was No. [...] in the Big Ten with 22 catches for 299 yards and two touchdowns. Richter was No. 2 with 21 catches for 273 yards and two touchdowns.

"The question you'd hear most often was, 'Who was going to be able to shut off the receivers?'" Richter remembered. "And we'd say, 'Okay, if they had Myers and Flatley, we felt Vandy and myself could match up with them.' We had a cadre of guys.

"I can't recall who their running backs were...."

(Bill Swingle and Steve Murphy were the fullbacks for the Wildcats. Willie Stinson, Larry Benz, and Dick McCauley were the halfbacks. Murphy was No. 2 in the Big Ten in scoring behind Wisconsin's Ron Smith, who had 36 points.)

"But we felt pretty good about the running backs we had," said Richter, listing Louie Holland, Gary Kroner, Ralph Kurek, and Jim Purnell. "That's where you see the real value of a balanced attack and what it can do for you."

As a team, the Wildcats led the nation in passing and total offense, while the Badgers ranked eighth and fifth, respectively, in those categories.

Sizing up the 19-year-old Myers—who had completed 88 of 134 attempts for 1,222 yards and 12 scores through six games—Bruhn told the *State Journal* that the Troy, Ohio, native has such a quick release, "It's difficult to penetrate and put a rush on him."

Northwestern coach Ara Parseghian had nothing but praise for VanderKelen and conceded, "We have to stop the pass-running option if we hope to win."

More than 3,000 students attended the "Yell Like Hell" rally Friday afternoon in front of the Memorial Union. The Homecoming game had been sold out weeks in advance.

Even though the Wildcats were the No. 1 team in college football—and the winner of Northwestern-Wisconsin would be declared the frontrunner for the Rose Bowl—there was little national interest. In fact, the game wasn't even televised from Camp Randall.

"It just wasn't the same kind of hype that you would get today for a No. 1-ranked team," Richter said. "But when you played No. 1, nobody wanted to be embarrassed. I know they were touted and we weren't necessarily highly-touted."

That was an advantage, according to VanderKelen. "Nobody figured Wisconsin was going to have a great year," he said. "They thought we'd be in the middle of the pack in the Big Ten or down in the lower level. But we played every game like it was the first game of the year. We knew who we were, and we went out and played our game."

Wisconsin had way too much game for Northwestern.

In the third quarter, the Badgers turned a modest 10-0 lead into a butt-kicking, scoring 21 points in the first seven minutes. The outclassed Wildcats had no chance of recovering from a humbling 31-0 deficit. At the very least they avoided being skunked with a consolation score, though Parseghian could find little to smile about after the 37-6 loss.

"They ran the same plays, they had the same defenses, they did everything we expected," Parseghian told the *State Journal*. "But they did it with greater execution and with greater determination. In a sense, they overpowered us. How did things get so far out of hand? I wish I had the answer to that."

As for the individual match-ups: Myers completed 16 of 26 passes for 181 yards and one touchdown. VanderKelen completed 12 of 22 passes for 181 yards and three scores. Flatley had 2 catches for 17 yards. Richter had 5 catches for 77 yards.

"VanderKelen was Wisconsin's big man," Dick Cullum wrote in the *Minneapolis Tribune*. "His passing was superb, but, in addition, he ran for crucial first downs and directed his team with daring and smartness...."

"The heralded passing duel between Myers and VanderKelen was strictly a one-sided affair, with the Wisconsin senior winning hands down," Roger Rosenblum wrote in the *St. Paul Pioneer Press*. "The big, fast-charging Wisconsin line rarely gave Myers a chance to set himself, and the Northwestern sophomore was a sitting duck for most of the afternoon."

Bruhn told the *State Journal*, "Our boy is a better runner, but there's no question about Myers being a good passer. But this was Vandy's day. He did everything well."

Yet it was Gary Kroner, not VanderKelen, who was named to UPI's National Backfield of the Week. Kroner caught two scoring passes from VanderKelen, kicked a 38-yard field goal and four conversions, and set up a score with a 45-yard kickoff return. Kroner had a hand, or a foot, in Wisconsin's first 17 points and accounted for 19 points overall.

"He was kind of a quiet person, but he always came through," VanderKelen said of Kroner, a senior. "If you needed a couple of yards, you got him the ball. He wasn't a spectacular, big-play guy like Louie Holland, but you could always rely on him."

Holland was spectacular against Northwestern—scoring three touchdowns, two by running. *State Journal* sportswriter Tom Butler wrote that Holland "ran like a midnight express, lowering the boom like a miniature Ameche when cornered."

Said VanderKelen, "Louie was so quick, if you could get him open on a short pass in the flat-or just give him the ball and let him run—he could break any play at any time."

Bruhn singled out the line play of Bowman, Underwood, Ron Carlson, Larry Howard, Roger Pillath, Andy Wojdula, Lee Bernet, Joe Heckl, and Dion Kempthorne.

"You kicked the hell out of 'em, Milt," a sportswriter volunteered to Bruhn during his post-game press conference. "Does that about sum it up?"

Always the gentleman, Bruhn replied, "We wanted them to play aggressively, and I think they did. The big thing was that we were never as healthy this year as we were today."

Bruhn dodged any Rose Bowl speculation. Taking a familiar stance, he said, "We think about just one game at a time. When you start thinking about Roses, you get into trouble."

That thought had crossed VanderKelen's mind—in 1959—while he was riding the pines in Pasadena and the Badgers were getting clobbered, 44-8, by Washington. "I'm a sophomore and I thought, 'Wow, wouldn't that be wonderful to go back to the Rose Bowl,'" he related. "But when you're playing sports, you never try to project too far out."

In the AP poll, Northwestern dropped from No. 1 to No. 9 (Alabama climbed into the No. 1 spot with USC ranked No. 2). Wisconsin moved up to No. 4 in both polls.

When asked if the Northwestern win was the turning point to the '62 season, VanderKelen said, "Absolutely. Any time you play the No. 1 ranked team in the country and beat them pretty badly, you've got to start believing you're a pretty good team. For a lot of people I think it built up their confidence. It was like, 'Hey, we're good, we can do this.'"

Entering the regular season finale against Minnesota, the Badgers were virtually assured of getting the official bid to Pasadena—regardless of the outcome—when the Big Ten athletic directors were polled. That's because Wisconsin couldn't drop lower than second place, and the Gophers were ineligible for the Rose Bowl after back-to-back trips.

Still, it was Minnesota-Wisconsin, the annual renewal of their rivalry. Both teams were 5-1 in the Big Ten. And what ensued in Camp Randall was the most controversial finish in the history of the series, the longest uninterrupted series in college football.

The Gophers were clinging to a 9-7 fourth quarter lead when the Badgers started to move the chains on what would be an 80-yard drive. VanderKelen found Richter for gains of 12, 18, and 12 yards before Minnesota's Jack Perkovich came up with a big defensive play. Perkovich intercepted VanderKelen. So he thought. So the Gophers thought.

But the turnover was washed out by a penalty flag. Bobby Bell had been called for roughing VanderKelen, giving the Badgers a first down on the Gophers' 28. After Minnesota coach Murray Warmath went ballistic—grabbing field judge Joseph Schneider—the Gophers were assessed another 15-yard penalty, putting the ball on the 13.

Three plays later, Kurek scored and the Badgers led, 14-9. With the help of two pass interference penalties and another flag for unsportsmanlike conduct, the Gophers stayed alive and drove to the UW 14 with 72 seconds remaining. But Jim Nettles preserved the victory with a clutch interception of a Duane Blaska pass in the end zone.

When Warmath was quizzed afterward on the 15-yard penalties and whether they had been the turning point, he bristled, "Who are you kidding? That should be damn apparent."

A small group of Minnesota fanatics took up Warmath's argument immediately after the game by confronting the officials as they ran off the field. The State Journal reported, "Police hurried to provide safe conduct [for the referees], but in the following melee a fan did break through the police ring and jump on the back of one of the officials."

The game was just as ugly. Minnesota had 14 penalties for 130 yards. Wisconsin was penalized 88 yards. So, did Bell rough VanderKelen?

"You learn in sports that you've got to go with what is called, and the referee (Robert Jones of Lansing, Michigan) called the penalty and we took it," VanderKelen said recently. He was very diplomatic—an understandable stance to take—given that he's working behind enemy lines in the admissions department of the University of Minnesota business school.

"They have pictures around here of Bell hitting me, and there are still some people up here who don't like me very much," said VanderKelen, who played five seasons for the Minnesota Vikings. "When Bell was taking me to the ground, he threw an elbow into my jaw, and the referee happened to be standing there and that's what he called the penalty for. It was a legitimate call."

A Minneapolis Star Tribune columnist wrote that Minnesota had been "cheated as no team in the history of competitive athletics had been cheated by bandits with striped shirts."

Butler remembered how another Star Tribune columnist, Sid Hartman, was so angered by the call that he left the press box, ran down to the field, and confronted an official.

Underwood was responsible for blocking Bell, an All-American.

"I remember Carl Eller was on the other side of the ball and Bell gave me nothing all day," Underwood said. "I'd say I went up against him 10 times and he wasn't playing hard."

Except there was an 11th time.

"When he came that last time, he was playing hard," Underwood said. "He was so quick, I didn't even touch him. I remember it was like I was blocking a totally different guy. He gave me an inside look, I went inside, he went outside and it was all over."

What Underwood remembers the most, though, was VanderKelen's poise under pressure. "He showed so much leadership," he said. "He was always cool and collected, telling us in the huddle, 'Don't worry, we're going to get out of this.' He was always composed and had everything under control. That was the hallmark of his performance."

And that drew a hand signal from Underwood.

A thumbs-up.

Wisconsin 24 Penn State 3
November 21, 1998

"Just looking around at the crowd [in Camp Randall Stadium], it was unbelievable. I'd say it was a great Wisconsin effort-the fans, the team and the coaches. This is what football is supposed to be all about and the nation saw it today."
— UW defensive end John Favret

Philadelphia Eagles offensive coordinator Brad Childress had a flashback to his previous life as a college assistant the first time that he was introduced to Jon Sandusky, one of the organization's pro scouts. Sandusky is the son of Jerry Sandusky, who was Joe Paterno's defensive coordinator for 31 years at Penn State.

Since Childress spent seven years as the quarterbacks coach and offensive coordinator at Wisconsin, it was inevitable that when he bumped into Jon Sandusky—a back-up safety and a special team-er for the Nittany Lions in the late '90s—a certain topic would come up in conversation: the '98 game between Penn State and the Badgers at Camp Randall.

"Jon kind of takes me back to what an unbelievable atmosphere that was, and it really was—it was a charged atmosphere," said Childress. "You remember things like the tradition of 'Jump Around' before the start of the fourth quarter, and Jon talks about that, too."

If you're Childress, you remember things like going to your second Rose Bowl with the Badgers and third Rose Bowl overall (including a trip to Pasadena with Illinois).

And he talked about that, too.

"To go there once in a lifetime is a dream come true,"

Courtesy of Craig Schreiner/Wisconsin State Journal

Inside linebacker Donnel Thompson (44) wraps up Penn State quarterback Kevin Thompson. As a youngster, Thompson grew up a few blocks from Camp Randall, and hawked soft drinks on game days. He played for his dad at Madison West and worked his way up the ladder: from unsung walk-on to the team's leading tackler and a two-time captain.

Courtesy of Craig Schreiner/Wisconsin State Journal

Opposite page: Badger wide receiver Chris Chambers hauls in a 26-yard scoring pass from quarterback Mike Samuel.

Childress said. "But I only had a short period of time to enjoy it [a third time], and I probably didn't get to enjoy it as much as I would have liked because three weeks later I'm here in Philadelphia."

At a January 13, 1999, press conference, Childress talked about the opportunity to coach at the highest echelon of his profession—the National Football League—in explaining the reasons behind leaving a solid and secure college job. With the Eagles, he was taking over as the quarterbacks coach for Andy Reid, a longtime friend.

Childress later recounted this story. On his first night in Philadelphia as a member of the Eagles' staff, he went out to dinner with Reid, a Mike Holmgren protégé, who coached on the same staff with Childress at Northern Arizona in 1986.

They had no trouble getting a good table at a popular Philly restaurant because the town was being pelted by an ice storm. It didn't take long for the plump, round-faced Reid to be recognized, either. "Give 'em hell, Andy," shouted a voice from an adjoining table. "I'll tell you what, you're going to do a great job."

Reid, the first-year head coach, waved and acknowledged the boisterous words of encouragement. Minutes later, Philly Fan toasted Reid again and, along with his buddy, gave him a standing ovation before suggesting Reid deserved a real Philly welcome.

"Boooooooo..."
"Boooooooo..."

Childress swore it was a true story. "They started booing us from across the room," he contended. "That's my first night in town, and I got the picture right away. Tough crowd."

That first year in Philly did not go well for Reid, Childress, or the Eagles.

"Anytime you start with a new program, there are growing pains, not unlike what we had at Wisconsin," Childress said recently. "So you go through a period of getting your fanny beat and that's the

Courtesy of Craig Schreiner/Wisconsin State Journal

Quarterback Mike Samuel tucks in the ball and heads up field following the lead block of #89 Eric Grams.

hardest thing —the losing. Here we are going 5-11 that first year in Philadelphia and trying to lay the groundwork for where we are now [NFC champs] and Wisconsin is going back to the Rose Bowl in '99.

"And you're casting a glance [toward Madison] and you're kind of thinking, 'Geez, did I do the right thing? Here we are in the basement of the division, getting our tails beat and playing in the Vet, where the rats are chasing cats, and they've got that great physical plant at Wisconsin and they're winning....But all's well that ends well."

Over the last five seasons, the Eagles have won 11, 11, 12, 12, and 13 games, and Childress has become a hot NFL commodity—so hot that in early February 2005, the Eagles extended his contract through the 2008 season.

But there's no question that Childress still has special memories from his hitch with the Badgers, not the least of which was that '98 regular season finale against Penn State.

"1998, huh?" Childress posed coyly. "Was that the game that was played kind of late in the afternoon in Madison? The game that Mike Samuel ran over LaVar Arrington?"

Childress knew the answer. "Later that year," he said, "Arrington made a comment in a Florida paper that the hardest hit that he got all year was from Mike Samuel."

That opened the door to one of Childress' favorite topics: Samuel.

"For all the things people wanted to say about him, Mike was one of the toughest-minded guys that I've ever been around, and you can couple that with his physical toughness, too," Childress said. "Mike was like a giant bruise after every game. He really got beat up. But he still wasn't afraid to lower his shoulder if he had to bowl you over."

Even if the tackler was Superman. Did we mention that LaVar Arrington could fly? As a prep, he was clocked in 10.78 seconds over 100 meters. As a collegian, he was timed in 4.4 seconds over 40 yards. But did we mention that he could really fly?

Ron Turner, then the Illinois coach, saw it with his own eyes during the '98 season. He saw film of Arrington flying through the air with the greatest of ease against Minnesota. "His vertical jump must have been 51 inches," Turner wagered. "I was like, 'Is that Michael Jordan?' I must have rewound the tape 10 times to see it again and again."

That year, Arrington was even scarier against Turner's team. In a single bound, the 6-foot-3, 233-pound Arrington leaped over the stunned Illinois offensive center and dumped the running back for a loss on a fourth-and-1 play.

"Everybody referred to him as LaVar 'The Superstar' Arrington when he was in high school," said Ben Herbert, then a UW freshman linebacker from McDonald, Pennsylvania. Arrington earned his frequent flyer miles with North Hills High School in Pittsburgh.

"I was at one of those games where he had everybody talking about him jumping over the offensive line. Everybody knew who he was. And everybody wanted to see him play."

UW coach Barry Alvarez, a former Nebraska linebacker, admired Arrington's skills to take on an isolation block by leaping over the top of the blocker. Asked if he could perform that feat in his playing days, Alvarez said, "I couldn't jump up on a Sunday newspaper."

When you used to think about Penn State linebackers, you used to think about Dennis Onkotz and Jack Ham; John Skorupan and Ed O'Neil; Kurt Allerman and Shane Conlan. You used to think burly and surly. Arrington was cut differently: sleek and swift.

"Penn State's linebackers may be the most athletic I've ever seen-they're thoroughbreds," said Alvarez, including Brandon Short in the discussion.

And the Nittany Lions' athleticism wasn't limited to the linebackers. Up front, Courtney Brown and Brad Scioli were big-time playmakers. So was David Macklin in the secondary. (Arrington, Short, Brown, Scioli and Macklin are playing in the NFL today.)

Michigan coach Lloyd Carr labeled Brown as "the best pass rusher I've seen in 10 years." Brown had five tackles behind the line of scrimmage, including a quarterback sack, against Northwestern. And that was in the first quarter alone.

As a defensive unit, the Nittany Lions were ranked No. 7 nationally against the rush. But they had been physically overmatched against the Wolverines and Ohio State-providing hope to Alvarez and Childress that the Badgers could establish the run either with tailback Ron Dayne or Samuel running options and quarterback draws.

First of all, Alvarez and Childress had to make sure Dayne and Samuel were back on the same page again after a disastrous roadie to Ann Arbor the week before.

The No. 8-ranked Badgers, unbeaten and winners of nine straight, went looking for respect and acceptance in the Big House. They got neither. Instead, they got a cold-hearted dose of reality during a humbling 27-10 loss to the Wolverines, still perfect in the Big Ten (7-0), and still on the rebound after season-opening losses to Notre Dame and Syracuse.

Defensively, the Badgers had been No. 1 in the nation against the rush (62.7). Michigan ran for 257 yards with Clarence Williams and Anthony Thomas each going over 100. "I was shocked they could run the ball like that," Alvarez said.

The Badgers also had been No. 4 nationally in total defense. Michigan had 476 yards of total offense—202 passing yards from Tom Brady—and averaged 6.1 yards per play.

"Sometimes, you're not going to play well on defense," Alvarez rationalized, "and that's the day when the offense has to step up, and ours sure didn't. We couldn't get anything going on offense. Zero. It was like banging your head against a wall."

The Badgers managed just 190 total yards, a season low. Dayne had 53 rushing, Samuel had 126 passing, 80 coming on a scoring throw to Chris Chambers. The most frustrating part of the game for Dayne and Samuel was their failure to communicate.

Three times they busted on the option, each going their own way. Whether it was Samuel going right and Dayne going left or Samuel going left and Dayne going right.

The Badgers have a "check with me" system for audibles. After reading the defense, Samuel will call out the direction the option will be run. Dayne didn't hear him. "I've got an ear infection and I can only hear out of one ear," Dayne said.

As a team, the Badgers heard nothing but criticism in Madison the following week as they got ready for Penn State. Now they needed help to get to Pasadena. They needed to beat the Nittany Lions, and they needed Ohio State to beat Michigan in Columbus.

Counting on a John Cooper-coached team can be risky business. Cooper was just 1-8-1 against the Wolverines. But the lone high-lights—the win and tie—were in Ohio Stadium. "Miracles happen all the time," said UW defensive end Tom Burke. "Don't they?"

They do. In 1993, the Badgers got help from Michigan when it upset Ohio State in Ann Arbor, clearing the path for Wisconsin to make its first Rose Bowl run under Alvarez.

"I just told the guys we don't control our destiny anymore," Alvarez said at his weekly press conference. "And I just told them that they handled winning well, now they have to handle a loss, and we'll see how they bounce back."

For starters, they got one back—starting inside linebacker Chris Ghidorzi, who missed the Michigan game after pulling his hamstring during the Wednesday practice. Ghidorzi's replacement, Roger Knight, wound up breaking his arm against the Wolverines and that forced more juggling, with Nick Greisen, a true freshman, playing the second half.

Everything was out of sync at Michigan. Because Ghidorzi called the defensive signals, Donnel Thompson inherited that responsibility

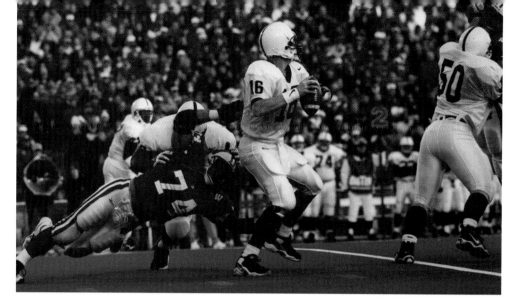

Courtesy of Craig Schreiner/Wisconsin State Journal

Penn State quarterback Kevin Thompson is about to be sacked by Wisconsin's Tom Burke, who races past offensive tackle John Blick. "I was going to throw the kitchen sink at 'em if I had to," Burke said afterward. "A couple of plays I did."

while Ghidorzi was sidelined—which, in turn, placed an additional burden on Thompson to perform in a much different role.

With Ghidorzi back, the focus shifted to another Thompson—Penn State quarterback Kevin Thompson, a lanky 6-5 drop-back passer who was not going to win any popularity contests in State College. The fans favored the backup, Rashard Casey. Don't they always? Asked about getting booed by the home crowd, Thompson said, "It's gotta motivate you."

Samuel could relate to self-motivation and the red hot glare of the spotlight. The week of the Michigan game, he and his brother got into a scrap outside a State Street bar.

"I knew Mike felt bad about that [incident] in terms of it being a distraction to the team that week," Childress recalled. "He had a lot of naysayers and that's a hard thing to deal with when people are pitching against you. But resiliency is an important part of the position. You have to have a short-term memory and you have to have confidence in yourself."

Childress brought up the 1997 Boise State game as an example of Samuel's mental toughness and resiliency. Samuel was benched midway through the second quarter after throwing two interceptions against the 36-point underdogs.

Samuel was back on the field for the second half, but after losing a fumble in the fourth quarter, he heard the boo's. ("I deserved to be booed," he said afterward.)

With time running out and the Badgers trailing 24-21, Samuel rallied the offense. On a third-and-12, he scrambled 28 yards for a first down. Five plays later, on a third-and-7, he was on the run again, running 12 yards for the go-ahead score with 49 seconds remaining.

"All I can say is that Mike is a soldier," UW fullback Cecil Martin told the *State Journal* after the Badgers survived the Boise scare. "He didn't give up and didn't let adversity or boo's or anything get in the way of his heart and his spirit and what he wanted to do. When crunch time came, he stayed poised and focused. That's what we expect from him."

That's why Childress felt good about the Badgers bouncing back against the Nittany Lions. That was the general sentiment in the Wisconsin locker room before the game. "It wasn't IF we were going to win," Ghidorzi said, "it was WHEN we were going to win. We knew that Penn State was no pushover. But I remember the confidence that we had."

With less than six minutes left in the first quarter, Ghidorzi remembered looking up to see what all the noise was about. "All of a sudden, the fans started cheering," he said, "and you realize that you're playing [Penn State] to go to the Rose Bowl. It was awesome."

Ghidorzi had made eye contact with the scoreboard at the south end of the stadium. The miracle that Burke was counting on was now official: Ohio State 31, Michigan 16. "It helps to know what you're shooting for," Burke said. "We needed help from [the Buckeyes] and we got it. So we just had to go out and help ourselves."

Joe Germaine threw for 330 yards and three touchdowns, David Boston had 10 catches for 217 yards, and Michael Wiley rushed for 120 yards as Ohio State shocked Michigan. That gave the Buckeyes, along with the Wolverines, a slice of the title. And by beating Penn State, the Badgers could make it a three-way tie with the tie-breaker going to Wisconsin.

(The only glitch would have been if Ohio State finished the season ranked first or second in the Bowl Championship Series, and that didn't materialize.)

Despite the wave of emotion that washed over Camp Randall when the Michigan-Ohio State score was posted, Penn State threatened to burst that bubble right away.

In a scoreless first quarter, the Nittany

Courtesy of Craig Schreiner/Wisconsin State Journal

Top & bottom: With 26 seconds left in a scoreless first quarter, Nick Davis reaches the end zone at the end of an 82-yard punt return and is mobbed by his teammates: Willie Austin (7), Tim Rosga (15) and Ryan Marks (30). "The first thing you have to do is catch the ball," Davis said, "and everything that happens after that is pretty much ad-libbed."

Courtesy of Craig Schreiner/Wisconsin State Journal

Lions had a first-and-goal from the Wisconsin 4-yard line. Who knows how things would have played out if they had gotten on the board first? (The Badgers were 12-30-2 under Alvarez when the opponent scored first).

On first down, Dan Lisowski dropped tailback Eric McCoo for a 3-yard loss. A 15-yard personal foul penalty marked off from the point of infraction pushed the Nittany Lions back to the 29. On second down, John Favret held Mike Cerimele to a 4-yard gain on a draw.

On third down, Jamar Fletcher broke up a Thompson pass intended for Corey Jones. On fourth down, the moonwalking Nittany Lions were forced to settle for a 42-yard field goal attempt. Travis Forney missed, letting the Badgers off the hook. "That was a huge defensive stand," Alvarez said, "because we started the game on our heels."

With 26 seconds remaining in the quarter, true freshman Nick Davis provided Wisconsin's first offensive spark of the game. Fielding a 54-yard punt off the foot of Pat Pidgeon, Davis remembered "catching it and taking a step back and making one move to my left. There was a flash and I saw an opening to the sidelines."

Davis picked up a block from Donte King and sprinted 82 yards down the east sideline—past a stunned Joe Pa—for the first score of the game, igniting the crowd.

"You could tell that return gave us the momentum because of the energy that went through the stadium," Davis said. "It was contagious, too. The offense felt it, the defense felt it, the fans got involved, and the game really opened up."

Less than five minutes into the second quarter, Samuel hit Chambers on a 26-yard scoring pass. Those points came compliments of a Penn State turnover as Bruce Branch mishandled a Kevin Stemke punt and King recovered on the Nittany Lions' 37. The Badgers converted another turnover into a Matt Davenport field goal and led 17-0 at halftime.

At that point everyone stopped to smell the Roses—because there was no way the Nittany Lions were going to dig themselves out of the hole, not against Burke and Co.

"I knew that I was going to have a good game because it was my last home game," said Burke, who had five tackles for loss (four sacks). "I'm not much of a talker, but I got together with the seniors and I reminded them that every minute that goes by on the field is one less minute we get to play here at Camp Randall. I said, 'Don't regret any minute.'"

Before the game, Arrington supplied this scouting report on the UW offense: "From the running back to the line, everybody at Wisconsin is big. Maybe it's the cheese."

Dayne tore his left pectoral muscle in the first quarter. At less than full strength, he still rushed 23 times for 95 yards. Samuel, though, was more than happy to pick up the slack. Mixing option keepers with draws, he rushed for a career-high 89 yards.

On one of his 13 carries, Samuel took on Arrington in a thunderous collision, mano-a-mano, that had Samuel popping up to his feet before the dazed Arrington. Say cheese, LaVar.

"We knew we had to stop the option, and we knew we had to stop Dayne," Paterno said. "We did a decent job on Dayne, but not on Samuel. He had a lot of yards."

Samuel put the exclamation point on his effort by closing out the scoring with a one-yard run in the fourth quarter, making it 24-3. By then, the celebration had already begun.

"These kids started two-a-day camp with one goal in mind and that was to go to the Rose Bowl," Alvarez said. "The two senior captains, Cecil Martin and Bobby Adamov, came up to me and said, 'Coach, we came here not just to go to bowl games. We'd like to go to the Rose Bowl.' I told them, 'Enough said, that's our goal.'"

In 1993, the Badgers were built around offense, a balanced, multi-dimensional offense that averaged 250 yards on the ground and 204

Courtesy of Craig Schreiner/Wisconsin State Journal

Badger players celebrate a return trip to the Rose Bowl.

yards through the air.

That "big play" team featured a pasty-faced quarterback, Darrell Bevell, who ended up as the school's all-time leading passer; a sticky-fingered receiver, Lee DeRamus; a reliable tight end, Mike Roan; and tag team tailbacks Brent Moss and Terrell Fletcher.

In 1993, the Badgers also featured an extremely opportunistic defense (23 interceptions, 11 fumble recoveries) that got timely contributions from a lot of different sources: Yusef Burgess, Reggie Holt, Eric Unverzagt, Lamark Shackerford, Carlos Fowler, Mike Thompson, Kenny Gales, Jeff Messenger, and Scott Nelson.

"Our defense was okay," Alvarez said of his first Rose Bowl team. "But it was a bend-but-don't-break defense. They got turnovers, but they weren't as smothering as this one."

In 1998, the Badgers were built around their defense, a punishing defense guided by Ghidorzi, the leading tackler, and fueled by Burke, who had an astonishing 31 TFLs and 22 quarterback sacks. "I didn't come to Wisconsin to go to the Outback Bowl or the Copper Bowl," Burke said, hitting on a familiar theme. "I came here to go to the Rose Bowl."

In 1998, the Badgers had top shelf specials teams—Stemke, Davenport and Davis-and an offense that rarely committed a mistake to compromise field position.

During the regular season, Samuel had four interceptions in 155 pass attempts. As a team, the Badgers had five picks, the lowest total in the last 52 years.

Dayne had the only fumble by a running back. And as a team, the Badgers lost just four fumbles in 552 rushes, also the lowest total in the last 52 years.

After the Michigan loss, Alvarez said, "All I wanted was our team back, our brand of football back—old school football—and that's how we played against Penn State."

And that's how it ended for Childress at Wisconsin.

With long-stemmed roses and post-game fireworks.

"Every year stands on its own merit, every team has its own personality," said Childress, fresh off a 2005 Super Bowl appearance with Philly. "People probably didn't think [the Badgers] were that talented, but they ended up being talented enough."

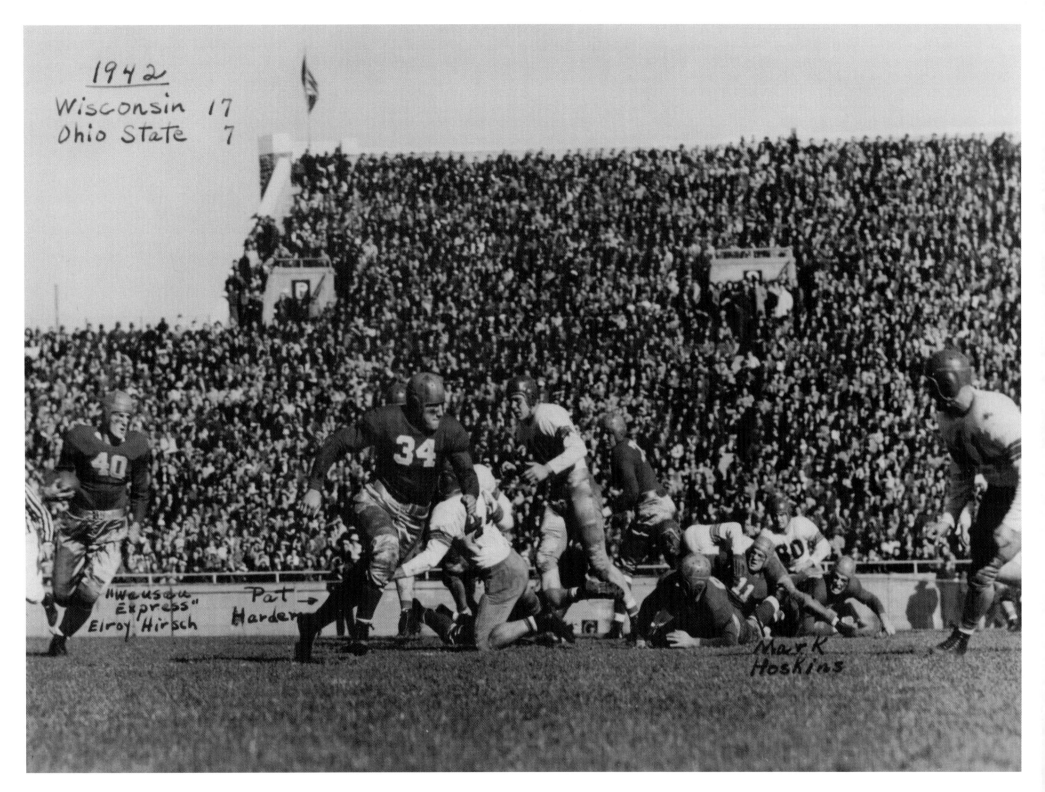

1942
Wisconsin 17
Ohio State 7

"Wausau
Express"
Elroy Hirsch

Pat
Harder →

Max K
Hoskins

Whether traveling down Regent, Monroe, Dayton, or some other campus artery, Otto Breitenbach has approached Camp Randall Stadium from a variety of directions during his lifetime. And today each trip past the renovated stadium takes him down Memory Lane. "When I drive by," he said, "I have a good feeling."

Growing up in Madison above his father's grocery on the corner of Williamson and Patterson Streets, Breitenbach paid 25 cents to get into his first game and watched from a seat in the north end zone as the Badgers walloped Coe College, 39-0.

That was in 1932.

Breitenbach took a liking to certain UW players from that era, like Buckets Goldenberg, Hal Rebholz and Howie Weiss. He wasn't completely biased. He also followed the exploits of the University of Chicago's Jay Berwanger, the first Heisman Trophy winner. (In 1935, the award honored the best college player east of the Mississippi River.)

Much later in life, as the ultra-successful Madison LaFollette head coach, Breitenbach lived on Edgewood Avenue, right across the street from his alma mater, Edgewood High School, and a straight shot down Monroe Street to Camp Randall.

Shortly after leaving the neighborhood and relocating to the east side of town, Breitenbach joined the staff of the UW athletic department as an assistant athletic director to Elroy Hirsch. For 14 of his 15 years on the job, Breitenbach worked side-by-side with Hirsch, rising to the title of associate director during his tenure at the school.

Breitenbach and Hirsch.

Blanchard and Davis.

Mr. Inside--the laid-back Breitenbach worked mostly behind the scenes.

Mr. Outside--the crewcut Hirsch was the face of the department.

"Elroy had a willingness to talk to everybody," Breitenbach recalled

fondly, "even if he didn't know their name from Adam. He was very outgoing."

The Breitenbach-Hirsch timeline goes back to 1941 and their freshman year at Wisconsin when Breitenbach, the townie, befriended Hirsch, the Wausau native.

"Back then, there was not the same publicity for coming to Wisconsin like a high-level recruit might get today," Breitenbach said, "but Elroy came with a name."

He meant Hirsch came with a reputation. But he chuckled at his choice of words, because, of course, Hirsch would later come by a name: Crazylegs.

"He was called a lot of different names," Breitenbach teased. Most credited *Chicago Daily News* sportswriter Francis Powers for coming up with the Crazylegs sobriquet.

"Hirsch ran like a demented duck," Powers wrote of Hirsch's 61-yard touchdown run in a 1942 game against Great Lakes Naval Station in Chicago. "His crazy legs were gyrating in six different directions all at the same time."

Madison sportswriters had coined another name for Hirsch: Ghost. As in Elroy "Ghost" Hirsch.

A Milwaukee writer referred to him as "The Wiggler." As in the Wausau Wiggler.

Crazylegs would stick.

"Any name is better than Elroy," Hirsch always joked.

Everyone had their own spin on the defining scoring run at Soldier Field which came in full view of nearly 60,000, half of which were unpaid admissions, soldiers and sailors.

The *Chicago Tribune's* Willard Smith, a seasoned and respected authority, wrote that Hirsch was "twisting and squirming perilously close to the sideline as he ran down the east side of the field, closely followed by an official watching his every step."

Hirsch later recalled, "One of my feet was going one way, the other one in another direction on the run. I must have been a sight running down the sidelines."

That was not the most spectacular run of the game, though. Jack Wink-who drew "Quick as a Wink" prose and doubled as the UW quarterback—returned an interception 101 yards for a touchdown,

Courtesy of University of Wisconsin Archives

Opposite page: Elroy Hirsch (40) has a firm grip on the football and his eyes fixed on Ohio State linebacker Gene Fekete (44) who has a knee down on the turf after fighting off a block. Wisconsin fullback Pat Harder (34), meanwhile, is focusing on Ohio State captain George Lynn (11), who has outside contain, while Mark Hoskins (11) already has his man down.

spelling the difference in Wisconsin's 13-7 win over Great Lakes.

"I never knew 100 yards could be so long," Wink told the *State Journal*. "Boy, I was tired when I got to that goal line. What, [it was] 101 yards? Was I actually behind the goal line on that pass? Will wonders never cease?"

After the game, Hirsch entered the Great Lakes locker room and visited with the player who had been hoodwinked—Bruce Smith, the former Gopher All-American and the 1941 Heisman winner. They first met during Hirsch's recruiting trip to Minneapolis.

"Hirsch can really lug that mail, can't he?" Smith posed rhetorically to the *State Journal*. "What's more, he's a great kid to get along with. I sure wish he was playing with Minnesota instead of Wisconsin. You know, we almost had him up there."

Hirsch was rapidly becoming a media darling and drawing extra attention.

"Elroy Hirsch was pleased as a youngster with a new drum," wrote *Capital Times* sports editor Hank Casserly. "He laughed and talked on the homeward trip Sunday morning from Chicago and made one statement which sounded logical.

"I learned not to let those ex-pros [playing for Great Lakes] get a good shot at you," he said. "They really put you down. It's far better to run away from them as I discovered."

The Badgers got a warm reception when they returned by train to Madison. The *Capital Times* reported that "hundreds of persons jammed the platform of the Milwaukee Road station....they turned loose loud bursts of cheering for Dave Schreiner, Pat Harder, and especially for Elroy Hirsch, but Wink was almost unrecognized.

"Hundreds were asking 'Which one is Wink' but the Badger quarterback hopped down the steps of the train and was well out into the crowd before his friends sighted him."

Such was the length of the shadows cast by Schreiner, Harder, and Hirsch.

Although Marlin "Pat" Harder—the Badger "Mule"—was injured and saw limited playing time in Chicago, he was expected to be ready for the Big Ten opener at Purdue. The preliminaries were now over. And, per usual, the sportswriters were looking ahead.

"The Wisconsin-Ohio State game here October 31 may settle not only the Western Conference, but the national title," Casserly opined. "Tickets for this game will be at a premium, and the biggest crowd of the season is certain to be here.

"Sports scribes were making reservations Sunday for accommodations in Madison for the Badger-Buckeye tilt, which now looms as a classic."

While the Badgers were winning in Chicago, the No. 1-ranked

Buckeyes were cruising in Columbus, wiping out Purdue, 26-0. Sophomore fullback Gene Fekete scored a couple of touchdowns as the Buckeyes rushed for over 300 yards. Defensively, they stifled the Boilermakers who failed to pick up a first down or complete a pass.

Wisconsin coach Harry Stuhldreher, who had revived the program after a bunch of lean years, recognized that the Badgers couldn't afford to look ahead to Ohio State or overlook anyone. After all, they already had a blemish on their record: a 7-7 tie with Notre Dame in late September at Camp Randall. Not that they had played poorly against the Irish.

"Fighting as gallant a battle against odds as any Wisconsin eleven you've ever seen, the Badgers turned in what amounted to a smashing upset," Henry J. McCormick wrote in the *State Journal*. "Notre Dame ran into an opponent that was asking and giving no quarter, the result being a savage, teeth-rattling battle that left each team plenty of honor."

The effort had to be pleasing to Stuhldreher, the former Gold Domer, who was immortalized as one of the Four Horsemen by Hall of Fame sportswriter Grantland Rice.

"Outlined against a blue-gray October sky," Rice penned after the 1924 Notre Dame-Army game at the Polo Grounds in New York City, "the Four Horsemen rode again. In dramatic lore, they are known as famine, pestilence, destruction and death. These are only aliases. Their real names are Stuhldreher, Miller, Crowley and Layden."

Stuhldreher was the quarterback, Don Miller and Jim Crowley were the halfbacks, and Elmer Layden was the fullback. Pretty dramatic stuff. Equally dramatic, and to the point, was McCormick's column following the Wisconsin-Notre Dame game.

"This is 'Anchors Aweigh' for the writer," he wrote. "Tomorrow, I leave for Norfolk, Virginia, and training in the United States Navy....Naturally, one has regrets in leaving a city where he was born, raised and worked. On the other hand, I am proud of the privilege of being in the U.S. Navy and I intend to do the best job at my command."

That was the spirit of the day—September 26, 1942.

McCormick's patriotism must be kept in context with another date—December 7, 1941—Japan's attack on Pearl Harbor which pushed the United States into World War II.

"I keep picturing the boys who are playing for me as they may be a year from now, pattling a Jap or a Nazi with a bayonet," Stuhldreher told *Columbus (Ohio) Citizen* sports editor Lew Bryer. "The story also ran in the *State Journal*. "There's a real parallel between football and modern warfare. And don't think the boys themselves don't realize it.

Courtesy of University of Wisconsin Archives

After playing the 1942 season for the Badgers, Elroy Hirsch was one of 11 UW athletes to move on to the University of Michigan in Ann Arbor as part of their commitment to the Marine Corps V-12 program during World War II. Hirsch helped lead the Wolverines to a 8-1 record in 1943 while the Badgers slumped to 1-9. Hirsch holds the distinction of being the only athlete in Michigan history to letter in four sports during one academic year (football, basketball, track and baseball).

"There's a difference in attitude this fall over anything I've seen either as a player or coach," Stuhldreher went on. "The boys are preparing themselves not only for the games to come but for their future in the armed services. Their imaginations are fired by what the Rangers and Commandos are doing to outsmart and out-gut the enemy. Eventually the present day football players will go a long way in helping to win this war."

That was the sobering reality of the day.

In parting, McCormick wrote, "There is no more beautiful spot in the world than Madison on an October afternoon when the leaves are beginning to turn, when a soft haze floats through the air, and when the lakes toss back the sun's rays like mirrors."

He could have easily been foreshadowing one October afternoon in particular—October 31, 1942—when the Buckeyes and the Badgers clashed at Camp Randall Stadium.

Wisconsin had momentum, coming off a 13-0 win at Purdue.

Ohio State had momentum, coming off a 20-6 win at Northwestern.

"There's a large red circle highlighting the Wisconsin locker room schedule," Marv Rand wrote in the *State Journal*, "and a large emphasized 'must' written in the margin. The bold encircled figures say, 'Oct. 31 — Ohio State Homecoming.'

"It's one of the dates every member of the undefeated Wisconsin football team has been looking forward to since reporting for practice September 1. This is THE GAME..."

The Buckeyes were still ranked No. 1, and gaining support. In the Associated Press' first poll of the 1942 season, Ohio State picked up 25 first place votes and 636 points.

The week of the Wisconsin game, the Buckeyes had garnered 80 first place votes and 1,029 points. Georgia, Alabama, Notre Dame, and Georgia Tech rounded out the top five. The Badgers were ranked No. 6 in the AP poll with one first place vote and 574 total points.

"Fiction writers—even Joe Goebbels—couldn't make up a story which would match the Badger-Buck battle for plot and potentialities," Harry Sheer wrote in the *Capital Times*. (Joseph Goebbels was Adolph Hitler's propaganda minister in Nazi Germany.)

"Sometime Saturday afternoon either coach Harry Stuhldreher or Ohio State coach Paul Brown will probably clap his hand to his head and yell, 'I shoulda stood in bed.'"

Stuhldreher and Brown both hailed from the gridiron hotbed of Massillon, Ohio, accounting for one of the storylines. But it wasn't like they had a secret handshake. "Let's just say they weren't very chummy on the field or anything," Breitenbach said.

Courtesy of University of Wisconsin Archives

During the 1940 season opener, a couple of sophomores from Lancaster — Mark Hoskins (seen here) and Dave Schreiner — each scored in their collegiate debut and from that point on they were known as the "Touchdown Twins."

As the game neared, the fullbacks got the most hype: Harder vs. Fekete.

The *Capital Times* reported, "Maulin Marlin is at full strength after a troublesome ankle injury and is not giving away his [scoring] title without a battle." Fekete (pronounced Feckitty) was still leading the Big Ten and ranked third nationally in scoring with 60 points.

Fekete's nickname was "Big Bertha." According to a Columbus newspaper, it was "not without just cause for Fekete is about as gentle with enemy lines as a whole panzer division....He hits like a thunderbolt, climbs out from beneath the pile, gives his sleeves another push up to the elbow and trots back for more."

Another storyline revolved around the halfbacks: Wisconsin's Hirsch and Mark Hoskins vs. Ohio State's Paul Sarringhaus and Leslie Horvath, who won the 1944 Heisman. The Badgers got a scare on Wednesday when Hirsch was confined to the infirmary with a sore throat. But Stuhldreher assured the local media that he would play on Saturday.

Earlier in the week, Stuhldreher announced that Dave Schreiner, the senior All-American end from Lancaster, would be Wisconsin's captain against Ohio State. (Hoskins also hailed from Lancaster and made up the other half of the "Touchdown Twins.")

Everybody had good things to say about No. 80, Schreiner.

"I remember in our scrimmages against the varsity when I was a freshman," Breitenbach said, "if I had to block Schreiner, it was an easy task because he always made you look good. He treated everyone as equals, even though we were much younger. I had just turned 17, and I felt like a novice and kind of awe-struck.

"But there was no harassment or intimidation or anything like that. Everybody treated me fine and part of that was due to the leadership of Schreiner and Hoskins. In my mind, they were the spiritual leaders of the team, and I don't mean religiously. They were the ones who set the pace for everybody else. And they were both outstanding people, on and off the field."

Added Bob Rennebohm, a sophomore end from La Crosse, "I've always said that Dave Schreiner was the best college football player for his position that anyone has ever seen."

Few would argue with that statement. After the Wisconsin- Great Lakes game, an Iowa scout asked Casserly, "Where do they get ends like Schreiner? He's the best end I've seen in years and not even three men can take him out of a play."

Casserly went on to quote former Minnesota star Bob Sweiger, a member of the Gophers' national championship teams in '40 and '41. "Shades of Bennie Oosterbaan (a three-time All-American receiver at Michigan)," Sweiger said of Schreiner. "Bennie might have been

Schreiner's equal on offense; in fact, Oosterbaan may get a slight nod. But on defense Schreiner was many times greater."

The UW receivers, Schreiner and Bob Hanzlik, and the 3-H backfield—Hirsch, Hoskins and Harder—were indebted to the strength in the offensive line. From left to right, Bob Baumann, Evan Vogds, Fred Negus, Ken Currier, and Paul Hirsbrunner.

Negus was a good recruiting story. As chronicled by the *State Journal*, his brother showed up unannounced one day in Stuhldreher's office at the Field House.

The introductions went like this: "My name is John Negus, Mr. Stuhldreher, and I represent Johnson & Johnson," the stranger said.

"Sorry, Mr. Negus," replied the Wisconsin athletic director and coach, "but we are purchasing all of our training room apparatus from another firm."

"I am not here to sell you a bill of goods, but to turn over a good football player to you," Negus answered.

Asked the identity of the player, Negus said it was his kid brother, Fred.

"Oh, oh," thought Stuhldreher to himself, "I've got a pest on my hands."

John Negus went on to explain he had just been transferred to Madison from Cleveland and his brother was going to come and live with him. Fred Negus prepped at Kisky High School in Saltzburg, Pennsylvania. Stuhldreher was suddenly all ears. That was his high school.

Stuhldreher summarily arranged for Negus to enroll at Wisconsin, the *State Journal* story goes, "and pats himself on the back frequently for the good fortune that brought him the best sophomore center in the Big Ten."

Friday afternoon, Brown met with the Madison media after conducting a short workout in a steady drizzle on a practice field adjacent to Camp Randall. Brown claimed that his 1942 team wasn't as good as the 1941 Buckeyes who beat the Badgers, 46-34, in Columbus. Brown dismissed the polls and No. 1 ranking for a lack of credibility.

"We don't take that rating seriously, for, after all, the five teams that we have beaten have won only a total of five games between them this season," Brown told the *State Journal*. "On the other hand, Wisconsin has beaten some mighty tough competition. It wouldn't surprise me at all if the Badgers won Saturday."

Early Friday evening, some 9,000 people attended a 40-minute "We Can't Lose" pep rally on the lower campus. Stuhldreher informed the crowd that the Ohio State-Wisconsin game would have the largest radio coverage ever. NBC's Bill Stern would handle the play-by-play of the broadcast which was to be carried by 184 stations in the United States.

In addition, the Homecoming game was to be short-waved to 11 South American stations, two in England, two in Ireland, two in Alaska, one in Hawaii, and one in Australia.

Schreiner spoke at the rally and so did Madison mayor James Law.

In 1942, Dave Schreiner added to his lore by repeating as an All-American. He was also the Most Valuable Player in the Big Ten. Before heading off to the Marine Corps, he played in the East-West Shrine game. Schreiner was killed in Okinawa, while his close friend, Mark Hoskins, spent nearly a year as a prisoner of war after his plane was shot down over Hungary.

There was no sighting of Wisconsin Governor Julius P. Heil. But, then, nobody had seen him lately.

(Under the boxed headlined "He's Gone" the *Capital Times* reported weekly on Heil's whereabouts. In this case, "Gov. Heil was not in the office yesterday. Since January 1, Gov. Heil has appeared at the executive office exactly 48 out of 253 working days.")

The Halloween pep rally was definitely a "feel good" experience. But everything turned sour shortly thereafter as an estimated 5,000 rioted in the downtown area. Thirty-two were arrested for disorderly conduct, destruction of property, and shooting fireworks.

Tear gas was used in some instances to disperse the mob. Police chief William McCormick told the *State Journal*, "It was the worst crowd we've had. It was certainly un-American. A bunch of German youths couldn't have been worse."

A large group of youths began marching towards the capitol, according to the *State Journal*. Blocking their path was the police public address car at Gorham and State.

"The United States is at war," an officer pleaded. "You are acting like foreigners and you will be treated like foreigners. It will not be nice. Anyone remaining in the street past this intersection does so at his own risk."

The crowd was reported to have split to the sidewalks, passed the car, and closed back into the street." And so it went into the early morning hours.

The Buckeyes were bunking at the Park Hotel on the capitol square. And the street disturbance would be cited by more than one Ohio State apologist—including Brown himself—for preventing the players from getting a good night's sleep.

That and an outbreak of dysentery. Some blamed the drinking water in Madison. Others believed the Buckeyes were exposed to contaminated water or food somewhere on their train ride between Columbus and Madison, which included an overnight stop in Janesville. Ohio State loyalists still refer to it as "The Bad Water Game."

"I never head that story verified," pooh-poohed Breitenbach. "I think it was just spin out of the Ohio State camp. No, I'm still not buying it."

A record-breaking crowd of over 45,000 jammed into Camp Randall Stadium for the long-awaited game. "It was a bright sunny day," Breitenbach remembered, "with women in their hats and dresses and high heels and men in their suits and ties."

And the WAVES and sailors in their blue jackets and white caps. They sat in Section A. Soldiers from the Army Air Forces Technical School were a solid mass of khaki in Section X, according to the *State Journal*. And led by director Ray Dvorak and his 150-piece Wisconsin band, the WAVES, soldiers, and sailors marched across the field before the game.

There was some gamesmanship before the kickoff, too.

"Ohio State's squad was on the field at 12:45 in civvies," Casserly wrote. "They walked about inspecting the turf, and Fekete noticed the huge spool on which the field telephone wire is wound. It was directly on the goal line. 'Do they keep this here during the game? They'd better not for I'll be down here quite a bit,' he said. He wasn't cocky, just confident."

That was an apt description for Wisconsin. Confident, not cocky. And the game played out that way with the underdog Badgers grabbing a 10-0 first half lead and parlaying their confidence and momentum into a memorable 17-7 win.

Here's how some of the "fishhacks" saw it.

The *Chicago Tribune's* Irving Vaughn: "A previously unbeaten Ohio State machine was blasted off the highway....its wheels gone, its cylinders sputtering and its heretofore brilliant chauffeurs completely dazed. The Badgers simply whipped the speedy, supposedly invincible Ohioans at their own game-wild, fearless running."

The *Chicago Herald-American's* Leo Fischer: "'On Wisconsin' may well be the theme song for the rest of the war-torn Big Ten schedule if the Badgers can play more football like they did out here today. Perfect coordination on defense, brilliant blocking, bone-crushing tackling and brainy selection of plays sent Ohio reeling after the first few minutes of action and kept the Buckeyes completely out of the picture for the entire afternoon."

The *Milwaukee Journal's* Oliver Kuechle: "Wisconsin rose to its greatest heights....Ohio State left here crushed and bedraggled and physically punished....A lot of things dazzled this crowd and set it to screaming until the capitol dome probably shook. None dazzled it quite as much, however, as Elroy Hirsch's individual brilliance."

The *Milwaukee Sentinel's* Stoney McGlynn: "Hirsch and Harder, the two best backs in the Big Ten in my book, were nothing less than terrific. They so far outshone the Buckeye duo of Sarringhaus and Fekete for explosive, breakaway abilities there is no basis for comparison....Wisconsin was everything a great club should be."

The Badgers held Fekete to 65 yards and Sarringhaus to 55. Harder rushed 21 times for 97 yards and Hirsch had 13 carries for 118. A signature 59-yard Hirsch run—triggered by a key block thrown by Harder on Ohio State's George Lynn—set up the first score of the game, a Harder plunge, in the second quarter. Harder would add a field goal before halftime.

The *State Journal's* Willard R. Smith wrote that Hirsch ran "like a scared jackrabbit on the desert with only sagebrush and cactus to hinder him."

Wrote Casserly, "Hirsch showed the fans one of his famous 'fakes' during this run, which left an Ohio State man floundering in his wake."

On Wisconsin's only score of the second half, Hirsch also decoyed the Buckeyes. Faking a run around the end, he drew the defense up and passed to a wide open Schreiner who juggled the ball before crossing the goal line. That took away the momentum from the Buckeyes, who had just executed a 96-yard scoring march capped by a 4-yard run by Fekete.

Courtesy of University of Wisconsin Archives

Mark Hoskins sprints away from the defense. Decades later, Hoskins told the Wisconsin State Journal, "I don't think there's any question the fellows today are probably bigger and better. They just grow'em that way now. But so many people remember that (1942) team because so many things happened. It was like a curtain dropped down. The war came along and everything was (judged) before 1942, and after 1942."

During his post-game press conference, Stuhldreher said, "What I liked best about the game was the way the boys came back to score after Ohio State had ground out 96 yards for its touchdown. That proved extreme poise." Outlined against a blue-gray October sky (go ahead and pretend), he then conceded, "That's the greatest victory of my football career."

Staying in character, the unassuming Schreiner told the *State Journal*, "I don't believe we could have won if it hadn't been for coordinated teamwork. This was distinctly a team victory, and that's the way games should be won."

Brown was less engaging and revealing than Stuhldreher or Schreiner. After extending half-hearted congratulations to the victors, he grumbled to the local writers, "Wisconsin's got a fine team. That's all. You saw the game as well as I did."

What could be fairer? As such, this was how the *State Journal's* daft magpie, Roundy, called it: "The Ohio dressing room was the sickest one I was ever in. All you had to do was name the pallbearers and you would have been ready for the procession."

On the lighter side, Casserly dutifully followed up with this game note:

"Bill Stern, NBC's well-known sportscaster, was given the well-known 'bird' at the close of the fourth quarter by the 50-yard line cheering section just below the broadcasting booth. It seems Mr. Stern picked Ohio State to defeat Wisconsin earlier in the week."

A majority of the prognosticators whiffed the following week, too, by taking Wisconsin over Iowa. Seemed like the pick to click. But the emotionally-drained Badgers stumbled to a 6-0 loss in Iowa City, dulling some of the luster from their Ohio State win. The Buckeyes didn't lose again and were crowned the national champions.

Breitenbach still has warm feelings for that '42 team. And yet, there's a twinge of sadness when he thinks about Schreiner and Baumann, both of whom died fighting in Okinawa. Breitenbach doesn't get to Camp Randall much anymore. He gave up his season tickets in 2004 because it was getting too hard to get up and down the steps.

But whenever he does drive past the renovated stadium, he says, "I have a very good feeling for the whole environment, and nothing but good memories."

Wisconsin 41 Iowa 3
November 13, 1999

"I still run into people who were there that night. They remember the electricity, where they sat, who they were with. It was a night to remember for everyone involved. It's one of those things that's hard to explain. You just had to be there."
- Ron Dayne

Bret Bielema was there, and the Wisconsin defensive coordinator still has a hard time explaining what he saw and heard at Camp Randall Stadium. Bielema was dressed in Iowa colors - black and gold - that night. He was still a Hawkeye then, in charge of the linebackers for first-year head coach Kirk Ferentz.

"For the first time in my coaching career," Bielema confessed, "I felt like the crowd was an extra player on the field. It was an overwhelming experience as far as the sheer volume of the noise and the interaction between the fans and the players.

"I can remember Kirk making the statement when we got back to Iowa City that it was our goal to get our place (Kinnick Stadium) up to that type of setting and environment during a game. That really was college football at its finest."

As a player - a four-year letter-winner for the Hawkeyes - Bielema couldn't remember walking into any Big Ten stadium, including tradition-rich Michigan and Ohio Stadiums, and feeling the same way that he did that night in Camp Randall.

Courtesy of Craig Schreiner/Wisconsin State Journal

Courtesy of Craig Schreiner/Wisconsin State Journal

Opposite page: Tight end Dague Retzlaff (left) and offensive tackle Chris McIntosh (75) open up a gaping hole in the Iowa defense for Ron Dayne. After the game, McIntosh admitted, ``I just put my head down and cried. It was just a very emotional time.''

As an assistant coach, Bielema's frame of reference extended to the Big 12 Conference, where he spent two years on Bill Snyder's staff at Kansas State. During that stint, Bielema was exposed to some of the loudest and most intimidating venues in the country.

Still, nothing compared to what he saw and heard that night in Madison.

"As a coach, you talk to your players all the time about, 'Blocking out where you're at,'" Bielema said. "And I really believe that's true. But that's the one game, the only game, like I said earlier, where I heard the crowd noise and I heard the public address announcer and what was being announced during the course of the game."

Bielema still has one voice in his head: the mellifluous, haunting voice of Mike Mahnke, the PA announcer at Camp Randall Stadium since 1995. With his lyrical call, Mahnke turned each of Ron Dayne's runs into a celebration and singalong.

"It wasn't funny at the time," Bielema said, "but the next day, we're back home in Iowa City and we're all saying, 'Roooonnnn Daaayynne.'"

Bielema, by the way, does a barely passable Roooonnnn Daaayynne. Or rather, Bielema does a barely passable Mahnke doing Roooonnnn Daaayynne.

How many times has Mahnke had to put up with Mahnke impersonators?

"Dozens of times," he said. "I work for an ad agency, and I have hundreds of clients who know what I do - moonlighting (on the PA at Camp Randall) - and they'll come up and it's like, 'Say it for me, Say it for me.' Or they'll do their Ron Dayne for me, and it's like, 'What did that sound like?' Can I be up there (the press box) with you?"

The good-natured Mahnke is a Cheesehead from Racine, a UW grad, and the Vice-President/Creative Director of Roundhouse Marketing and Promotions in Madison. He takes everything in stride, though he has fielded some unusual requests.

"I had a guy who works for another agency call and ask for a favor," he related. "A girl in his office was having a birthday and he wanted me to pick up the phone, call her and say, 'Roooonnnn Daaayynne, Happy Birthday.' Weird stuff like that."

How did Mahnke's call evolve?

"It just kind of naturally happened the first time," he said of his personalized annunciation for Dayne. "Up until that point, I was keeping a relatively low profile, trying to be as unbiased as possible. But he just started taking off (as a big-time runner), the natural enthusiasm took over, and then I forgot about being an unbiased spectator."

As the oversized, bulldozing tailback grew in popularity and stature, so did Mahnke and his "Roooonnnn Daaayynne" to the point where the students began echoing the call - bouncing it right back at Mahnke. Only he couldn't hear them at first.

"Honestly, I didn't realize until the season wore on that the crowd was saying anything because in the booth I couldn't hear anything," he said. "Someone had to finally come up and tell me, 'Hey, they're saying it back to you.'" They were Ron Dayne-ing him.

When a speaker monitor was installed in the booth - to keep Mahnke from inadvertently stepping over the referee's voice on penalty calls - he was finally able to hear the product of his work, the Dayne echo. "And that's when I started playing with them a little bit," he said, "which kind of spring-boarded into a Matt Unertl thing as well."

Unertl was a reserve tailback from Sussex, a walk-on who went on to earn a scholarship with his steady play on special teams and reliable contributions as a backup. Whenever he carried the ball, Mahnke gave Unertl the Ron Dayne treatment.

Not that a Maaaatt Uneeeerrttl could ever top the original. But it was a nice touch, and especially nostalgic after Dayne had moved on to the National Football League.

For someone who's never heard the Dayne call, how would Mahnke break it down?

"As soon as he breaks through the line and has tacklers hanging all over him," he said, "the Ron part sounds like you've just been goosed and you're out of your seat."

That would be the Roooonnnn.

"The Dayne part," he added, "is when you sit back down."

That would be the Daaayynne.

Mahnke established some guidelines for his call.

"If he got 10-plus yards on a run, I'd usually give it a little bit of a goose," he said. "And if he rumbled for a touchdown, then it would be peel-me-off-the-ceiling time."

Like when Dayne rumbled 34-yards for a touchdown against Michigan in the 1999 Big Ten opener at Camp Randall. Classic Dayne. It looked like he was going to be stopped for a loss or no gain when he bounced off tacklers and accelerated into the open field, outrunning the pursuit to the end zone. Dayne had 14 carries for 88 yards in that first half.

And that's when the Wolverines hit the mute button on Dayne and Mahnke. "I don't recall a lot of the details from the second half of that game," Mahnke said. "I try to shut those things out of mind, because it's really hard for me to be quiet when we play Michigan."

The Wolverines decided that enough was enough and silenced Dayne on their own. "We told ourselves at halftime, 'Hey, we've got to stop him, he's getting too many yards," Michigan linebacker Ian Gold told the *Capital Times*. "We made an attitude adjustment. We came out and challenged ourselves to really get after him."

That they did. Dayne had eight carries for zero yards in the second half. He had three rushes for two yards each, two rushes for no gain, and three rushes totaling six yards in losses. "The coaches told me not to get frustrated," Dayne said afterward, sounding frustrated.

There was plenty of frustration to go around. A week earlier, the University of Cincinnati, a 26-point underdog, had upset the Badgers, 17-12, in the Queen City. And now the Wolverines had compounded Wisconsin's misery by leaving town with a 21-16 win.

The Badgers, who had been ranked as high as No. 8, dropped out of the Top 25. And Dayne, who had been the Heisman Trophy pre-season leader in the Scripps Howard News Service poll, dropped out of the top five. Florida State's Peter Warrick took the lead, followed by Purdue's Drew Brees, Georgia Tech's Joe Hamilton and Alabama's Shaun Alexander.

People were busting their ankles jumping off the Dayne bandwagon. There was one notable exception. *State Journal* columnist Andy Baggot cautioned against making hasty judgments on the Heisman based solely on Dayne's numbers from the Michigan game.

Baggot pointed out that Texas tailback Ricky Williams rushed 25 times for just 43 yards during a 41-point loss to Kansas State in the Big 12 Conference opener, and Williams still finished No. 1 on the 1998 Heisman Trophy ballot.

Baggot also noted that a handful of other Heisman winners were able to overcome an off-game during the season in which they won the award. The list included Bo Jackson (48 yards), Archie Griffin (46 yards), Billy Sims (36 yards), and Herschel Walker (20 yards).

That information might have eased Dayne's early season anxiety. But at the time, there was nothing anybody could write or say that would make Barry Alvarez feel better.

Following the Cincinnati game, the UW head coach decided that enough was enough. He had enough of the crutches that he used on the sidelines to prop himself up on a badly swollen right knee, a football knee and a souvenir from his playing days at Nebraska.

And he had enough of the sleepless nights and the excruciating pain, so excruciating that he had broken down in the privacy of his home and wept in front of his wife, Cindy.

"Never been sick a day in my life," Alvarez said. "I've been involved with football since I was 9 years old, and I don't think I've ever missed a football game or a practice."

But that streak was coming to a screeching halt. "Right now, I'm in so much pain, I'm scared to death," Alvarez said. "I don't sleep, and it's just taken its toll."

Five days before the Big Ten opener, Alvarez consulted with doctors at Mayo Clinic in Rochester, Minnesota, and scheduled knee replacement surgery for Tuesday, October 5.

That was the week after the Wisconsin-Ohio State game in Columbus, and the week of the Wisconsin-Minnesota game in the Metrodome. He would coach against the Buckeyes but turn over his team to John Palermo and the staff for the Gophers.

"The closer I get to this surgery, I know the more serious it is," Alvarez said. "We've tried to gradually work into it, and our kids are just going to have to deal with it."

Despite this predicament, Alvarez was in surprisingly good spirits leading up to the Ohio State trip. Surprisingly good because the Badgers were on a two-game losing streak and listed as a seven-point underdog. Surprisingly good because Wisconsin had won just twice in the 77-year history of Ohio Stadium, and hadn't beaten the Buckeyes in Columbus since 1985.

Turns out Alvarez was full of surprises.

One was Bollinger, a redshirt freshman who was taking over as the starting quarterback. "Some people may not have recognized the job he did against a great Michigan team," Alvarez said. "And I wanted to see if he could keep that momentum."

Late in the Michigan game, Bollinger replaced Scott Kavanagh and scored on a 13-yard run culminating an 80-yard drive. "He brought a different dimension to the game with his running," said Alvarez. "And I thought he made some exceptional throws, too."

The real surprise was Alvarez's confidence going into Ohio State. And much of it had to do with what he had seen from his team and Bollinger during practices that week.

"We're going to win this game," Alvarez volunteered on Thursday from his office in Camp Randall Stadium. "And it might not even be close."

151

Dayne joined Alan Ameche as the only Badger players featured on the upper deck facade at Camp Randall.

It wasn't close for a while. The Badgers trailed 17-0 in the second quarter at Ohio State. But they got a couple of field goals before half-time and kept scoring and scoring in the second half. The Badgers scored on six straight possessions. And by the time it was over, they had scored 42 unanswered points against the Bambi-in-the-head-lights Buckeyes.

Dayne scored four times, and of his 161 rushing yards - catapulting him back into the Heisman race - 125 came in the second half when he was at his finest, his punishing finest.

On one possession, three different Ohio State players - Ahmed Plummer, Jason Ott and Na'il Diggs - had to be helped off the field. "When you see people getting up slow," Alvarez said, "that's because they're tackling somebody who's 255 pounds and they're tackling him time and time again. And he just keeps getting stronger and stronger."

Alvarez also had strong words for Bollinger's debut as a starter. "What an awesome performance," he said. "He creates a lot of problems for a defense. He managed the clock, he managed the noise, he moved the sticks, and he made play after play after play."

Bollinger was a quick learner, a coach's kid. His dad, Rob, was an assistant coach at the University of North Dakota. His grandfather was also a coach and he left a family treasure - a Grantland Rice poem - which had been passed from Bollinger generation to Bollinger generation. And it would ultimately become Brooks Bollinger's anthem.

"Football's Answer"
They reform me each new season as they point to each new fault.
And their hands are turned against me as they crowd me to the vault.
But amid the growing clamor, they know around the clan;
I'm the soul of college spirit and the maker of a man.
Oh, I know I'm far from perfect when the autumn leaves turn red,
when the tackle's neck is furrowed by the halfback's heavy tread;
but you hear them still admitting as they put me on the pan,
he's the soul of college spirit and the maker of a man.
Perhaps I'm more important than a mere game ought to be;
but with all the sins they speak of, and the list is quite a span,
I'm the soul of college spirit and the maker of a man.

After a Monday meeting with his players, Alvarez turned over the team to his assistants and flew to Rochester and checked into the Mayo Clinic. But there would be complications.

Tuesday, the medical team opened up his knee and came across signs of an infection, necessitating a lengthy surgery just to clean out the spurs and cysts. The actual knee replacement surgery would have to be delayed until the end of the regular season.

Alvarez was still restricted to his hospital room when the Badgers took the field against the Gophers in Minneapolis. He and Cindy watched the game on a small screen television. They watched as the Badgers overcame deficits of 7-0, 14-7 and 17-14. But Barry Alvarez couldn't watch when Vitaly Pisetsky lined up a 31-yard field goal attempt in overtime.

He turned away from the TV.

But after Pisetsky nailed it - his first game-winner at the collegiate or high school level - Alvarez couldn't hold back. "Just me and Cindy in the room - yelling," he said. "A nurse banged on our door and asked, 'Could you please quiet down?' They came in and took my blood pressure about 10 minutes after the game, and it was off the charts."

So was this 20-17 win - off the charts- given the circumstances. Alvarez talked to quite a few of the players on the phone. And again, he had strong words for Bollinger's impact. "He makes all the difference," Alvarez said. "He just spreads the field out for Ron."

During Palermo's post-game press conference, he got a question on the character of "his" team whereupon he quickly corrected the questioner.

"It's the character of Barry Alvarez's team," Palermo insisted. "It's not my football team. I'm just one of the assistants who have followed the plan that he set forth for us. This is characteristic of an Alvarez team - the kids fought and fought and never gave up."

Palermo admitted that when he got on the phone with Alvarez, they didn't have a lot to say. "We were just so happy, I think we were both crying a little bit."

Nobody was happier to get back with his team than Alvarez, whose main concession to the bothersome knee was getting off the sidelines on game days and watching from the press box. He joked that he felt a lot smarter already, cloistered among the media representatives.

Those first two weeks in October - those two road victories in two hostile environments, Ohio Stadium and the Metrodome - were the most telling and critical to Wisconsin's goal of capturing back-to-back Big Ten championships, and to Dayne's aspirations to break Williams' NCAA rushing mark and win the Heisman Trophy.

There was another source of motivation for Dayne. In the October 18 issue of *Sports Illustrated*, he was ranked on a list of the top 10 disappointments in college football. Dayne didn't say anything. He just cut out the list and taped it to his locker.

On October 23, matched against the No. 1 rushing defense in the nation, Dayne bulled for 34 carries and 214 yards in a decisive 40-10 win over Michigan State at Camp Randall. Dayne had 72 yards on the first possession, including a 51-yard touchdown.

"We relied on the big guy," said Alvarez, who became the winningest coach in school history with his 66th career victory. "We wanted to get on his back and ride him."

Dayne had to share top billing with cornerback Jamar Fletcher, who had demanded earlier in the week the assignment of covering Michigan State's Plaxico Burress. "If your mouth writes a check," Alvarez warned Fletcher, "your fanny better be able to cash it."

Fletcher picked off two passes and suffocated the 6-6 Burress, who managed just five catches for 58 yards. "It's never bragging," Fletcher said, "if you back it up."

Two weeks later, in what was billed as a Heisman showdown - Dayne vs. Purdue quarterback Drew Brees - Dayne was a first-ballot winner, rushing 32 times for 222 yards. His 41-yard touchdown run in the fourth quarter was a masterpiece, his 17th career run of 40 or more yards and his 69th career score, a Big Ten record.

There was another run - an 11-yard run when the Badgers were running out the clock - that was so severe, so Ron Dayne, it had UW offensive coordinator Brian White standing and screaming his approval from the press box in Ross-Ade Stadium. "I haven't seen Ron with that much spring," Alvarez said, "or that excited in a long time."

The excitement was justified. He was within 99 yards of breaking Williams' record. For the first time, Dayne conceded that he was now prepared to think about becoming the all-time leading rusher. But he stressed that a win over Iowa was the first priority.

As it was for his teammates, who had traveled a considerable distance from the frustration and second-guessing after back-to-back losses to Cincinnati and Michigan.

"It was a pretty dark time back then," said UW offensive tackle Chris McIntosh. "But everyone believed we'd get better week to week, and we'd fight and claw our way back up. We've come a long ways and it says a lot about this team. We've got a lot of believers."

Dayne made believers out of the Heisman voters. After the Purdue game, he moved back into the No. 1 slot in the Scripps Howard poll. Hamilton dropped to No. 2, and Brees stayed at No. 3 on the list. Speaking of lists, Dayne finally got around to publicly addressing his inclusion on *Sports Illustrated's* list of the top 10 disappointments.

"I'm not going to lie about that," Dayne told the *Capital Times*. "That really motivated me to go out and play harder. I've still got the list up in my locker."

After *SI* published its story, Dayne became the storyline, rushing for 214, 162 and 222 yards. "His numbers speak for themselves," Alvarez said. "He came back for a fourth year when most people thought that he wouldn't. And he's what our program is all about - blue-collar, hard-nosed, not doing it the easy way, and doing what you have to do to win."

In Iowa City, Bielema had watched a ton of tape on Dayne.

"He wasn't about just putting the head down and running over people," he said. "I thought he was very good at finding the open angle, sliding a couple of steps and coming down-hill on the tacklers. Usually when running backs are going sideways, they don't have as much power. But that was unique about him. He had power going sideways or forward.

"What we wanted to do was overwhelm him at the point of attack. You had to swarm tackle and basically put more numbers on him than he could handle. With the record on the line, we knew that he was going to be featured. So we wanted to do everything we could to commit to the run. But, unfortunately, at the time, our horses didn't add up to their horses."

The horses were McIntosh and Mark Tauscher at tackle, Bill Ferrario and Dave Costa at guard, Casey Rabach at center, and Dague Retzlaff and John Sigmund at tight end.

"We never really varied much when Ron was playing," said UW offensive line coach Jim Hueber, who coordinated the running attack. "We had a game plan, we had experienced linemen, and we were going to tweak the running plays - the outside runs and the hard dive inside - that he liked. We knew what we were going to do and we felt like we were physical enough to handle people, and we felt like Ron really trusted the way those guys blocked things. We set up the angles for him, and we changed the way the plays were designed because he liked the ball tighter. That's why we ran more of an up-and-down inside play."

Ron Dayne was always known as a finisher, a strong runner who finished each of his runs. And that's what he did on his record-smashing run — powering through teammate Chris Chambers and a tackle attempt by Iowa cornerback Joe Slattery. "When Ron broke the record, it was such a weight lifted off my back and I'm sure everybody else's, too," said UW offensive guard Dave Costa. "Once he got the record, it was like, 'We can just go out and play now and not worry about anything. Let's win the Big Ten title.'"

A commemorative white towel - bearing Dayne's No. 33 and a congratulatory message - was handed out to every fan entering Camp Randall. And just before the 2:36 p.m. kickoff, four F-16 jets from the Wisconsin Air National Guard's 115th Fighter Wing provided a fly-by salute to America's veterans. By 5 p.m., the temperature climbed to 69 degrees. For this time of the year, mid-November, the normal high was 45.

And the momentum just kept building. Michigan's 31-27 victory at Penn State put the Badgers in a position to lock up an outright Big Ten championship.

Welcome to the Jungle (cue Guns N' Roses and the House of Pain).

"Simply stated, it was the best atmosphere I have ever seen at any sporting event in my life," Bollinger said from the training camp of the New York Jets. "My first-year roommate with the Jets was on that Iowa team, and we have talked about that game a few times. He was amazed - as were his teammates and coaches - at the electric atmosphere.

"Personally, I think it was the best I ever felt before and during a game. I felt like I had a bounce in my step, and I felt sharp and confident. Things went well for us offensively early and I racked up a few rushing yards, but they were doing a fairly good job of stacking the box to stop the run and they were slowing down Ron."

(Bollinger rushed 11 times for 113 yards and one touchdown.)

"After one of my runs, I remember saying to Ron, 'You better hurry up and get going or I'm going to have more yards than you.' It was kind of a little joke, because we all knew that he would break the record, come hell or high water."

What was Dayne's anxiety level going into the historic game?

"I didn't have any idea, in terms of plays, how the record would fall," he said from the training camp of the Denver Broncos. "But I was confident prior to the game that it would fall. What I do remember is in the second quarter, as I was nearing the record, Chad Kuhns said, 'You know, you can't break the record without me being in there.' And not only was he in there when I broke the record, but he threw a crucial block as well."

With 4 minutes and 32 seconds left in the first half, Bollinger got the signal from the sidelines, stepped into the huddle, and called a "23 zone."

"I thought I was going to break the record when that play was called," Dayne said. "I felt like Coach White had read my mind when he chose that play. I also remember the look Chad Kuhns gave me. I think he knew, if he did his job, I would do mine. And I have always had nothing but confidence in my offensive line."

On the snap, Rabach fired out on Iowa's nose tackle Corey Brown, Costa slid off Brown and blocked middle linebacker Aaron Kampman, Tauscher locked up the defensive end Anthony Herron, and Kuhns kicked out on linebacker Fred Barr.

In the backfield, Dayne took the handoff from Bollinger and cut effortlessly from left to right - deftly executing his cutback skills into the hole.

The running seam opened up between Costa and Tauscher.

Once Dayne got into the second level of Iowa's defense, he used a nifty juke to freeze free safety Shane Hall, who was left swinging at air in the middle of the field.

Veering to the sidelines, Dayne slowed down long enough to allow wide receiver Chris Chambers to get a blocking angle on Iowa cornerback Joe Slattery.

Dayne didn't need the block.

Instead, he used another juke and cut back sharply inside, which left Slattery standing flat-footed and out of position. Dayne then muscled through Chambers and Slattery for extra yardage before being knocked out of bounds by the far-side cornerback Tarig Holman.

At the conclusion of the 31-yard run, Hall bounced over the top of Dayne, the freshly crowned all-time leading rusher in college football, the stadium exploded, and Dayne bounced to his feet to accept the hugs and chest bumps from his teammates.

"I think the whole week leading up to the Iowa game, everyone knew we were going to get Ron the record," Tauscher said. "But it took a little longer to get than we thought it would. I remember Coach Hueber saying, 'Relax, calm down' because we were just chunking two yards a carry in the first quarter. But, all of a sudden, Ron busted it over the right side, and I just remember all the excitement in the air and all the pictures being taken."

Mahnke's anxiety reached a personal high, too.

"I knew that it was going to happen, as did everyone, but I didn't know exactly what I was going to say or how I was going to say it," he remembered. "And there really wasn't a whole lot more for me to say other than 'Roooonnn Daaayyne.'

"Like everybody else, I had to be peeled off the ceiling when he finally did it. Looking around the stadium from the press box, and seeing all the flashbulbs going off was just incredible. And when the fans held up the No. 33 towels, the hair stood up on my arms."

During the fourth quarter, Alvarez left the press box and stood on the sidelines, basking in the glow of his team's effort. One by one, the players approached their head coach and exchanged hugs. "I remember telling myself to take it all in toward the end of the game because it was obviously special," Bollinger said. "It's one of those games that you hope somehow you'll get to experience something similar in your life. But it'll be tough to top."

The biggest and warmest hug was shared between Dayne and Alvarez as the sell-out crowd of 79, 404 roared its support. "I still remember the hug that he gave me," Dayne said. "It reminded me of the first time we met. He gave me a hug then, and it seemed only right that my time at Wisconsin would end the same way that it started."

On his 1996 campus visit, the recruit saw Wisconsin attempt 51 passes and only 20 runs in a 33-20 loss to Iowa at Camp Randall. The Badgers were out-rushed by 312 yards.

Sedrick Shaw led Iowa with 41 carries and 214 yards.

Aaron Stecker led Wisconsin with 13 carries and 25 yards.

After the game, UW assistant coach Brian White threw his arm around the recruit, sighed, and said, "See why we need you?"

The recruit nodded his head and replied softly, "Yeah, I do."

The recruit? Ron Dayne.

Courtesy of Wisconsin State Journal

The recruiter? Bernie Wyatt.

Thus began a chapter unlike any other that has been written at Wisconsin. The East Coast recruiter delivered the New Jersey recruit and the rest is history, NCAA history.

"I'll be real happy for him when he gets that record," said Wyatt, who was unwilling to share the spotlight. "He did it all - I'm just the guy who got him here."

In the 41-3 victory over Iowa, Dayne rushed 27 times for 216 yards and one score. That gave him a total of 6,397 career yards, 118 more than Williams.

"I don't really visualize that run," Dayne said of the record-breaker. "But I think about it when it comes on ESPN Classic or when somebody asks me about the pictures that I have of the run. And I still remember all the fans waving their towels. And I remember the unveiling of my name and number (on the upper deck façade).

"I do sometimes think about that night. And when I show them the game tape I'm going to tell my children - my daughter Jada was there and my son Javian was on the way - that was a very special night when daddy became the NCAA's all-time leading rusher.

"Playing at Camp Randall was a wonderful, unforgettable experience. And when I retire from football, I'll have more time to reminisce about those special moments."

Special moments, great moments.

And this was the greatest of the great.

You just had to be there.

UW athletic director Pat Richter (far left) and Barry Alvarez (breaking down in tears) celebrate another Big Ten championship with the team captains: Ron Dayne (behind Richter), Chris McIntosh, Jason Doering, Donnel Thompson (44) and Chris Ghidorzi (16).

Other Titles From KCI Sports

TOP DAWGS:
UW-Stevens Point's 2004-2005
National Championship Season

BRUCE WEBER:
Through My Eyes

Available at your local bookstore or by calling 1-800-697-3756

GREATEST MOMENTS

1941

1998

**Like Camp Randall, UW Health has experienced
many great moments over the years.**

From development of the Mohs Surgery Technique to
remove skin cancer in 1941, to Dr. Jamie Thomson's
isolation of human embryonic stem cells in 1998, there
have been many great moments.

Some may have affected only one patient, in need of critical
care at a critical time. Others have helped extend the lives of
countless people through the nation and world.

Here's to future greatest moments.

uwhealth.org